ADVENTURES of GOD

Volume 1

by Corey & Teo

Layout assists by Nicholas Hogge

Rocketship Entertainment, LLC

Tom Akel, CEO & Publisher
Rob Feldman, CTO
Jeanmarie McNeely, CFO
Brandon Freeberg, Dir. of Campaign Mgmt.
Jed Keith, Social Media

rocketshipent.com

ADVENTURES OF GOD originally published digitally at WEBTOON

ADVENTURES OF GOD VOLUME 1
ISBN: 978-1-952126-04-8

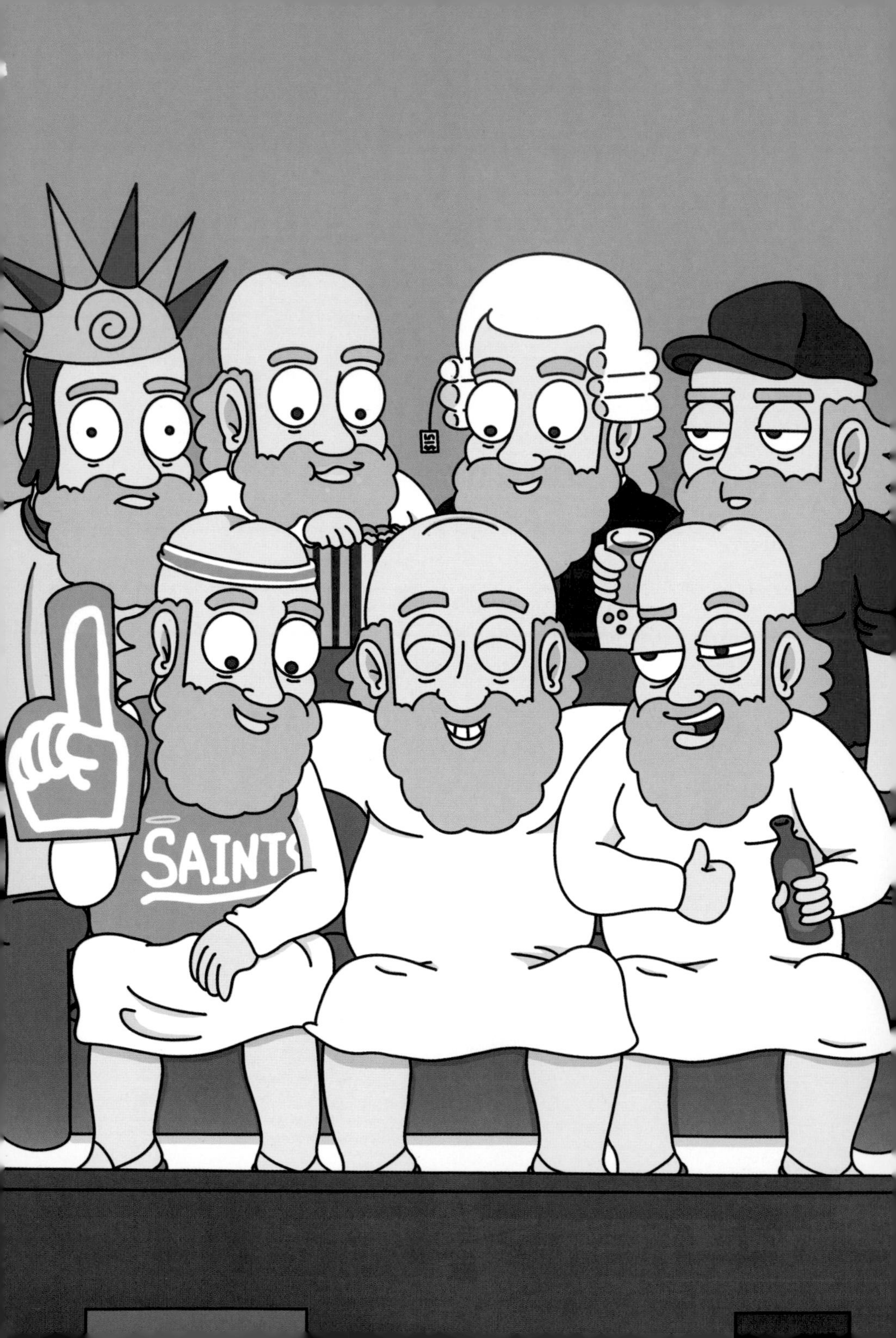
$15
SAINTS

Tablet of Contents

Answering Prayers

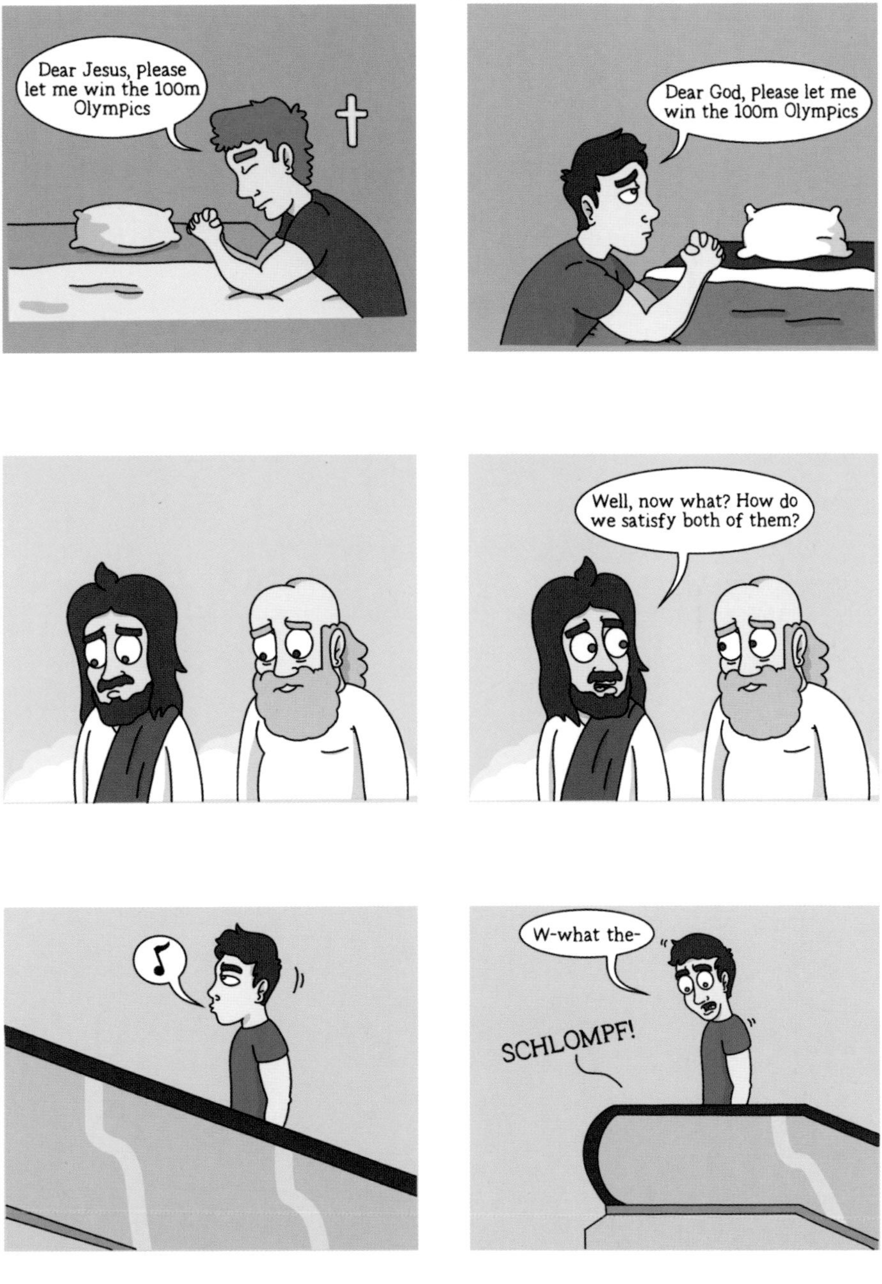
Dear Jesus, please let me win the 100m Olympics
Dear God, please let me win the 100m Olympics
Well, now what? How do we satisfy both of them?
W-what the-
SCHLOMPF!

OH - NO - NO - NO! AGH!!
CRUNCH!

GAAAH! MY LEGS!!
SNAP!
CRACKLE!
pop

Some time later...

7
5

You're welcome

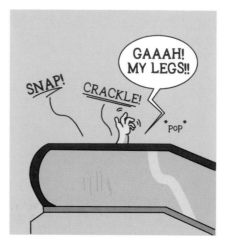

Where Fossils Came From

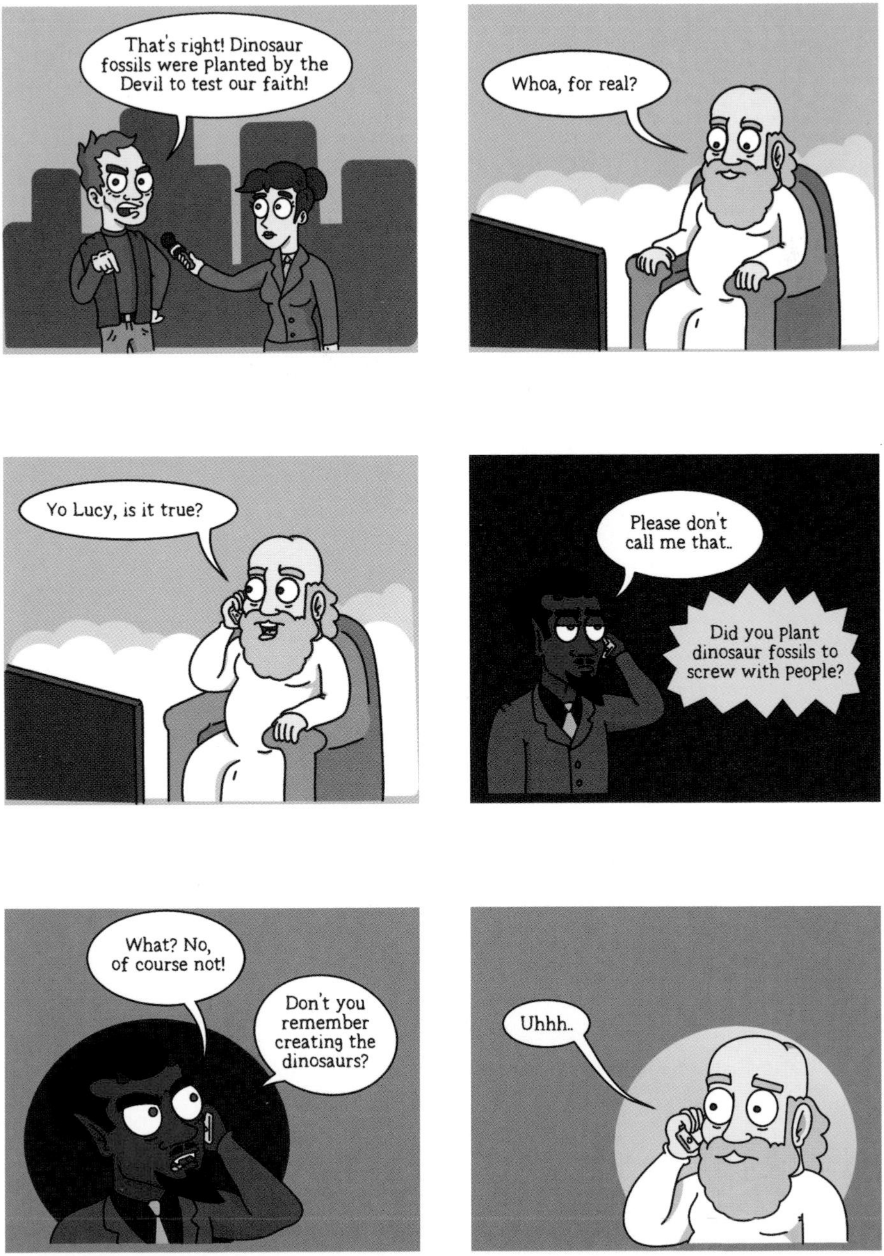
That's right! Dinosaur fossils were planted by the Devil to test our faith!
Whoa, for real?
Yo Lucy, is it true?
Please don't call me that..
Did you plant dinosaur fossils to screw with people?
What? No, of course not!
Don't you remember creating the dinosaurs?
Uhhh..

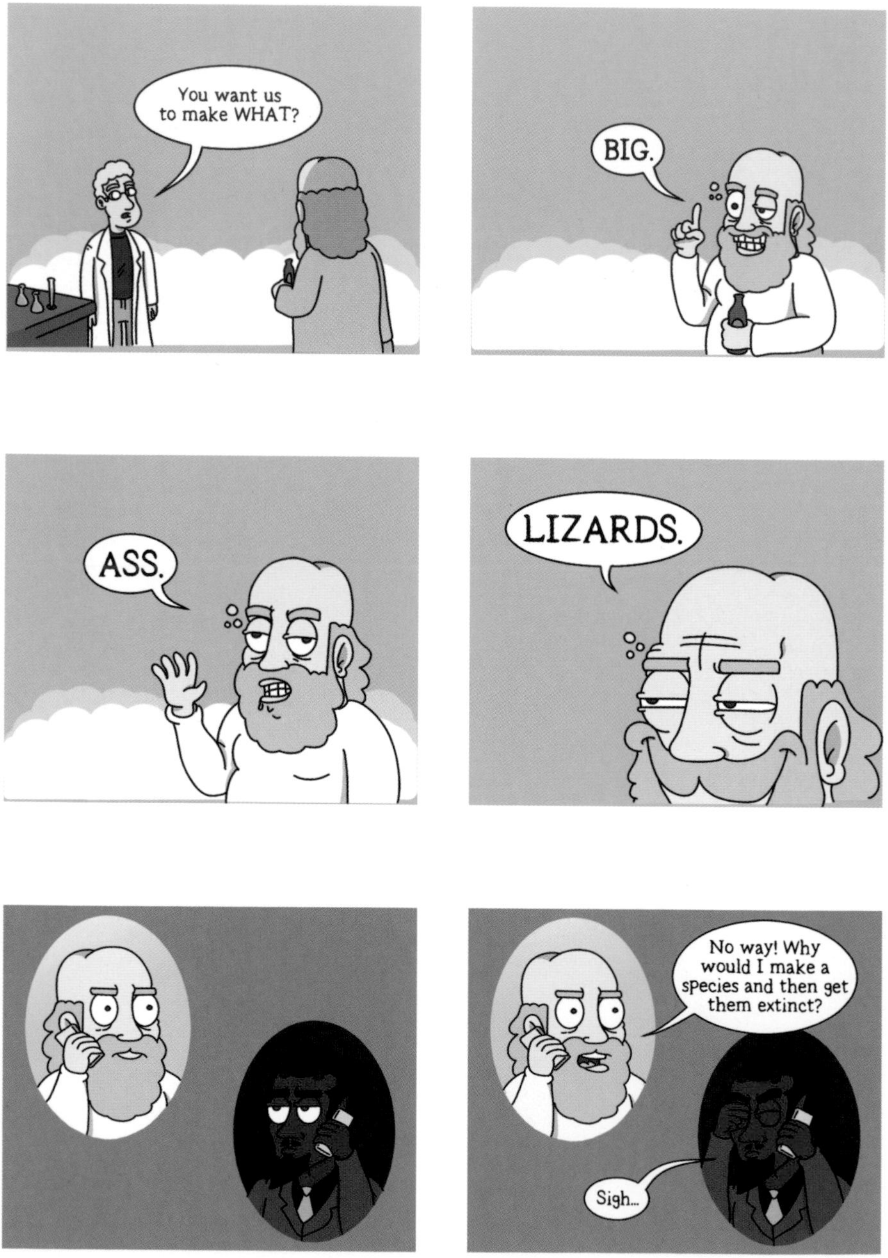
You want us to make WHAT?
BIG.
ASS.
LIZARDS.
No way! Why would I make a species and then get them extinct?
Sigh...

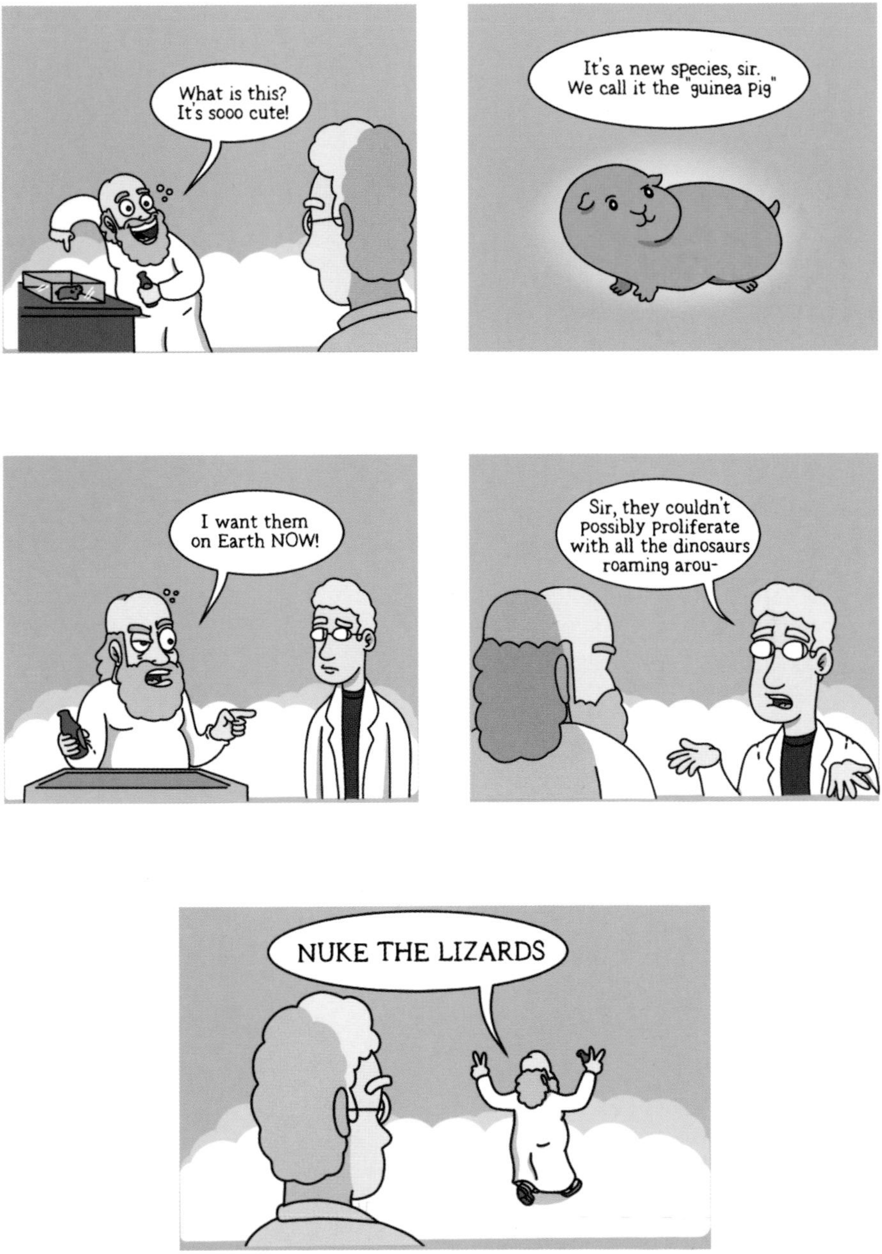
What is this? It's sooo cute!
It's a new species, sir. We call it the "guinea pig"
I want them on Earth NOW!
Sir, they couldn't possibly proliferate with all the dinosaurs roaming arou-
NUKE THE LIZARDS

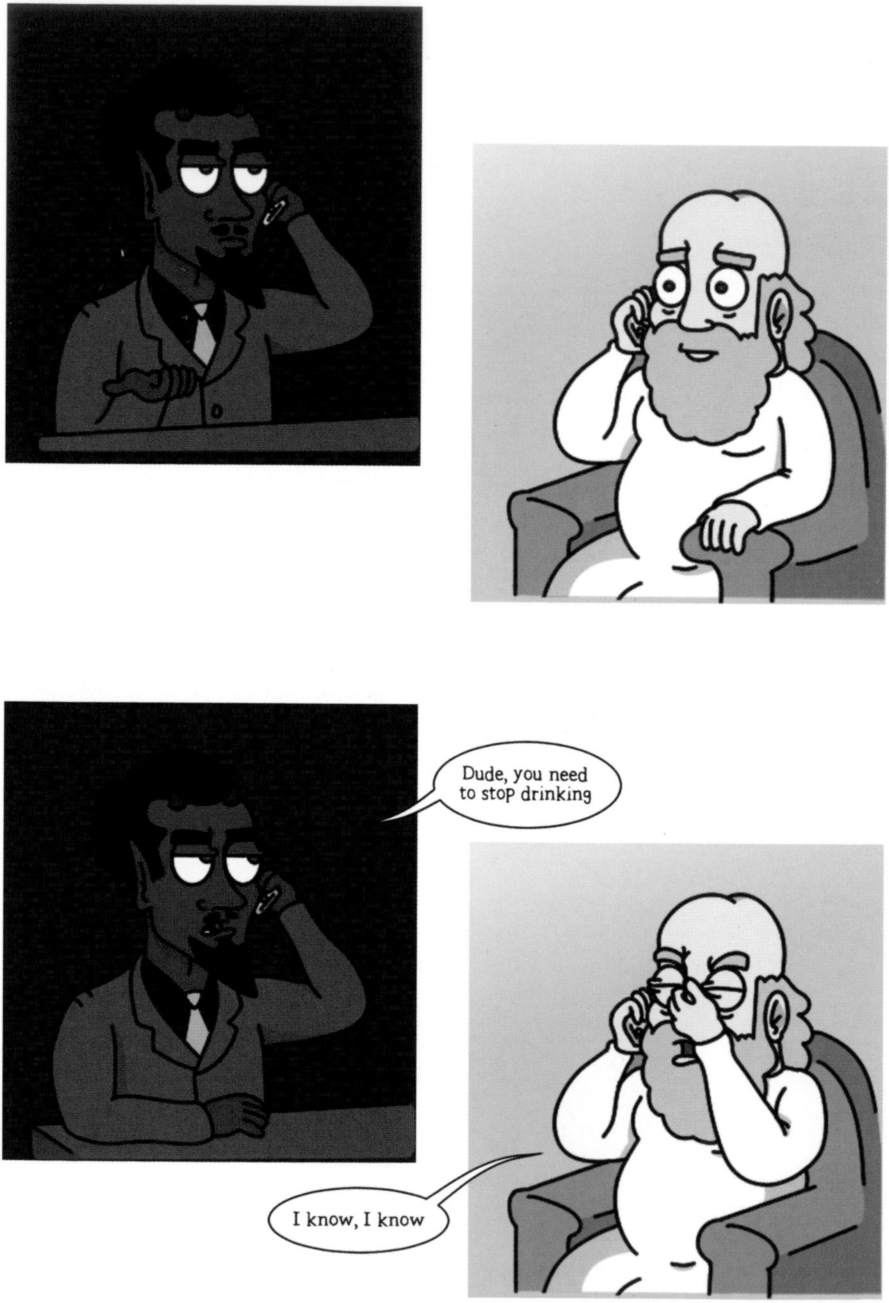
Dude, you need to stop drinking
I know, I know

Why He Went to Hell

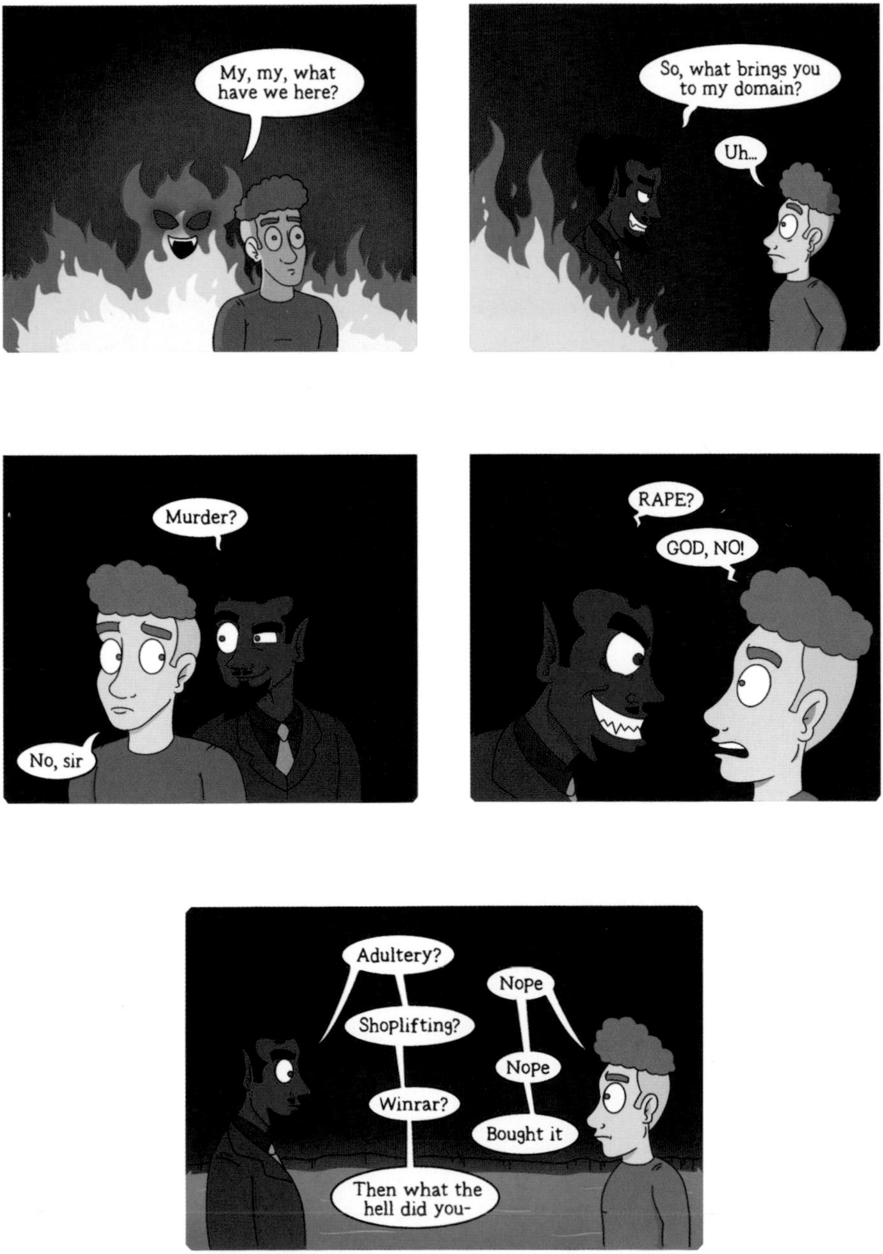
My, my, what have we here?
So, what brings you to my domain?
Uh...
Murder?
No, sir
RAPE?
GOD, NO!
Adultery?
Nope
Shoplifting?
Nope
Winrar?
Bought it
Then what the hell did you-

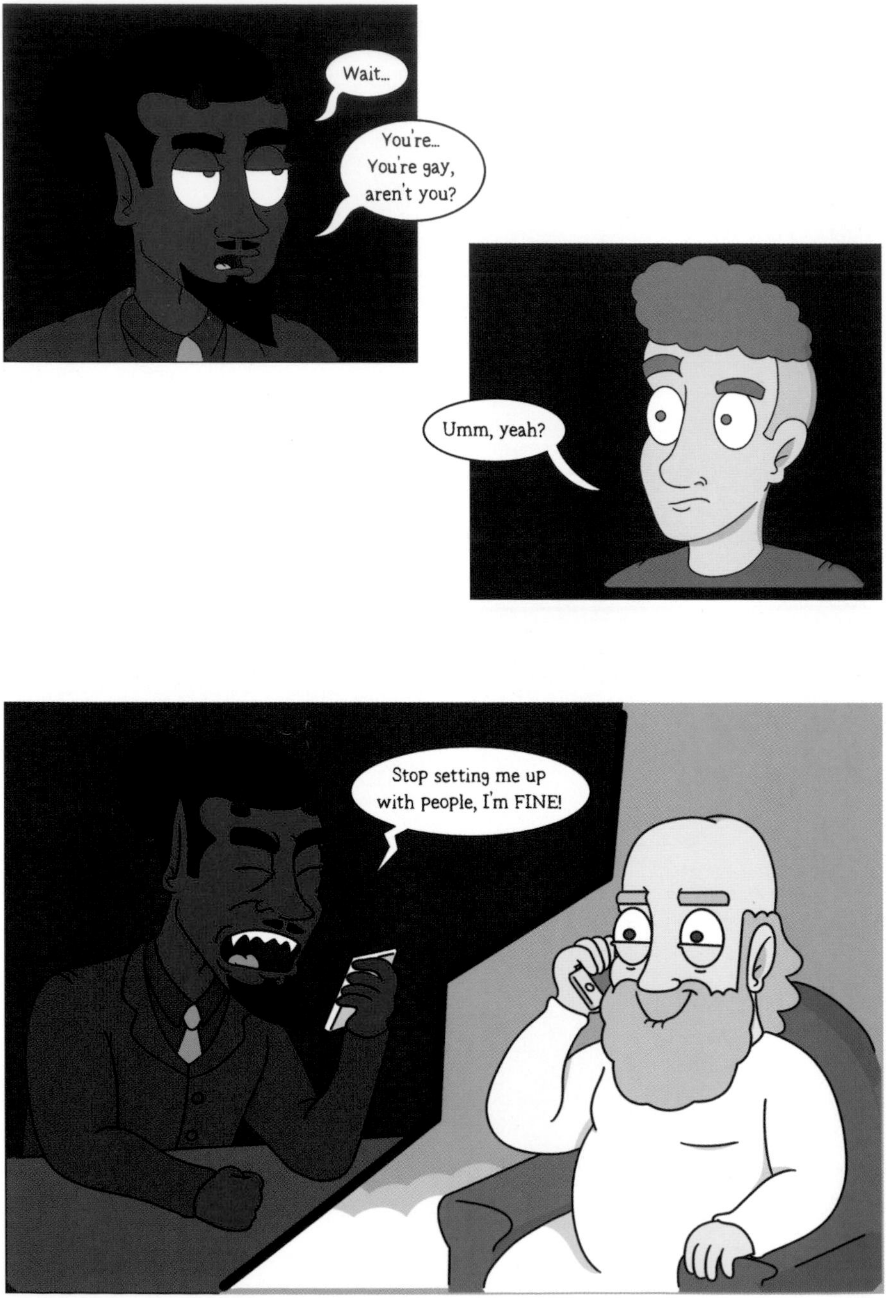
Wait...
You're... You're gay, aren't you?
Umm, yeah?
Stop setting me up with people, I'm FINE!

Why He Went to Limbo

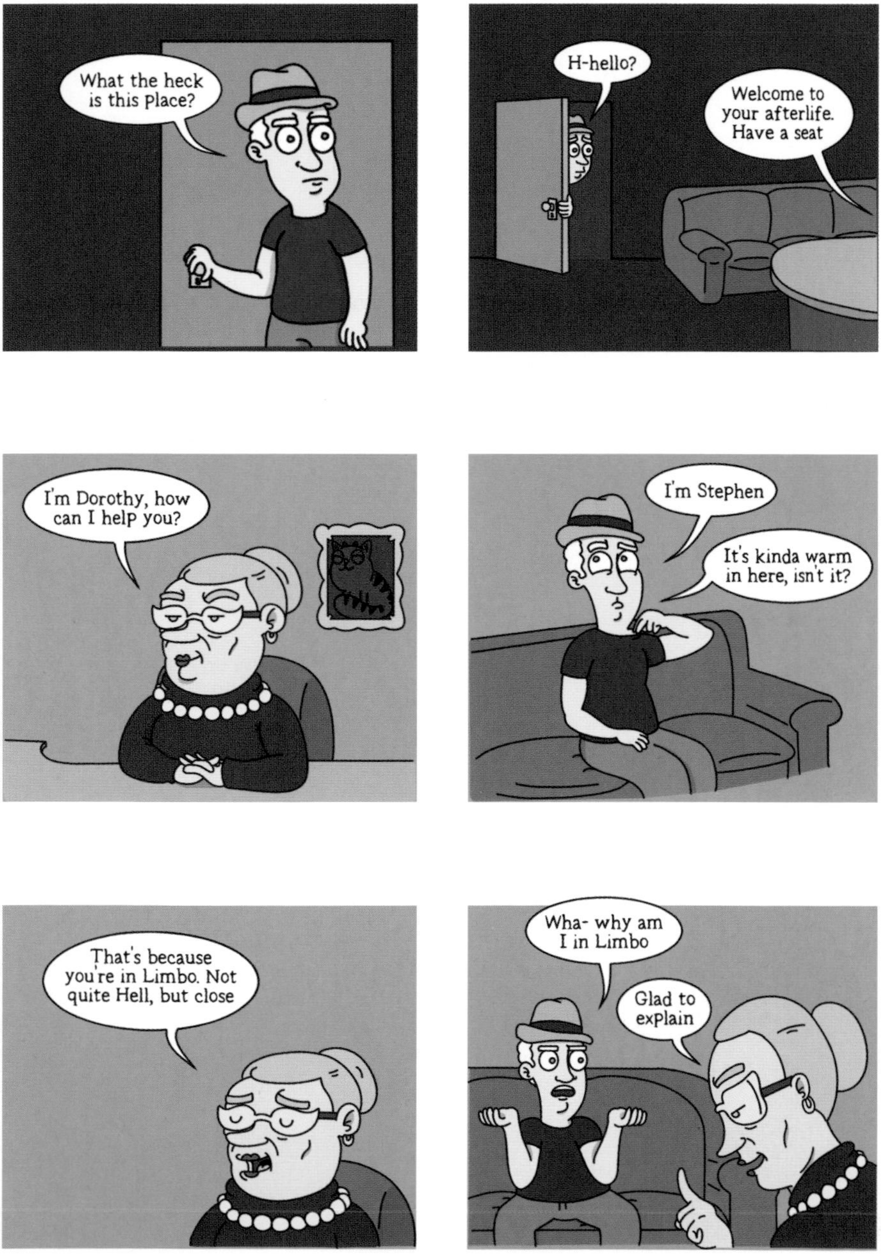

What the heck is this Place?
H-hello?
Welcome to your afterlife. Have a seat
I'm Dorothy, how can I help you?
I'm Stephen
It's kinda warm in here, isn't it?
That's because you're in Limbo. Not quite Hell, but close
Wha- why am I in Limbo
Glad to explain

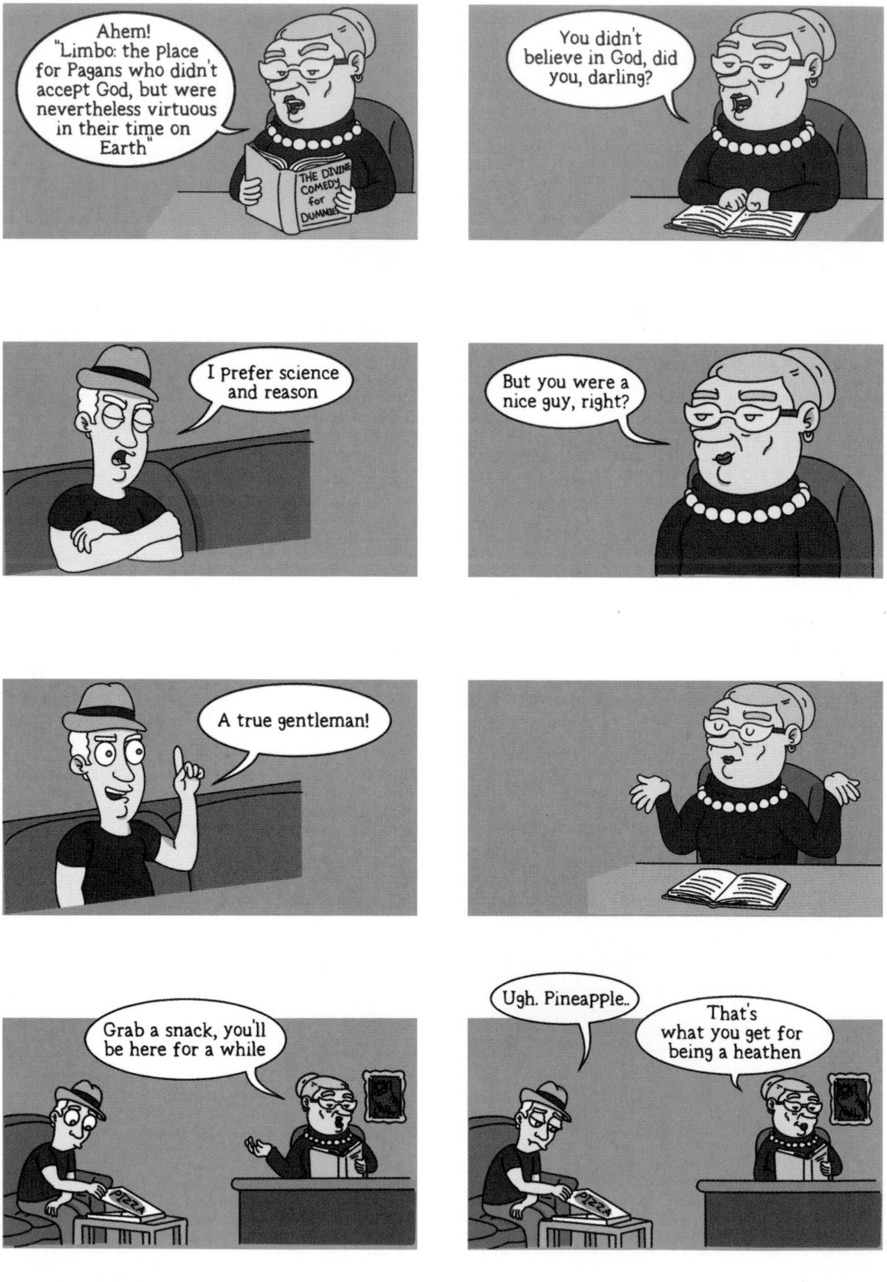
Ahem!
"Limbo: the place for Pagans who didn't accept God, but were nevertheless virtuous in their time on Earth"
THE DIVINE COMEDY for DUMMIES
You didn't believe in God, did you, darling?
I prefer science and reason
But you were a nice guy, right?
A true gentleman!
Grab a snack, you'll be here for a while
PIZZA
Ugh. Pineapple..
That's what you get for being a heathen
PIZZA

When You Thank God

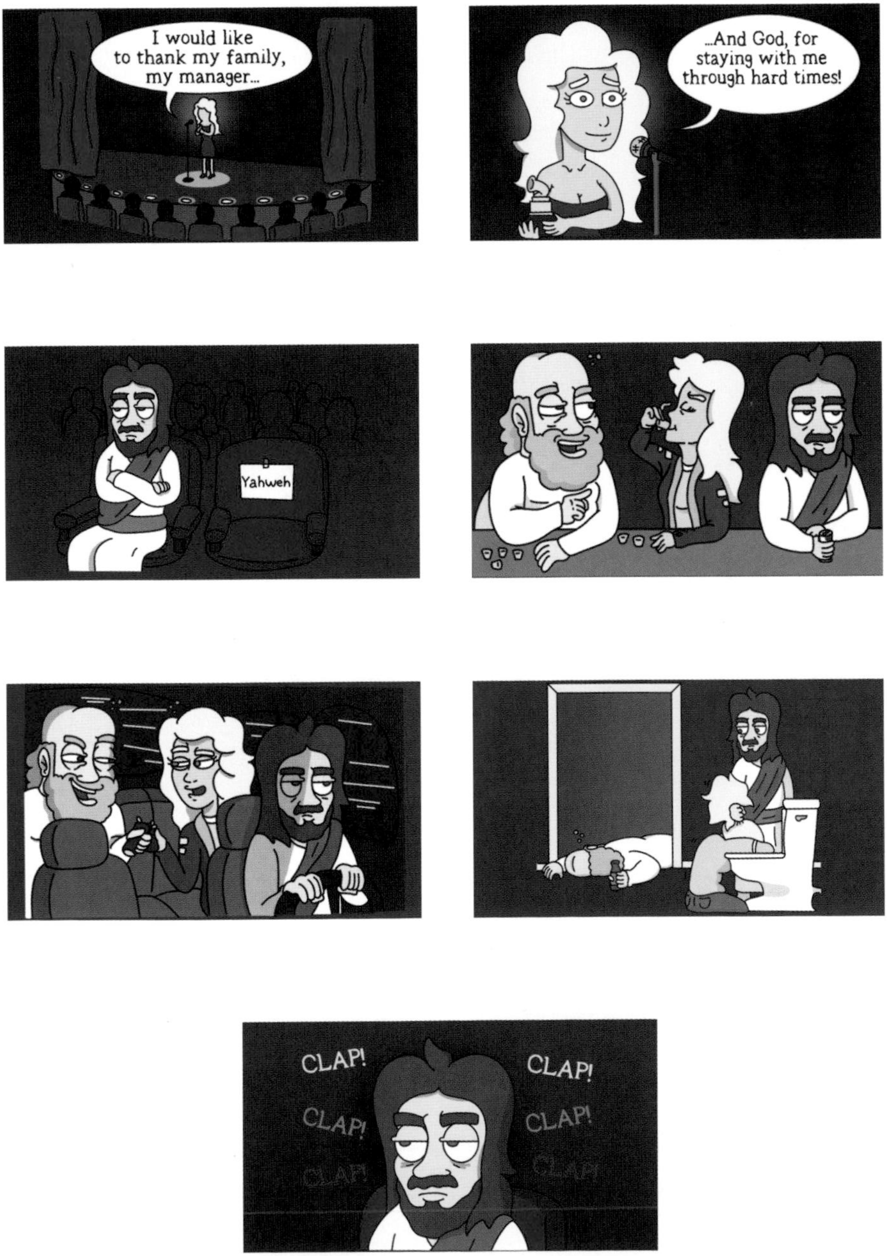
I would like to thank my family, my manager...
...And God, for staying with me through hard times!
Yahweh
CLAP!
CLAP!
CLAP!
CLAP!
CLAP!
CLAP!

The Old Testament

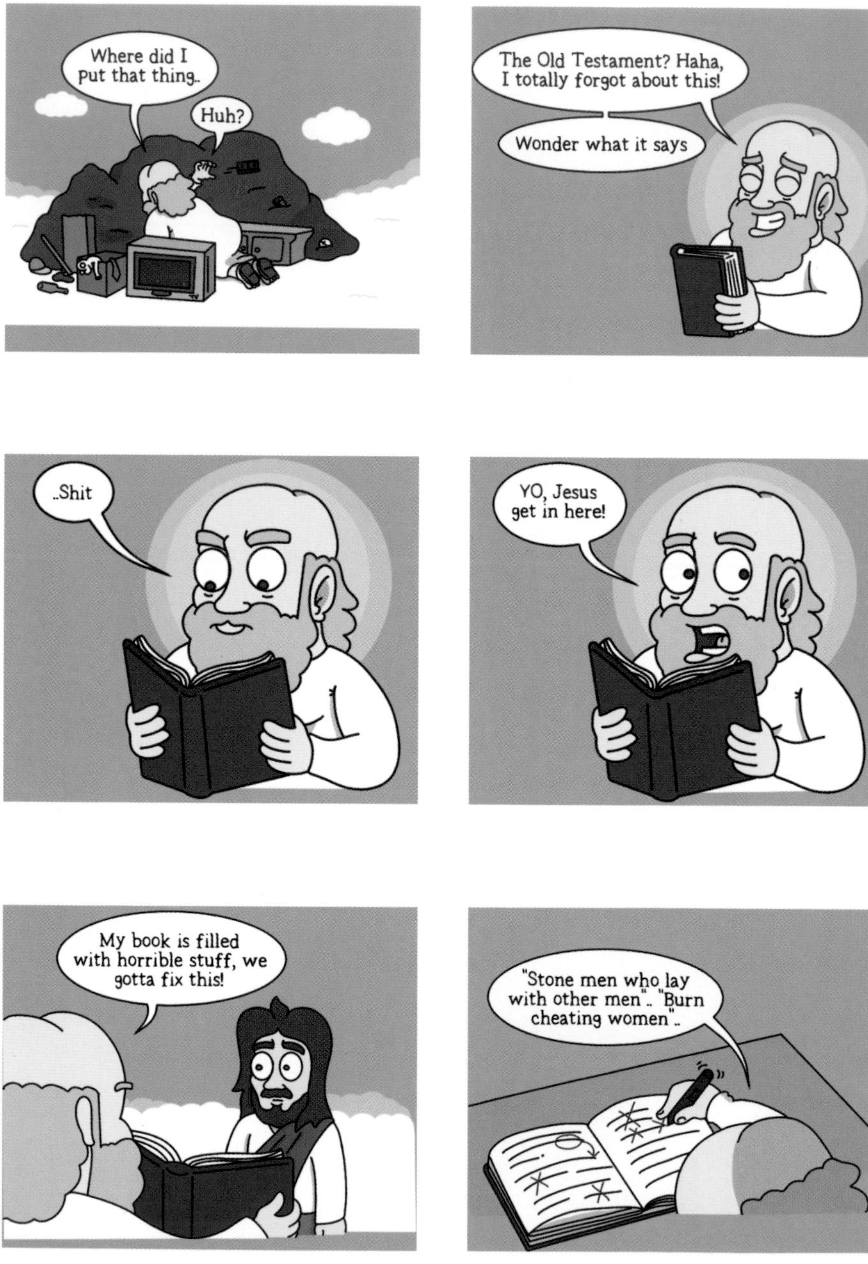
Where did I put that thing..
Huh?
The Old Testament? Haha, I totally forgot about this!
Wonder what it says
..Shit
YO, Jesus get in here!
My book is filled with horrible stuff, we gotta fix this!
"Stone men who lay with other men".. "Burn cheating women"..

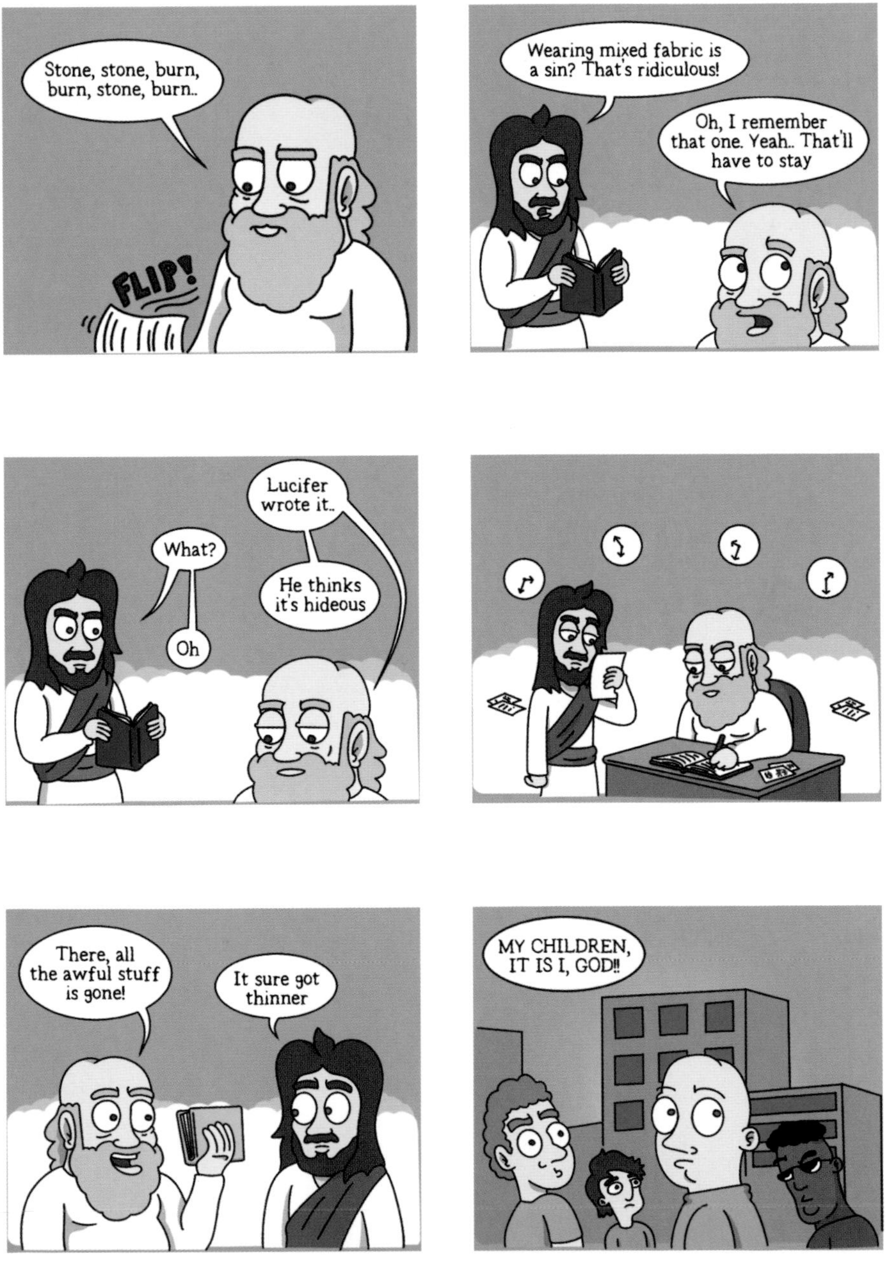
Stone, stone, burn, burn, stone, burn..
FLIP!
Wearing mixed fabric is a sin? That's ridiculous!
Oh, I remember that one. Yeah.. That'll have to stay
Lucifer wrote it..
What?
He thinks it's hideous
Oh
There, all the awful stuff is gone!
It sure got thinner
MY CHILDREN, IT IS I, GOD!!

And I bring to you, the NEW Old Testament!
Who the hell reads anymore?
The Bible is oppressive!
Is that a book?
I'm a Buddhist -and a vegan
>Shit-tier writing
>Calls himself "God"
0/10
And after this, the frogs!
Yessir.
A shit-ton of locusts

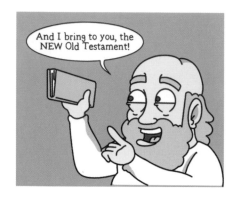

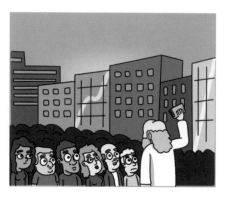

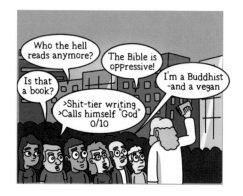

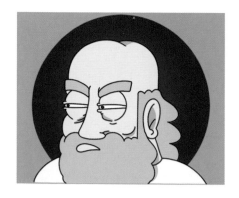

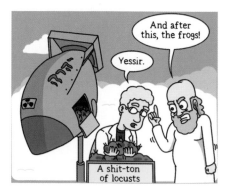

Why He Went to Hell 2

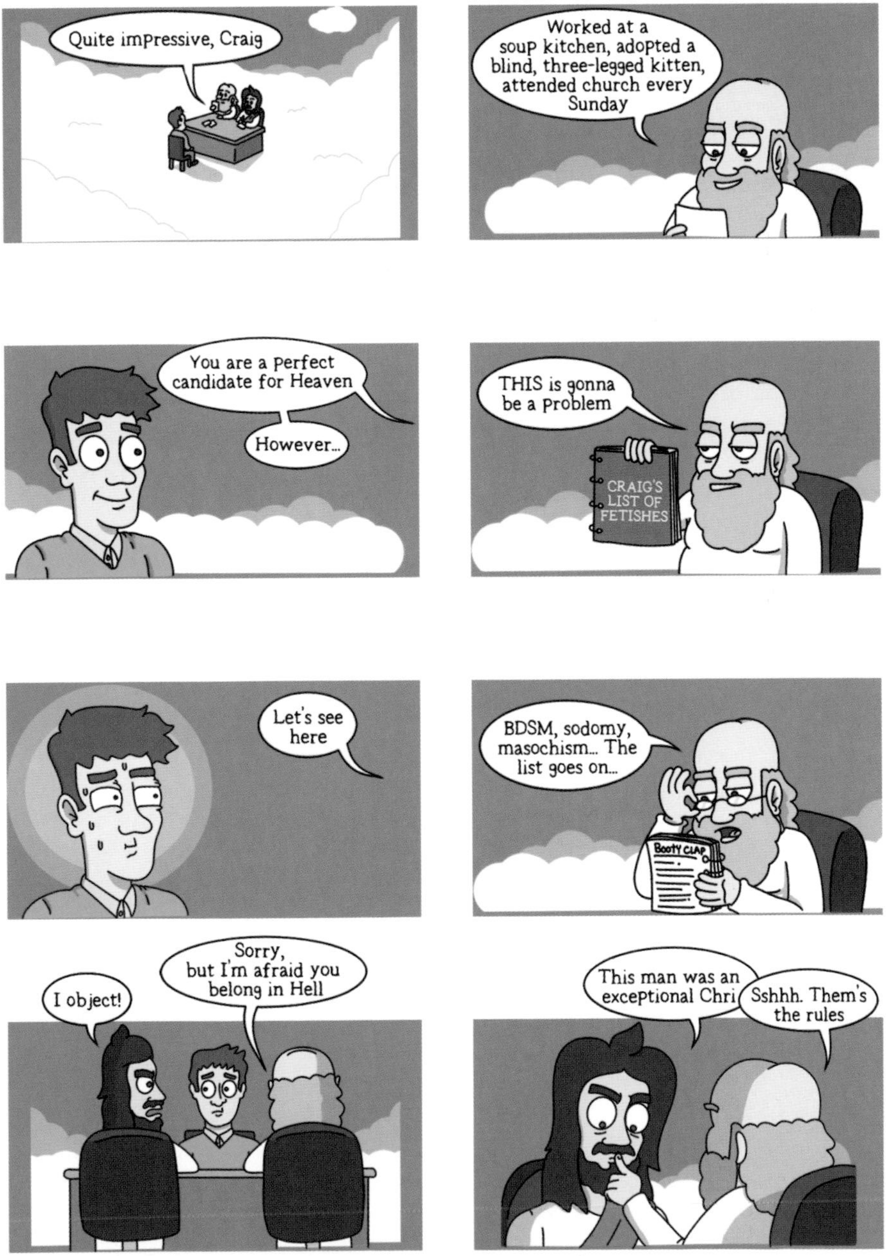
Quite impressive, Craig
Worked at a soup kitchen, adopted a blind, three-legged kitten, attended church every Sunday
You are a perfect candidate for Heaven
However...
THIS is gonna be a problem
CRAIG'S LIST OF FETISHES
Let's see here
BDSM, sodomy, masochism... The list goes on...
BOOTY CLAP
I object!
Sorry, but I'm afraid you belong in Hell
This man was an exceptional Chri
Sshhh. Them's the rules

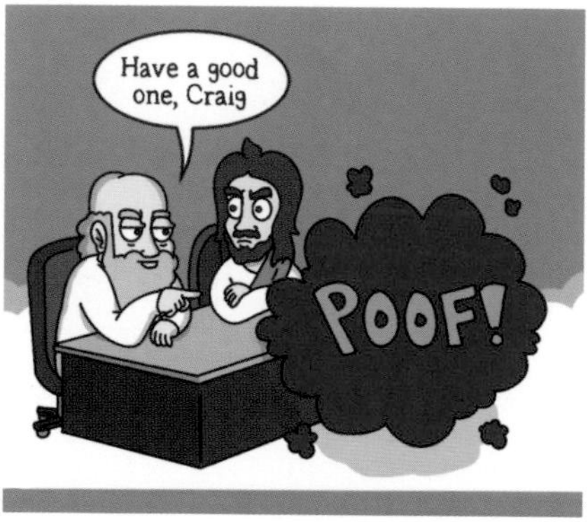
Have a good one, Craig
POOF!

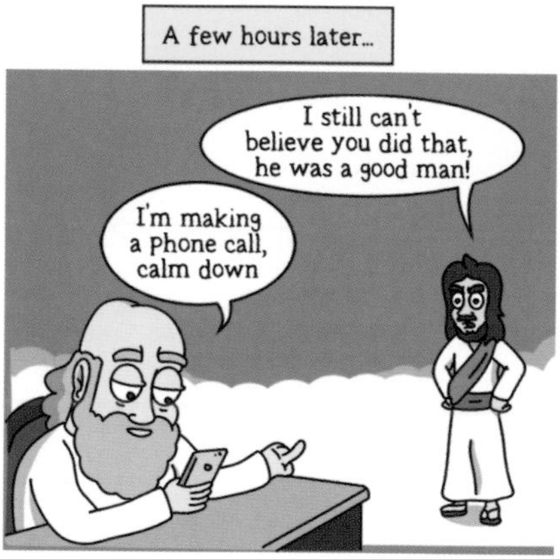
A few hours later...
I still can't believe you did that, he was a good man!
I'm making a phone call, calm down

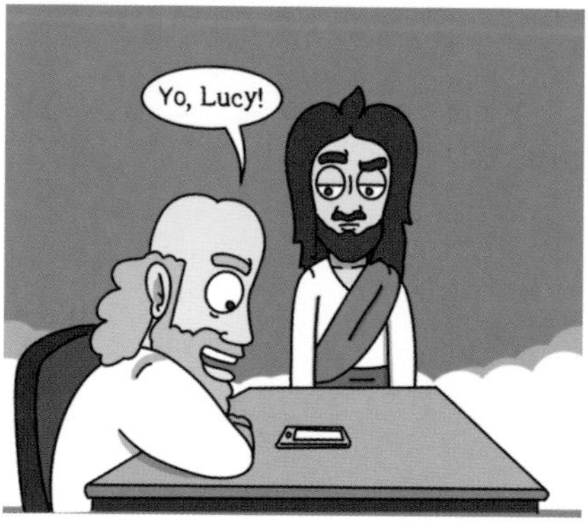
Yo, Lucy!

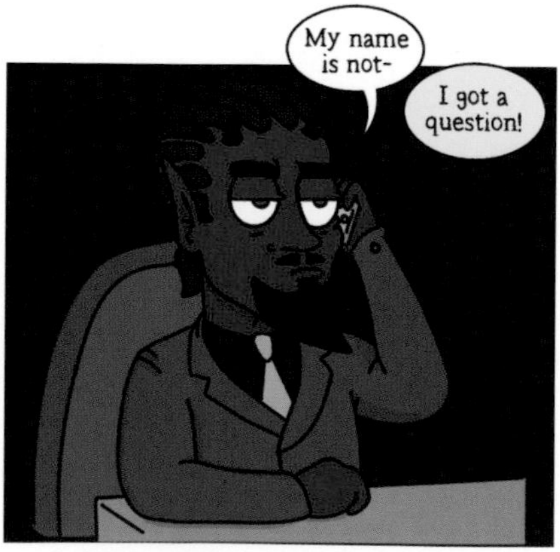
My name is not-
I got a question!

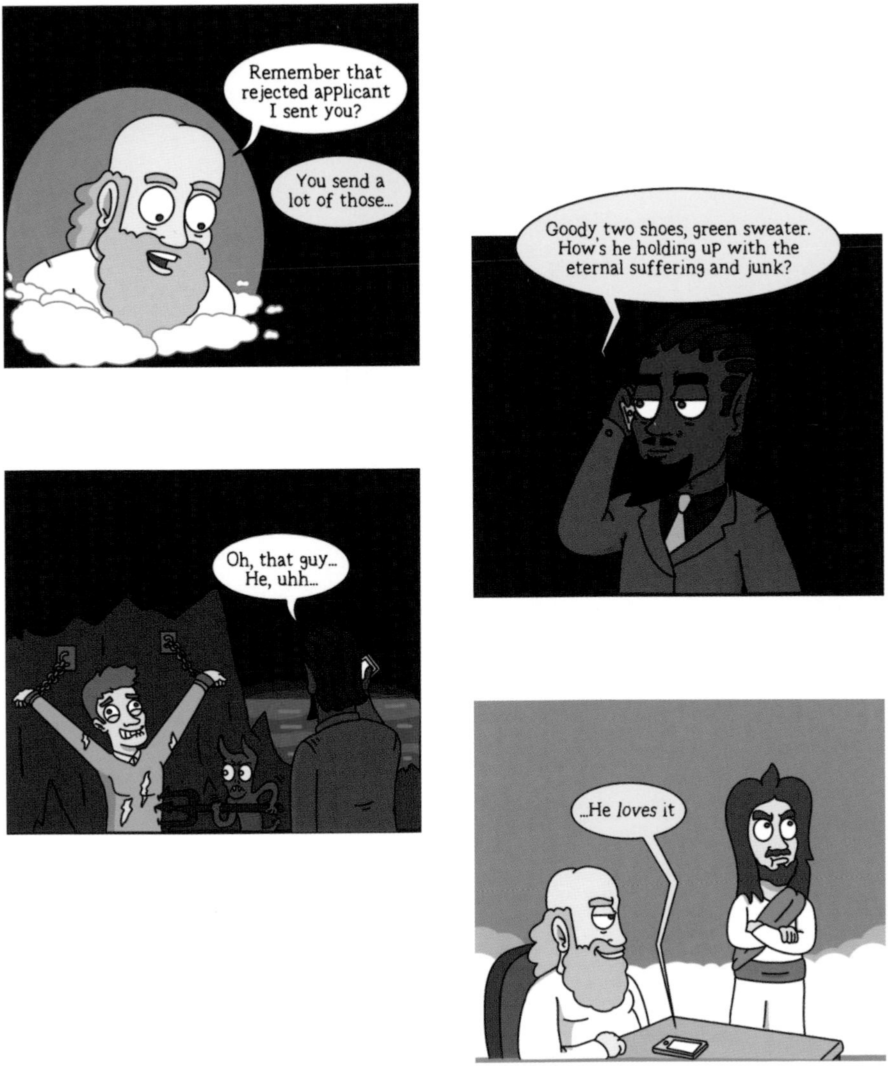

Remember that rejected applicant I sent you?
You send a lot of those...
Goody, two shoes, green sweater. How's he holding up with the eternal suffering and junk?
Oh, that guy... He, uhh...
...He *loves* it

Life Hack

Sir?
Mhm?
What's this pillow doing on the floor?
Oh that! I read an interesting life hack the other day
If you have something important to do in the morning, put an object in an unusual place.

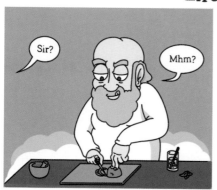

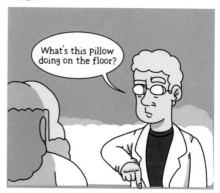

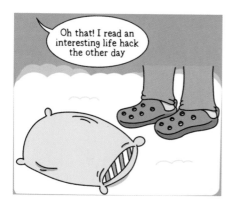

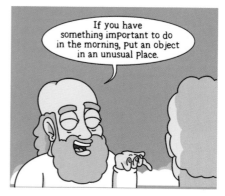

When you wake up, and you see the object, you'll instantly be reminded o-
ABRAHAM HOLD UP!!

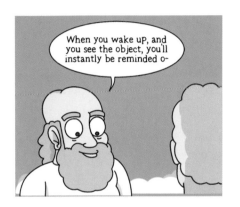

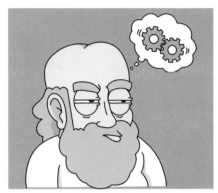

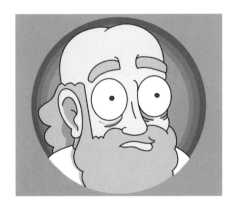

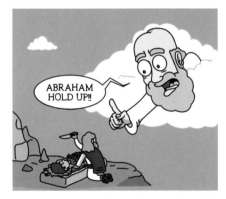

Talent

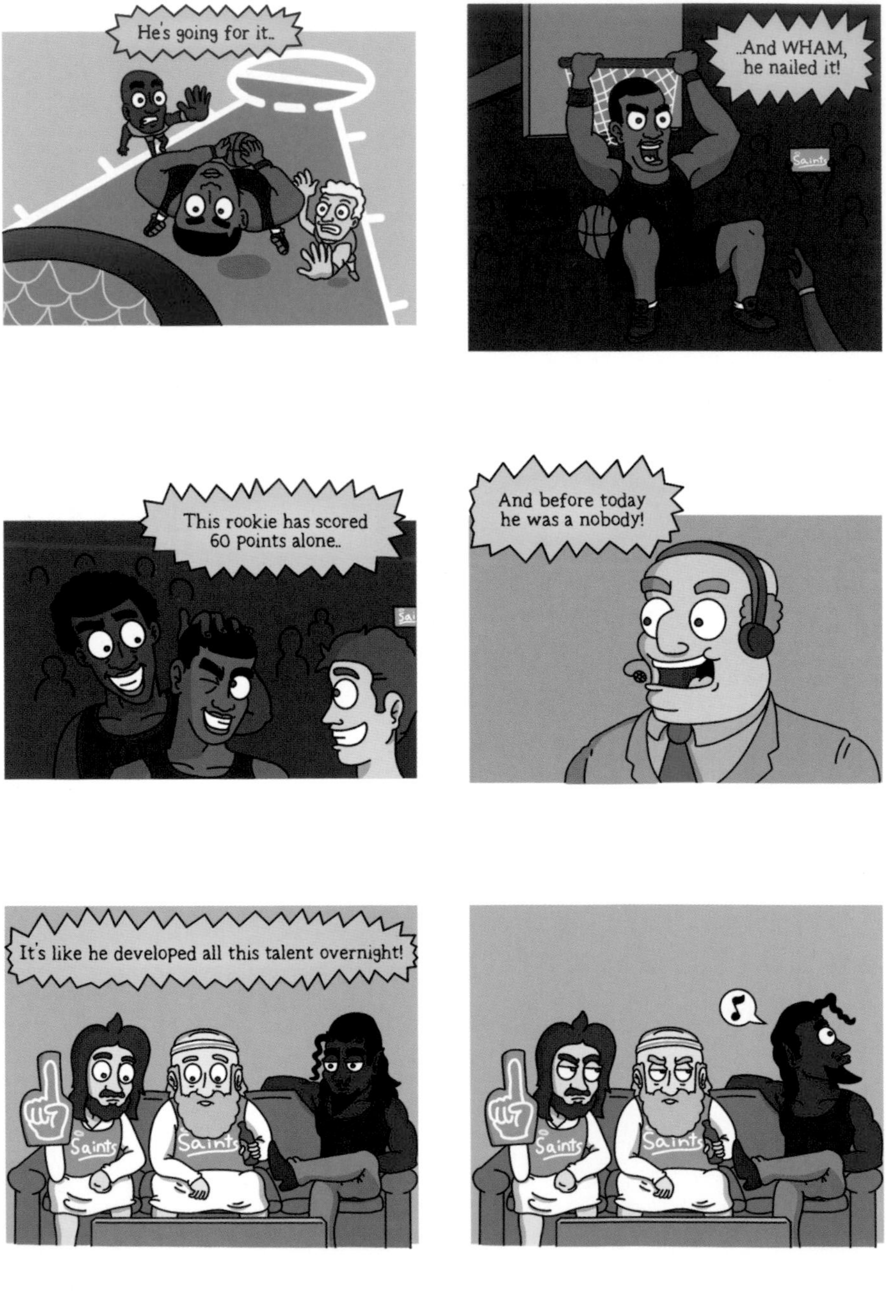
He's going for it..
..And WHAM, he nailed it!
Saints
This rookie has scored 60 points alone..
And before today he was a nobody!
It's like he developed all this talent overnight!
Saints
Saints
Saints
Saints

AA Meeting

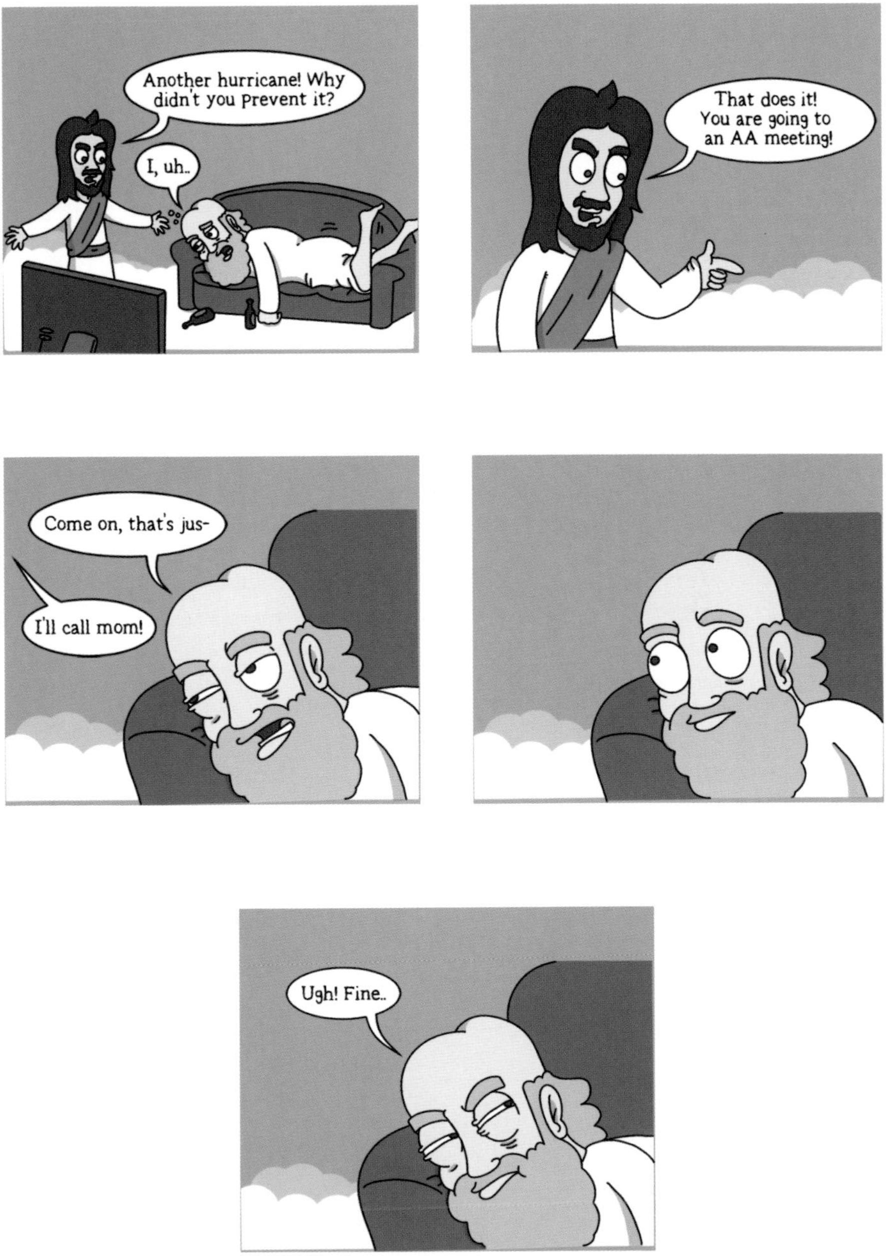
Another hurricane! Why didn't you prevent it?
I, uh..
That does it! You are going to an AA meeting!
Come on, that's jus-
I'll call mom!
Ugh! Fine..

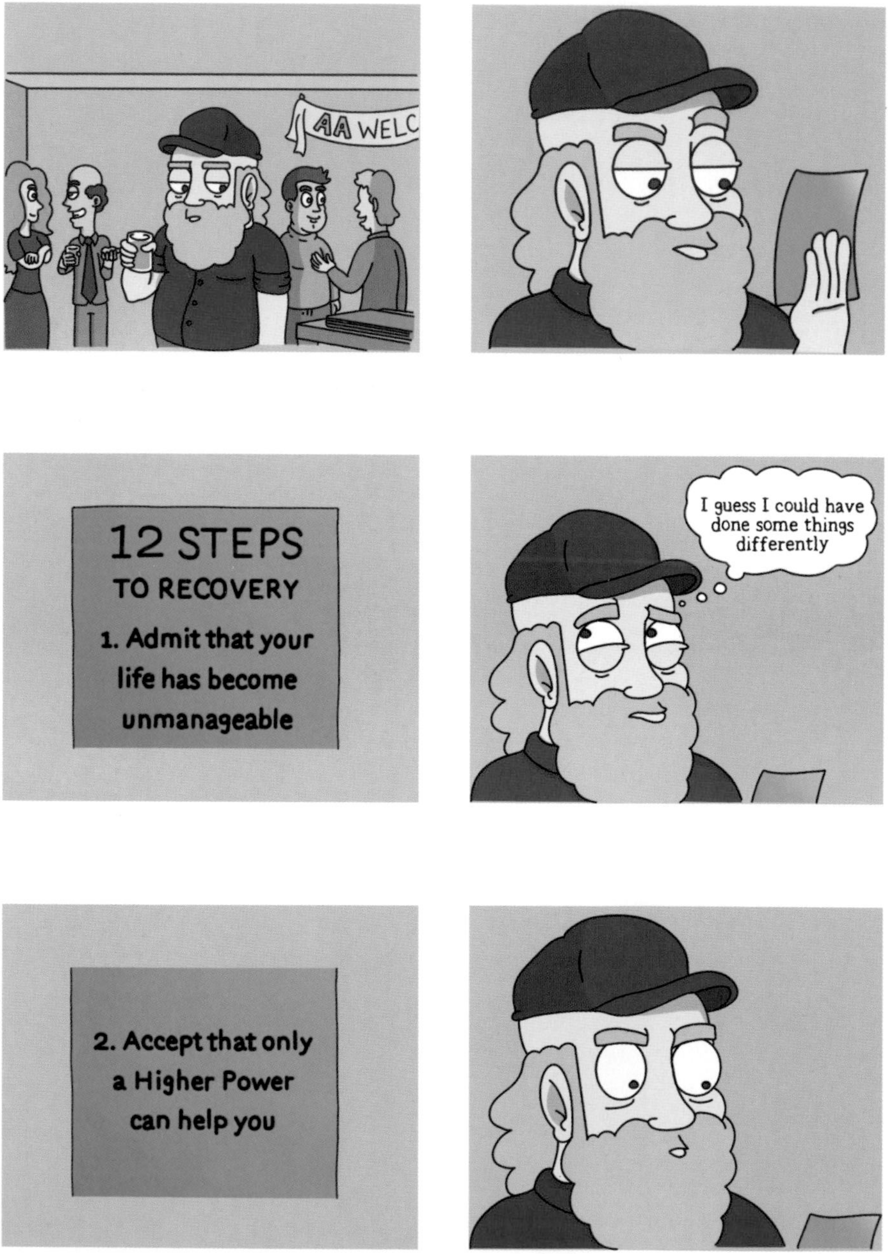
AA WELC
12 STEPS
TO RECOVERY
1. Admit that your life has become unmanageable
I guess I could have done some things differently
2. Accept that only a Higher Power can help you

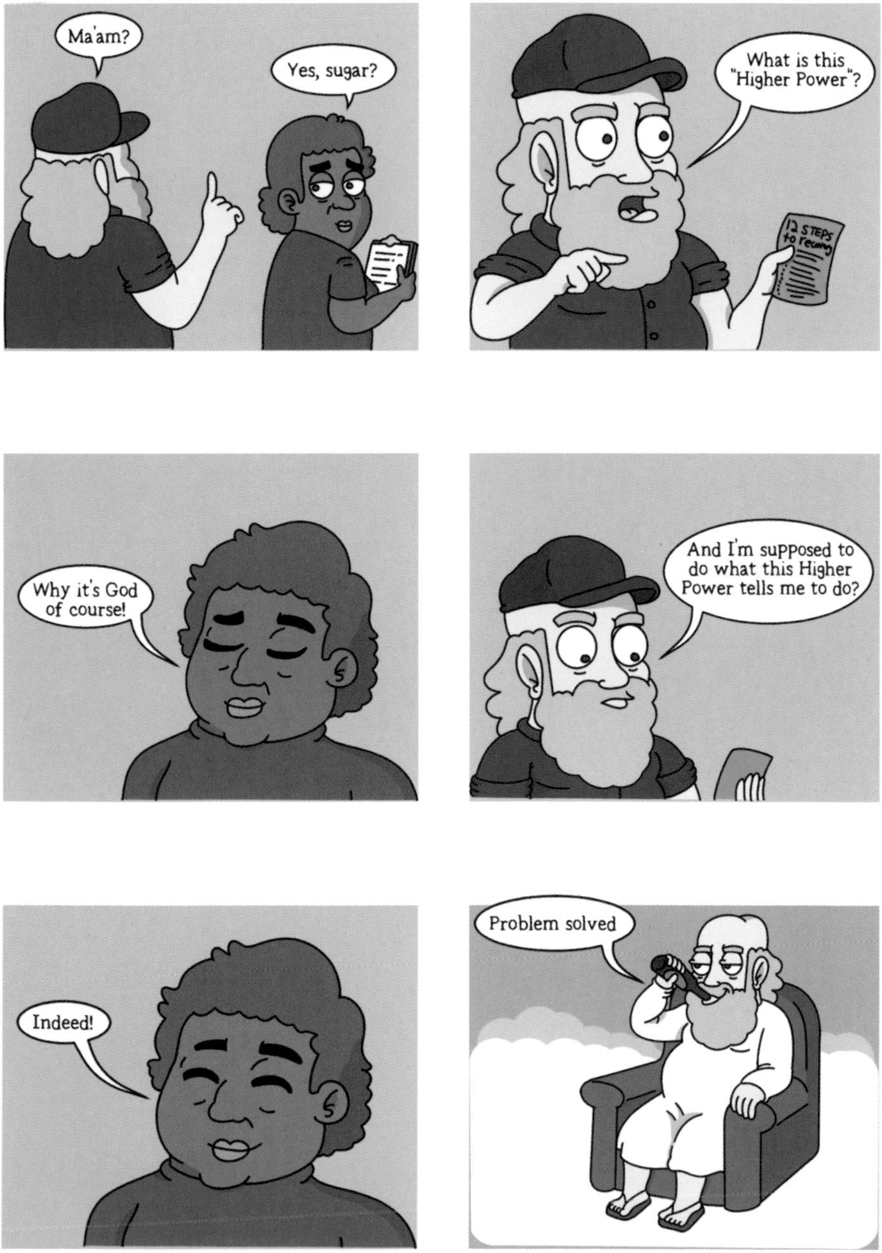
Ma'am?
Yes, sugar?
What is this "Higher Power"?
12 STEPS
Why it's God of course!
And I'm supposed to do what this Higher Power tells me to do?
Indeed!
Problem solved

Why He Went to Heaven

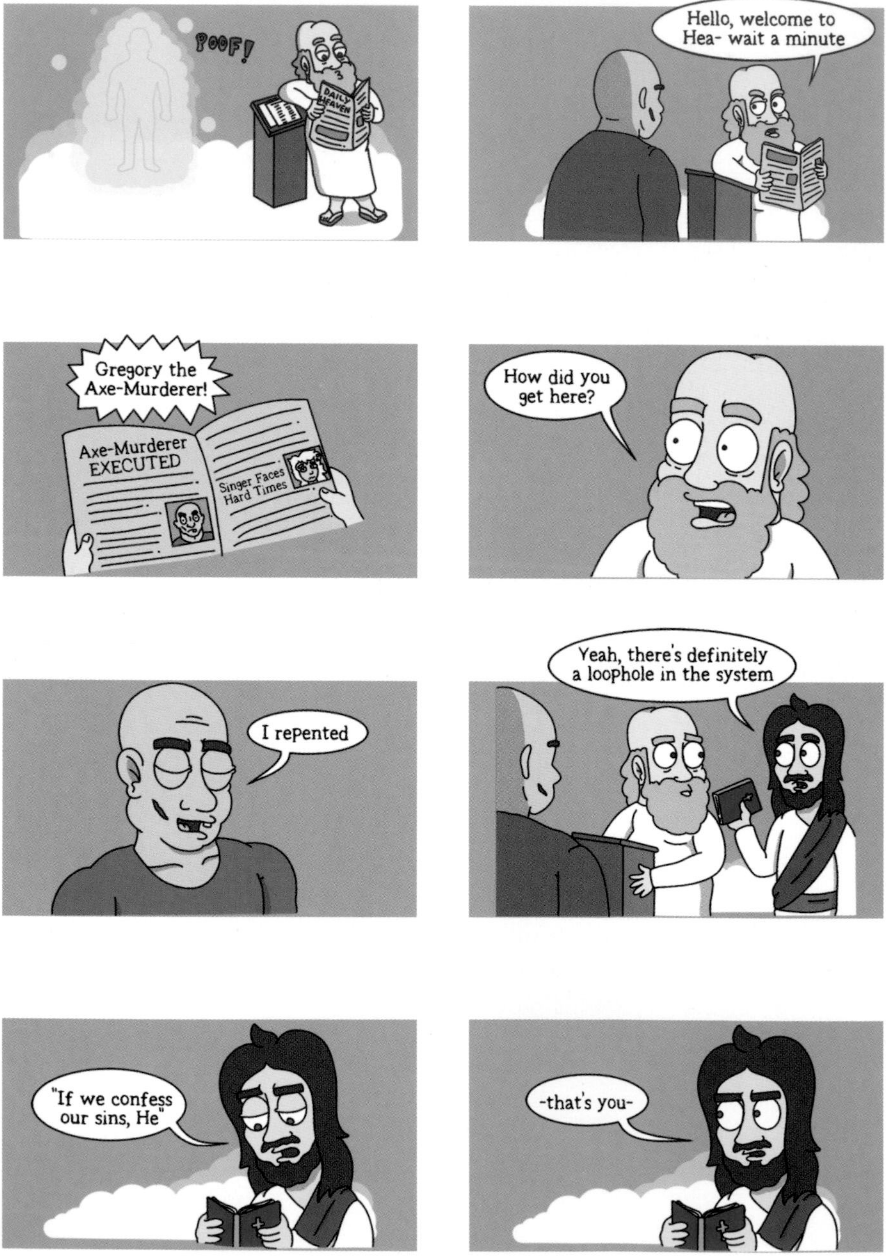
POOF!
DAILY HEAVEN
Hello, welcome to Hea- wait a minute
Gregory the Axe-Murderer!
Axe-Murderer EXECUTED
Singer Faces Hard Times
How did you get here?
I repented
Yeah, there's definitely a loophole in the system
"If we confess our sins, He"
-that's you-

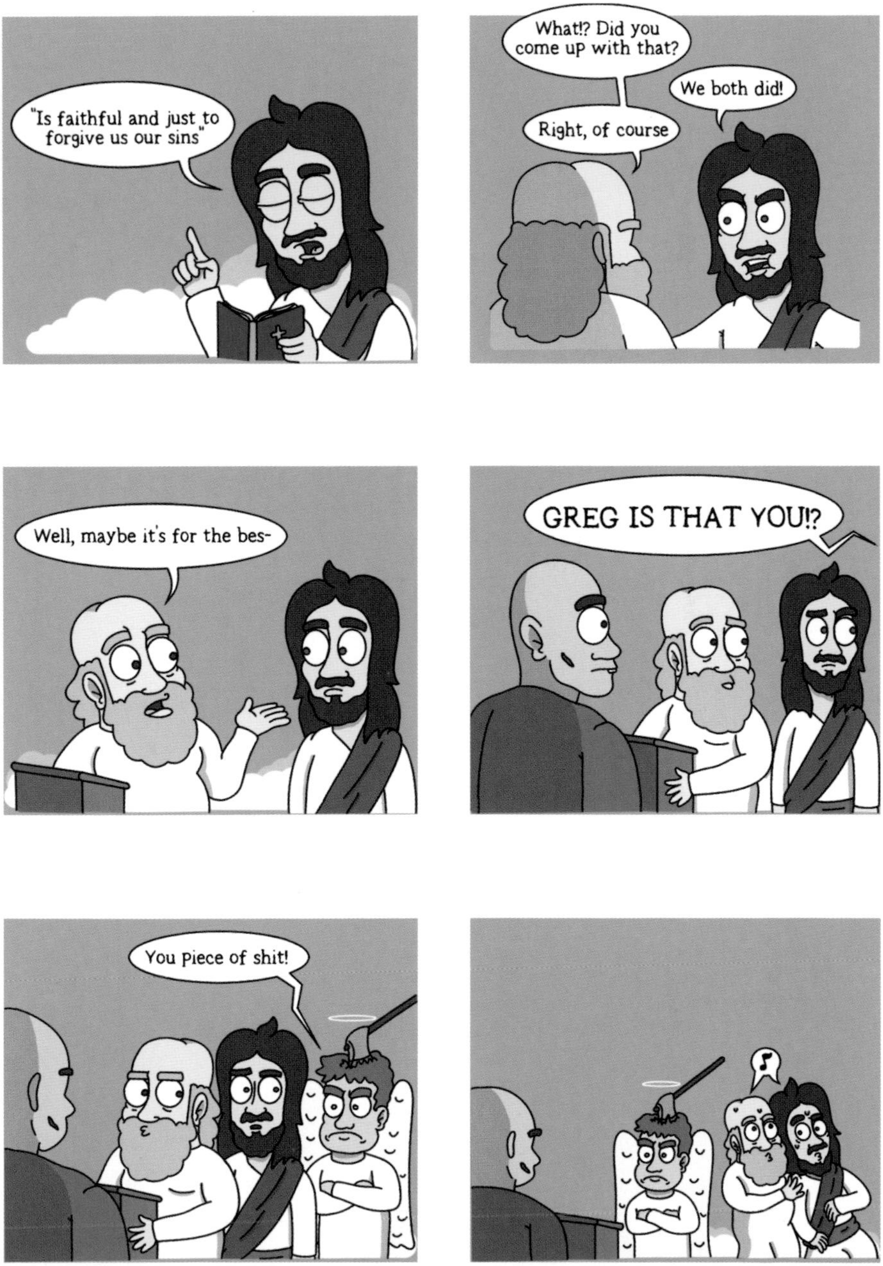
"Is faithful and just to forgive us our sins"
What!? Did you come up with that?
Right, of course
We both did!
Well, maybe it's for the bes-
GREG IS THAT YOU!?
You piece of shit!

Miracle

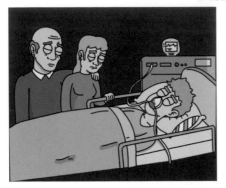 

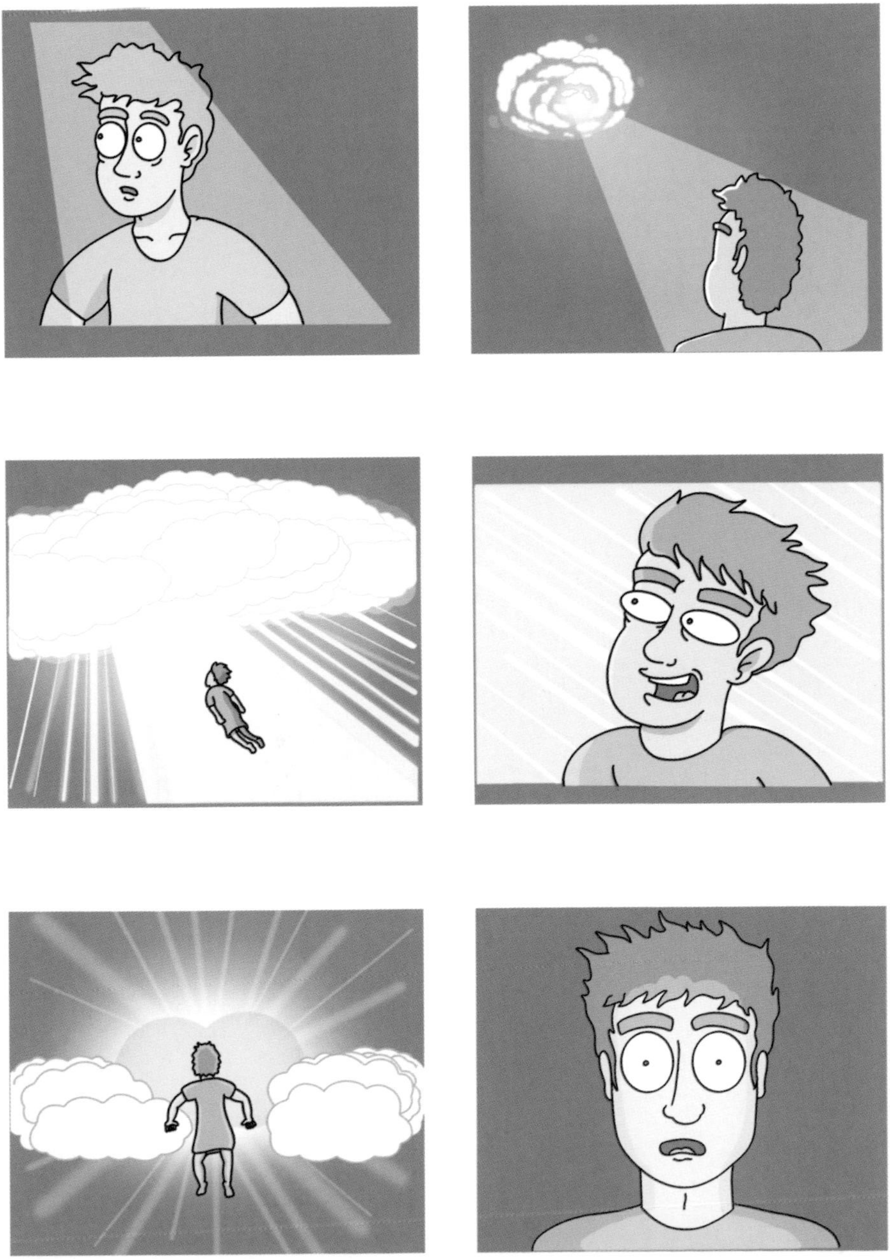

It's a miracle!
He was too young to die, man

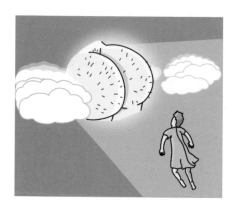

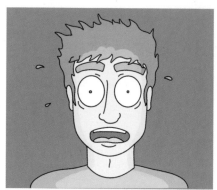

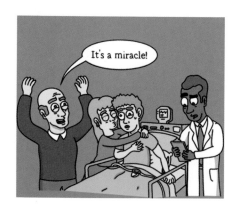

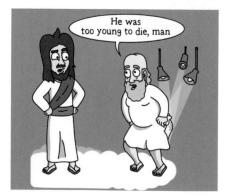

Noah's Ark

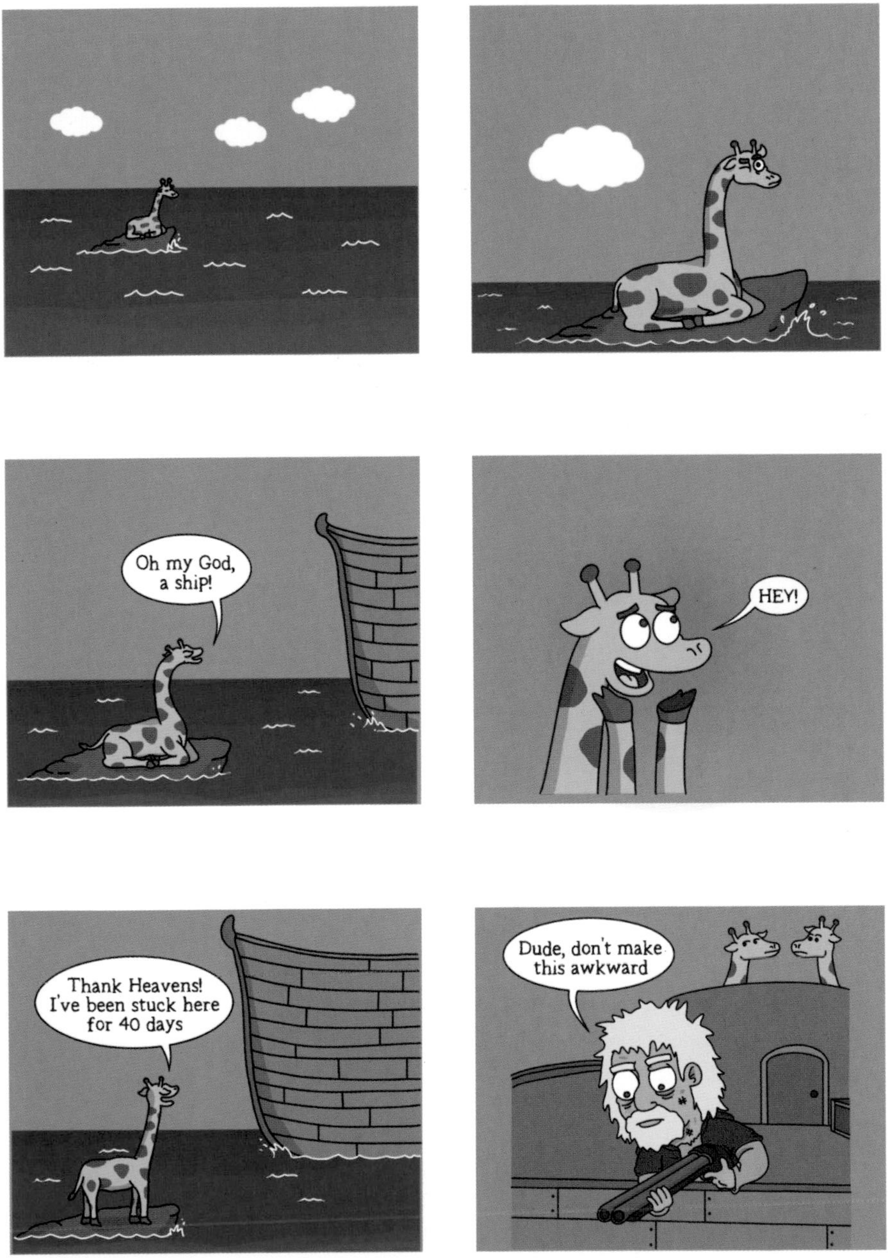
Oh my God,
a ship!
HEY!
Thank Heavens!
I've been stuck here
for 40 days
Dude, don't make
this awkward

The Ascent of Man

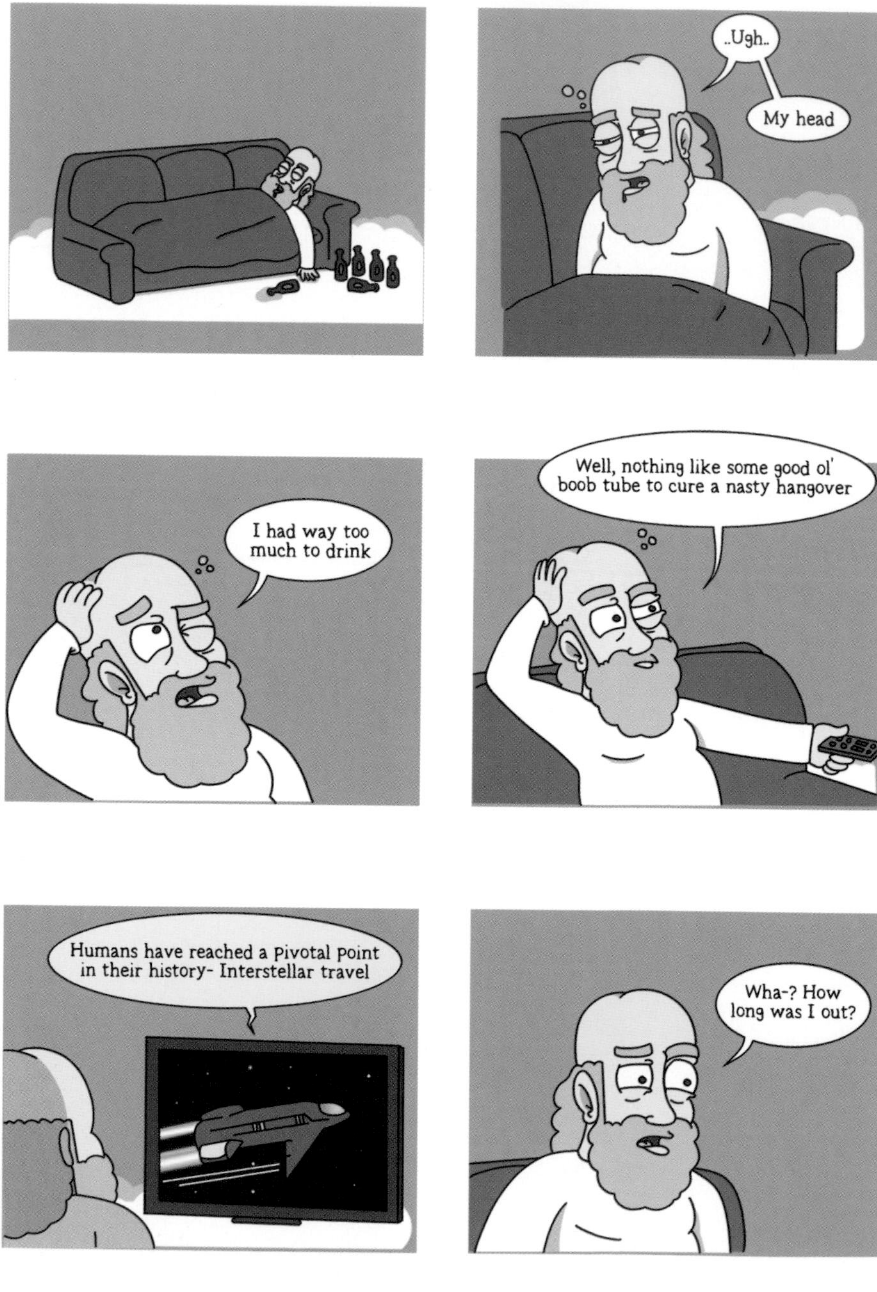
..Ugh..
My head
I had way too much to drink
Well, nothing like some good ol' boob tube to cure a nasty hangover
Humans have reached a pivotal point in their history- Interstellar travel
Wha-? How long was I out?

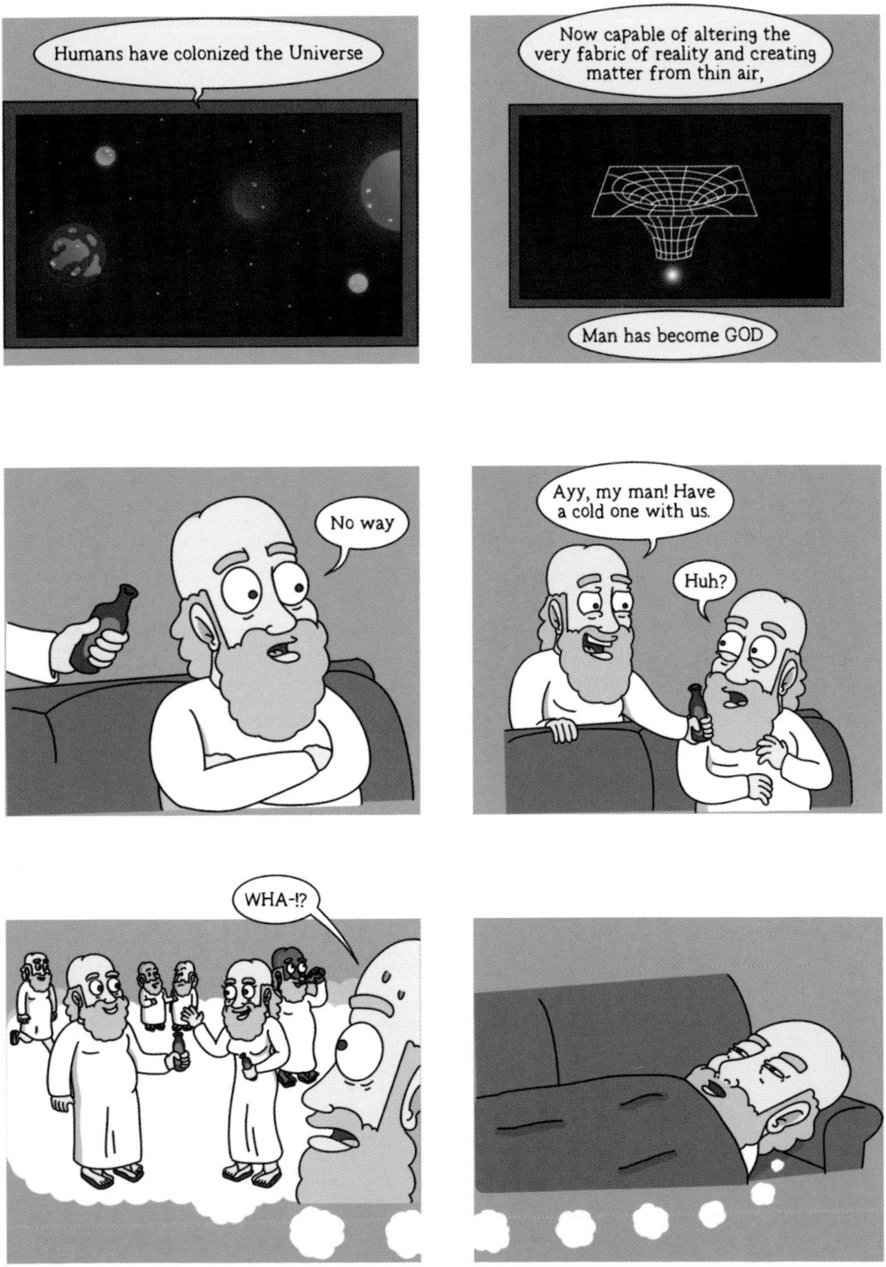
Humans have colonized the Universe
Now capable of altering the very fabric of reality and creating matter from thin air,
Man has become GOD
No way
Ayy, my man! Have a cold one with us.
Huh?
WHA-!?

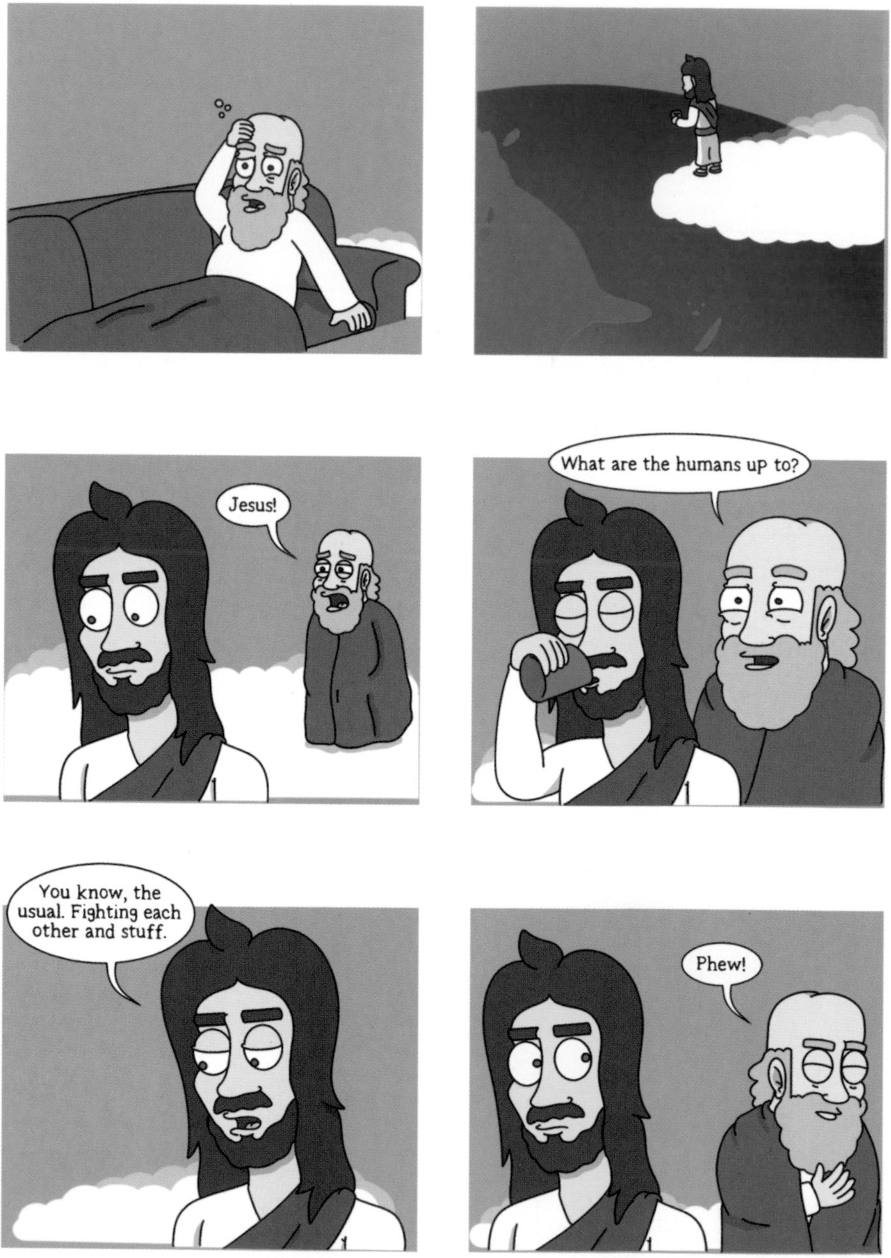
Jesus!
What are the humans up to?
You know, the usual. Fighting each other and stuff.
Phew!

God Wills It!

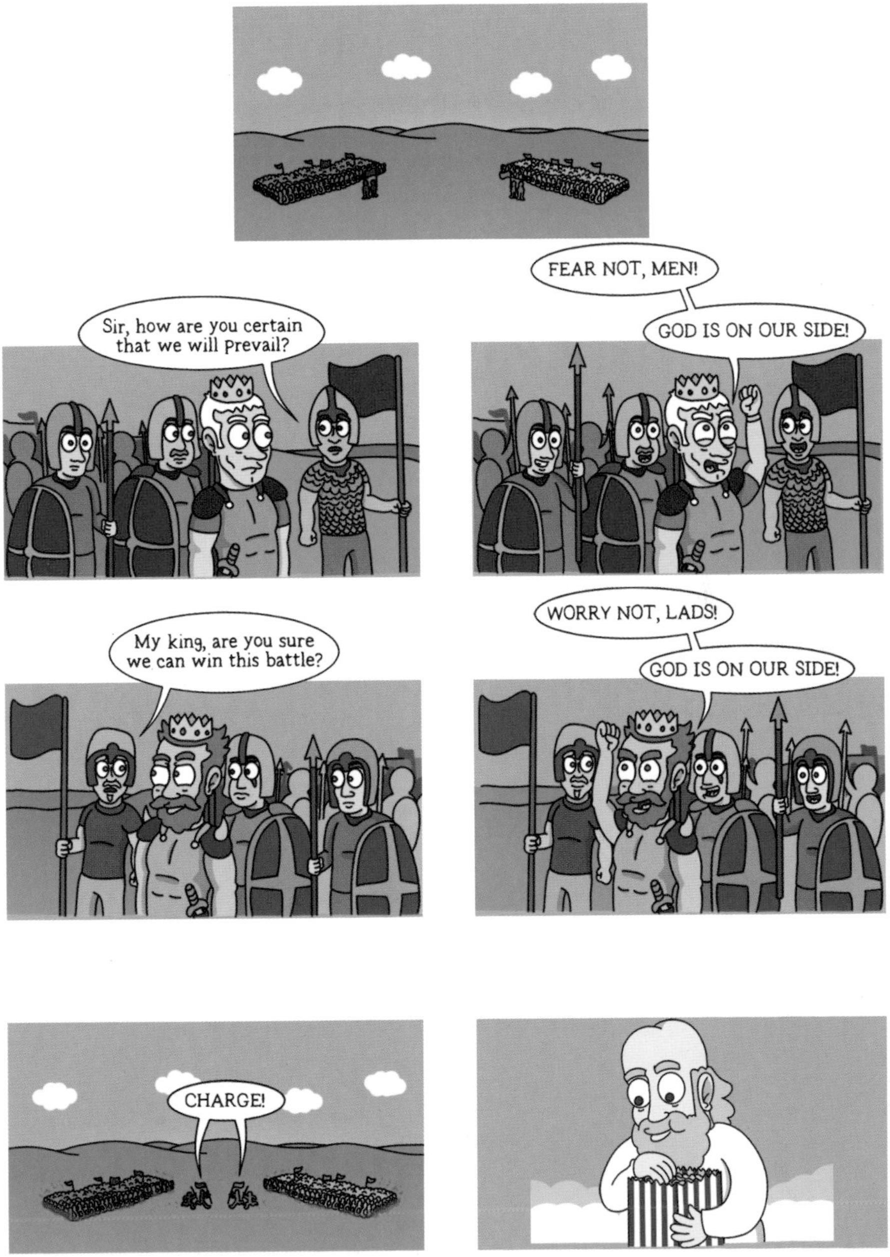
Sir, how are you certain that we will prevail?
FEAR NOT, MEN!
GOD IS ON OUR SIDE!
My king, are you sure we can win this battle?
WORRY NOT, LADS!
GOD IS ON OUR SIDE!
CHARGE!

Matthew 5:5

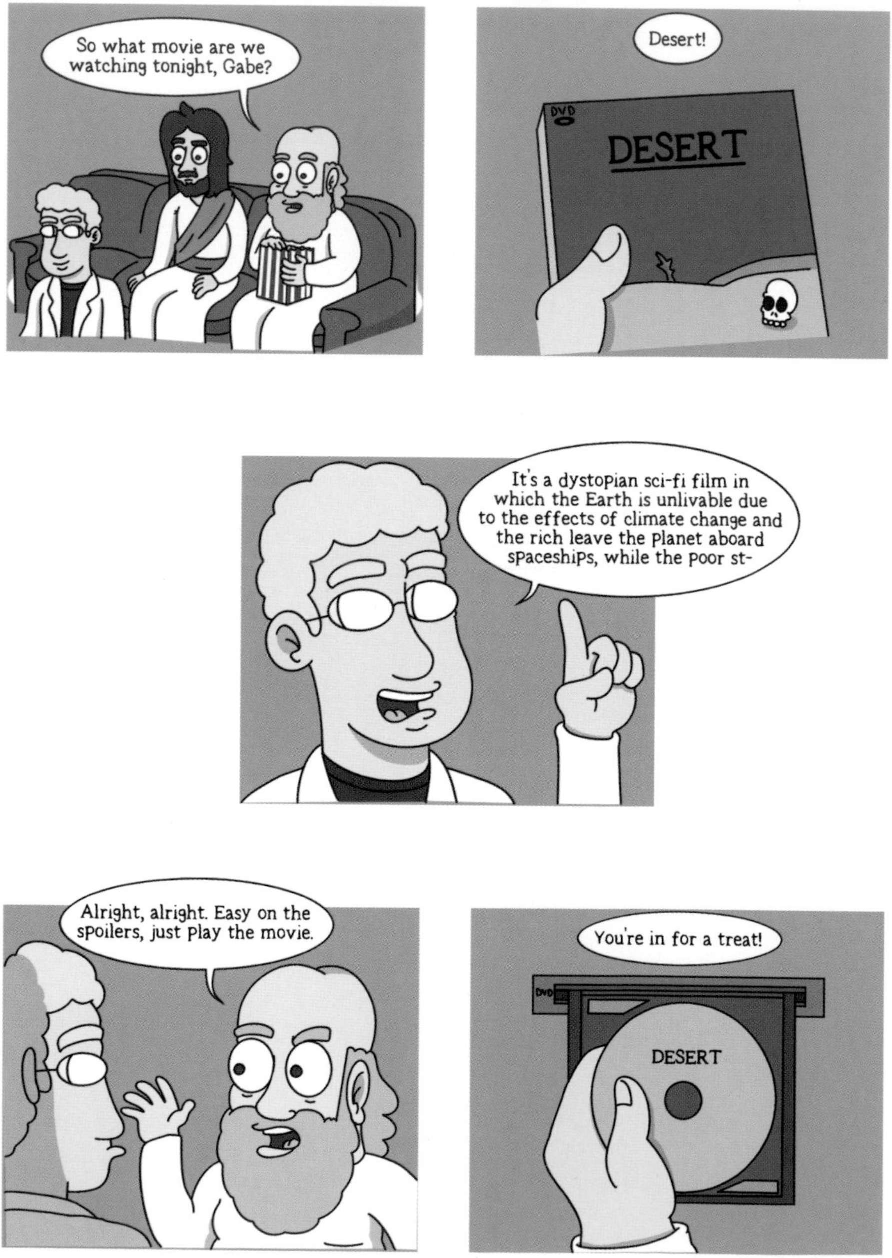

So what movie are we watching tonight, Gabe?
Desert!
DVD
DESERT
It's a dystopian sci-fi film in which the Earth is unlivable due to the effects of climate change and the rich leave the planet aboard spaceships, while the poor st-
Alright, alright. Easy on the spoilers, just play the movie.
You're in for a treat!
DVD
DESERT

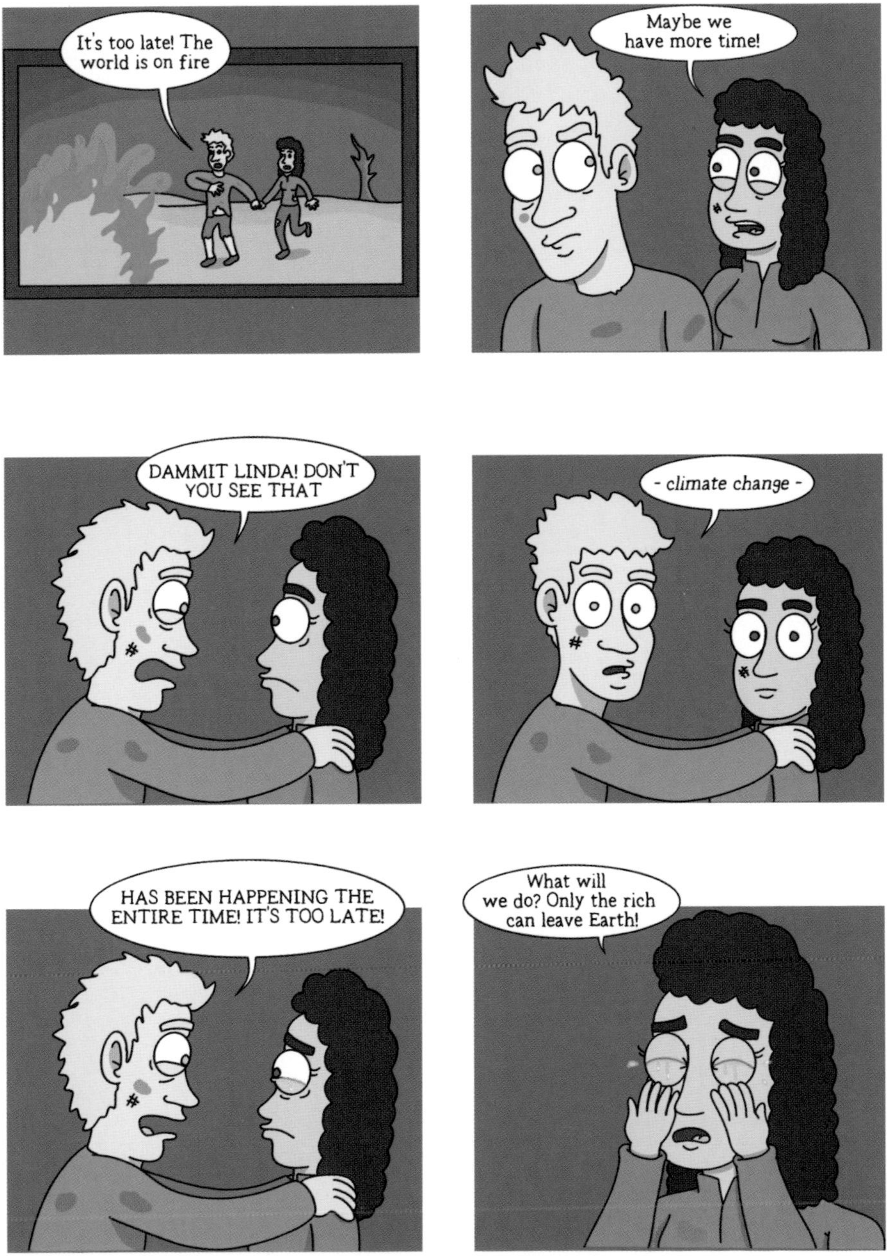
It's too late! The world is on fire
Maybe we have more time!
DAMMIT LINDA! DON'T YOU SEE THAT
- climate change -
HAS BEEN HAPPENING THE ENTIRE TIME! IT'S TOO LATE!
What will we do? Only the rich can leave Earth!

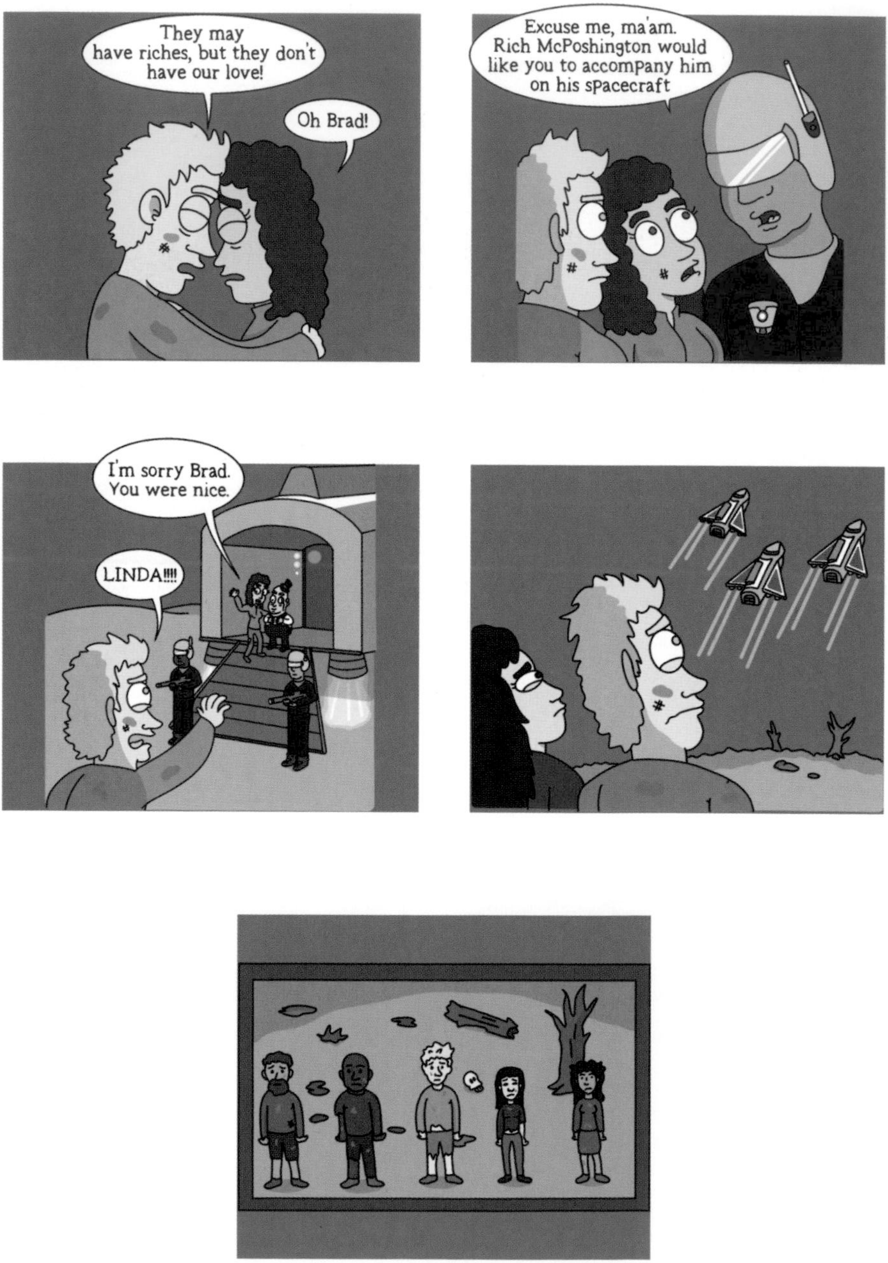
They may have riches, but they don't have our love!
Oh Brad!
Excuse me, ma'am. Rich McPoshington would like you to accompany him on his spacecraft
I'm sorry Brad. You were nice.
LINDA!!!!

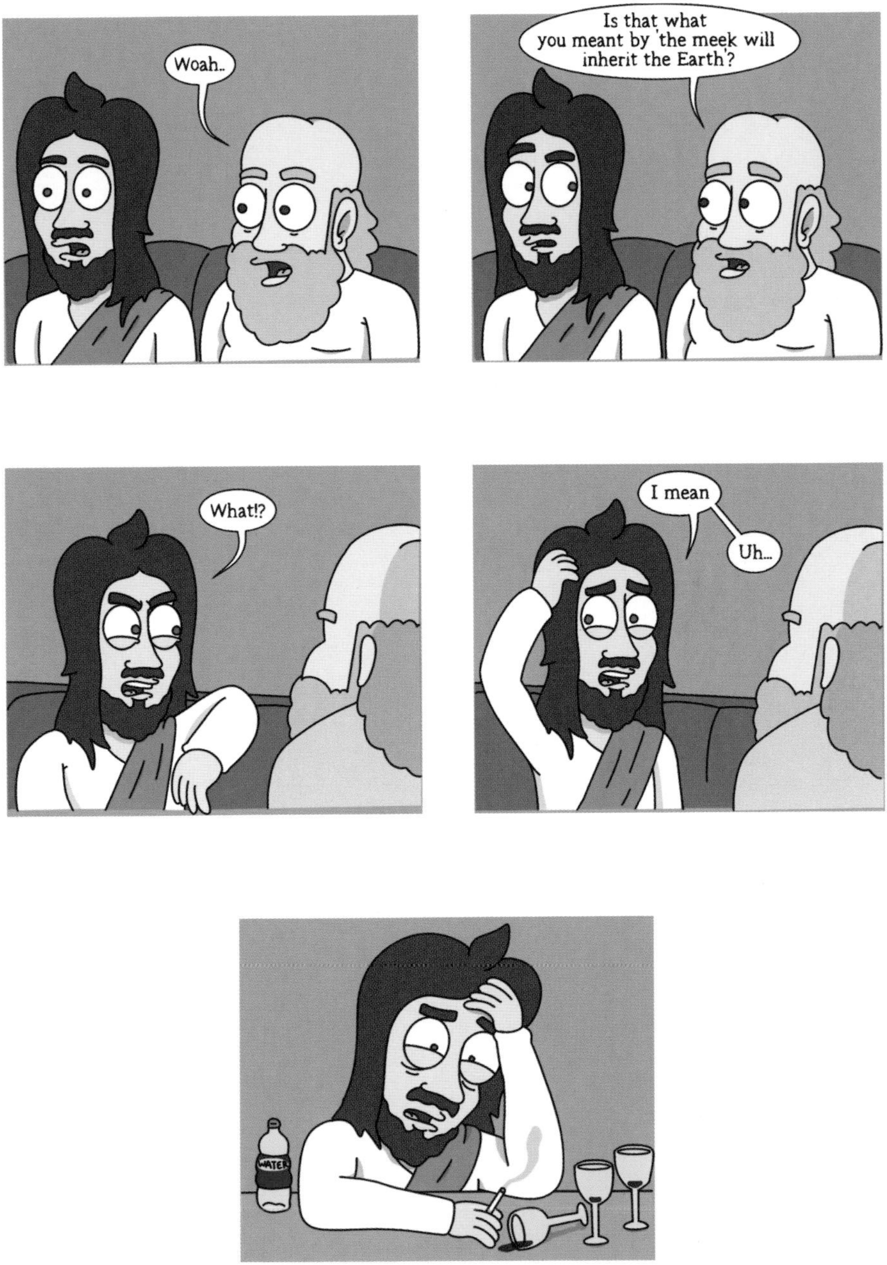
Woah..
Is that what you meant by 'the meek will inherit the Earth'?
What!?
I mean
Uh...
WATER

Purpose

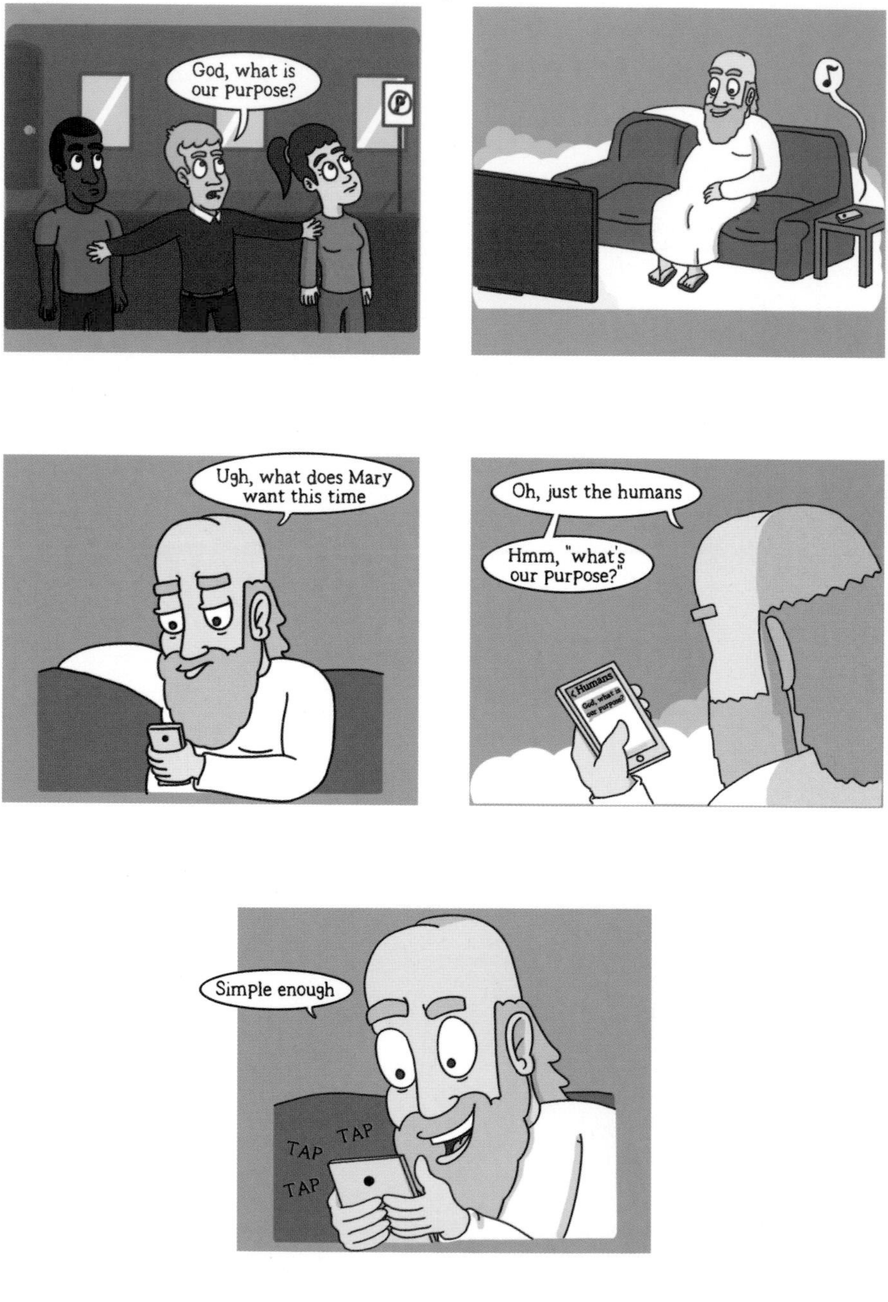
God, what is our purpose?
Ugh, what does Mary want this time
Oh, just the humans
Hmm, "what's our purpose?"
Humans
Simple enough
TAP
TAP
TAP

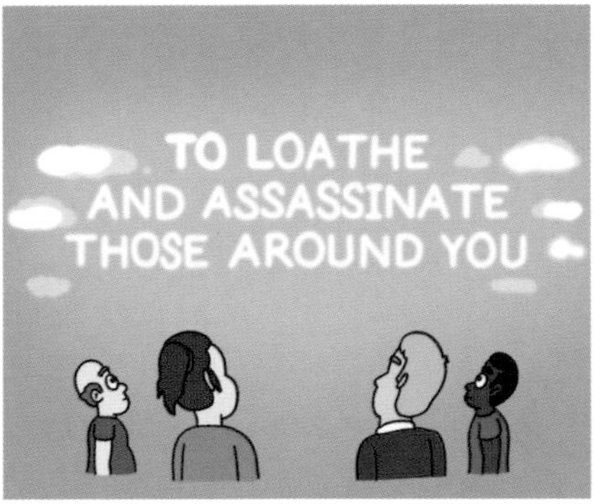
TO LOATHE
AND ASSASSINATE
THOSE AROUND YOU

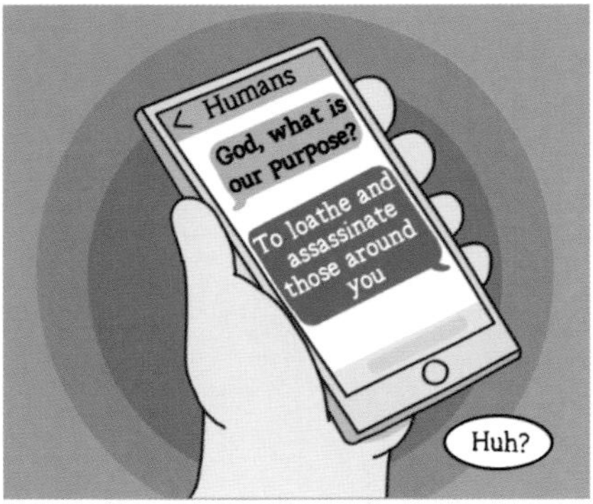
Humans
God, what is our purpose?
To loathe and assassinate those around you
Huh?

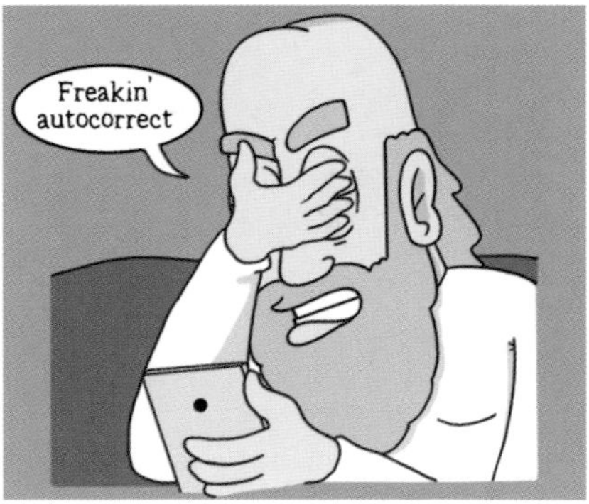
Freakin' autocorrect

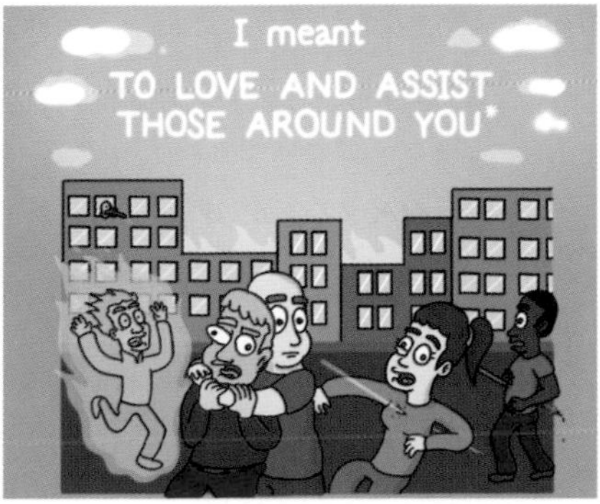
I meant
TO LOVE AND ASSIST
THOSE AROUND YOU*

WWJD

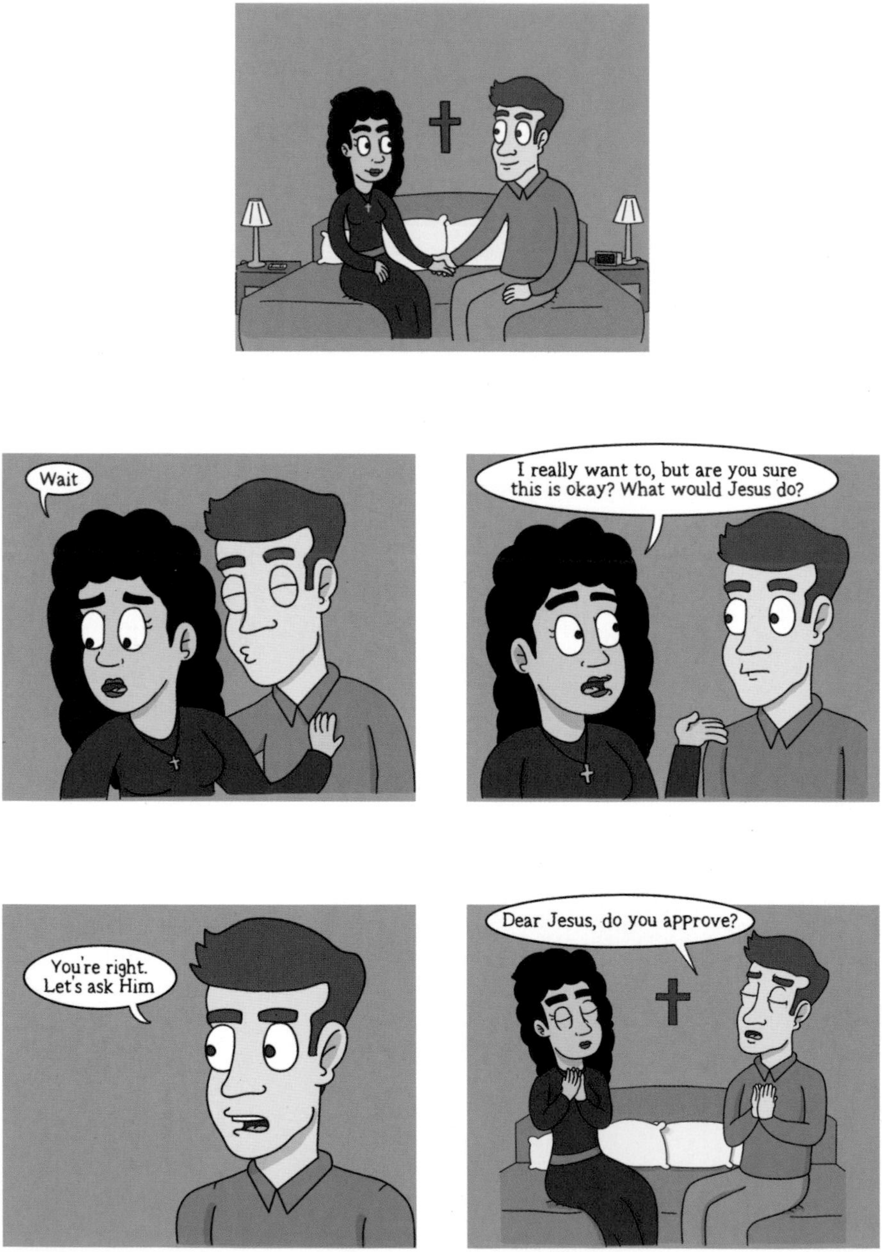
Wait
I really want to, but are you sure this is okay? What would Jesus do?
You're right. Let's ask Him
Dear Jesus, do you approve?

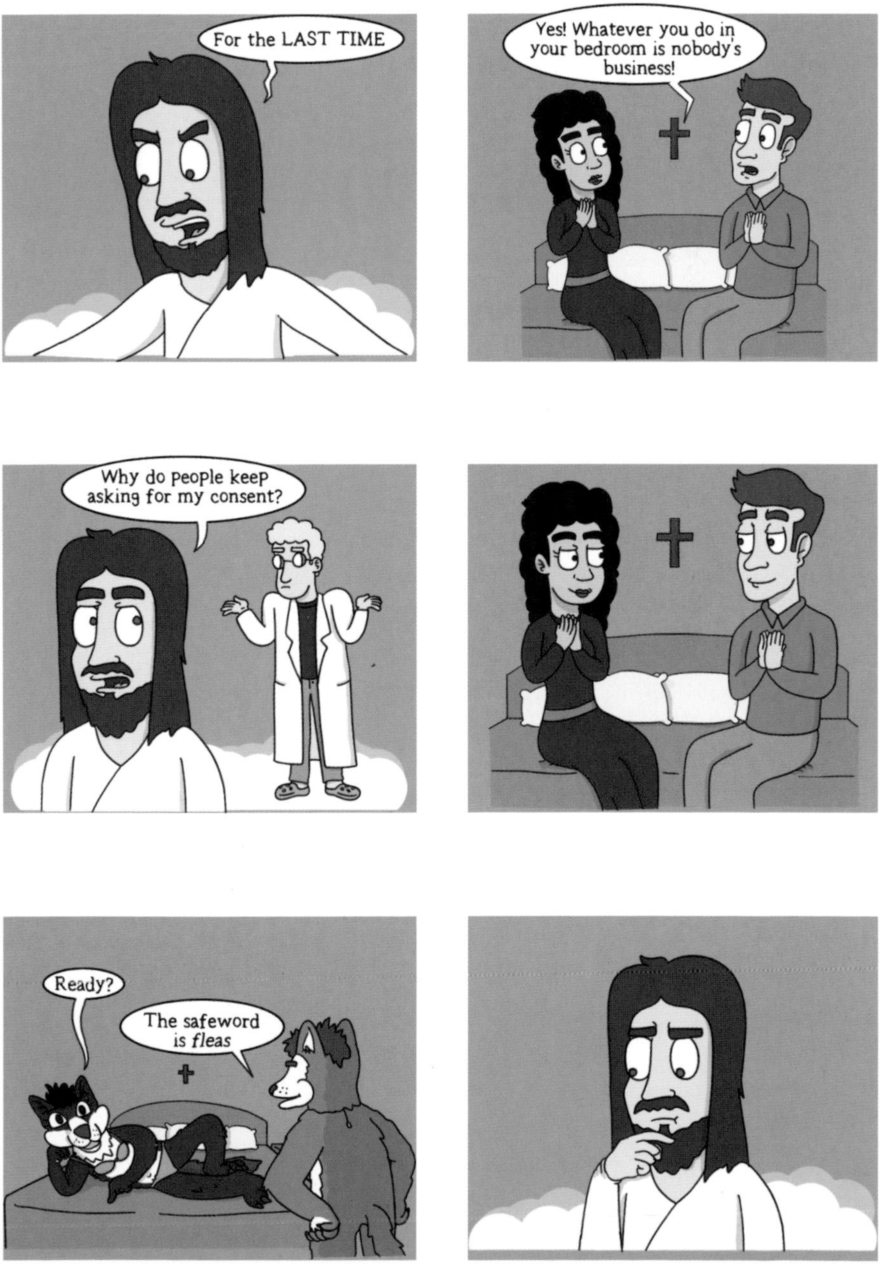
For the LAST TIME
Yes! Whatever you do in your bedroom is nobody's business!
Why do people keep asking for my consent?
Ready?
The safeword is *fleas*

Confession

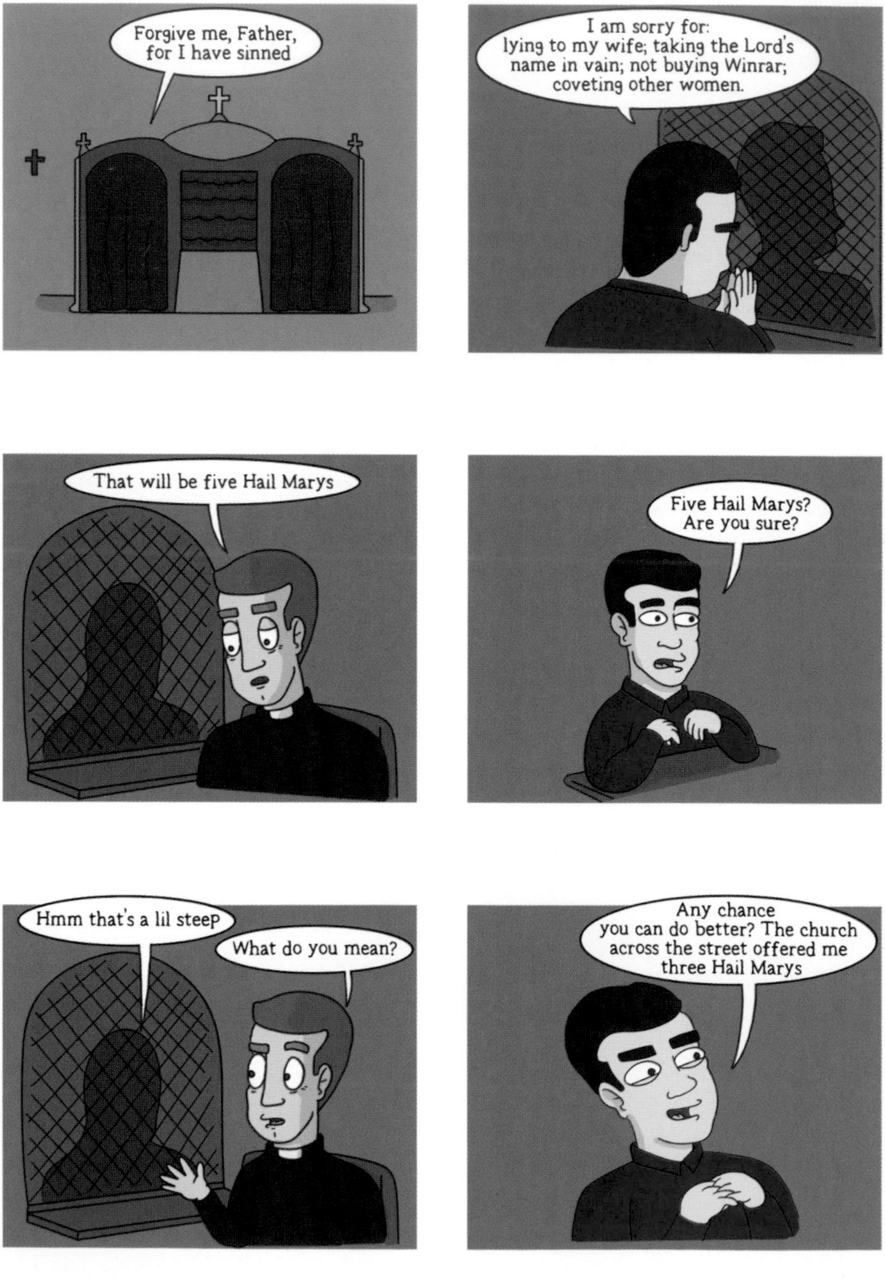
Forgive me, Father, for I have sinned
I am sorry for: lying to my wife; taking the Lord's name in vain; not buying Winrar; coveting other women.
That will be five Hail Marys
Five Hail Marys? Are you sure?
Hmm that's a lil steep
What do you mean?
Any chance you can do better? The church across the street offered me three Hail Marys

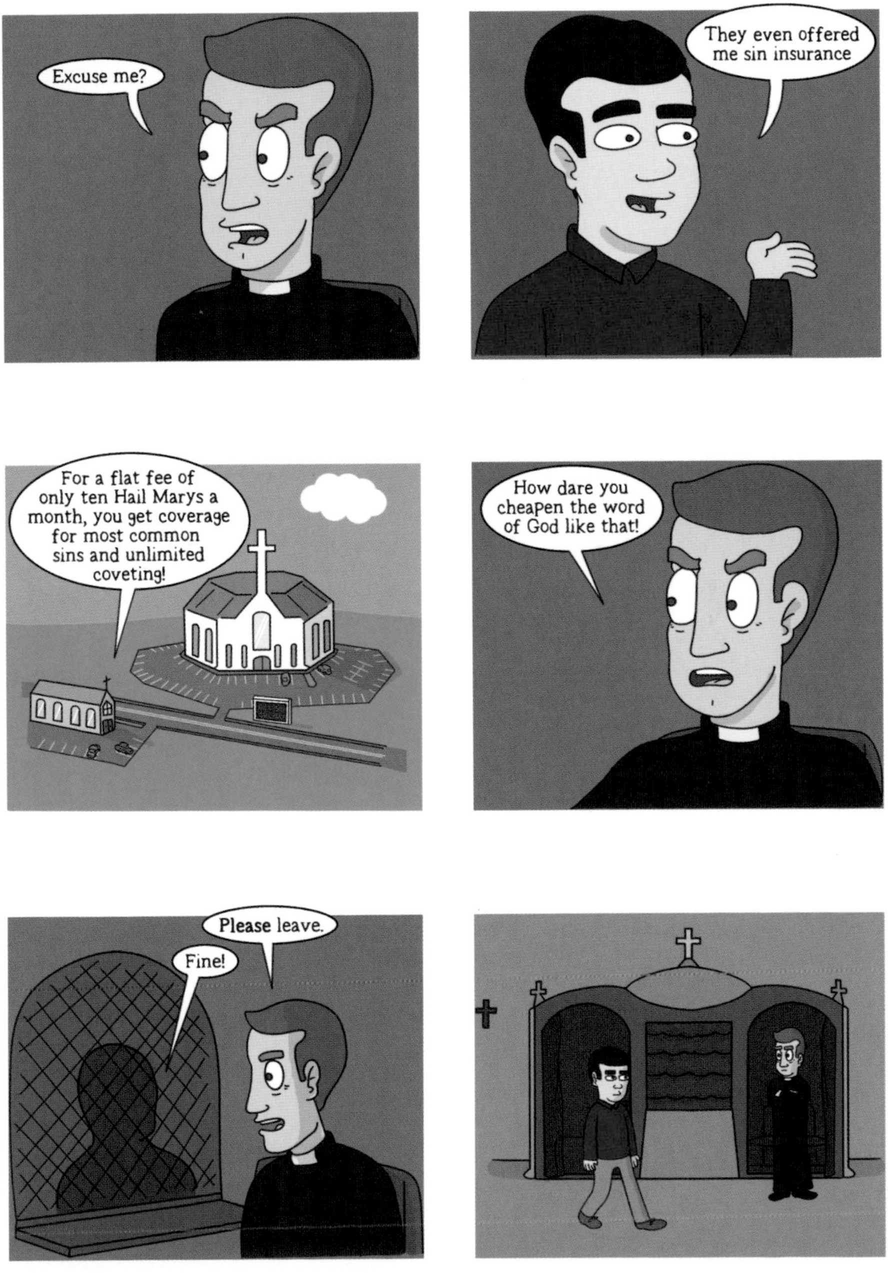
Excuse me?
They even offered me sin insurance
For a flat fee of only ten Hail Marys a month, you get coverage for most common sins and unlimited coveting!
How dare you cheapen the word of God like that!
Please leave.
Fine!

You're going in the wrong direction, sir
GIFT SHOP
The New NEW Testament
EXIT
Devil's Deal 66% off

BONUS

This is getting out of hand
Don't look at me! This is technically all your fault

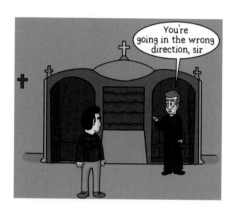

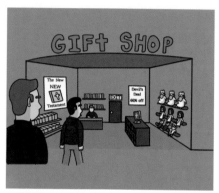

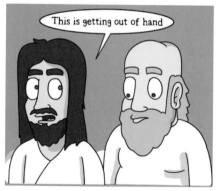

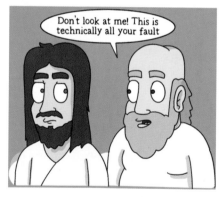

Holy Chip!

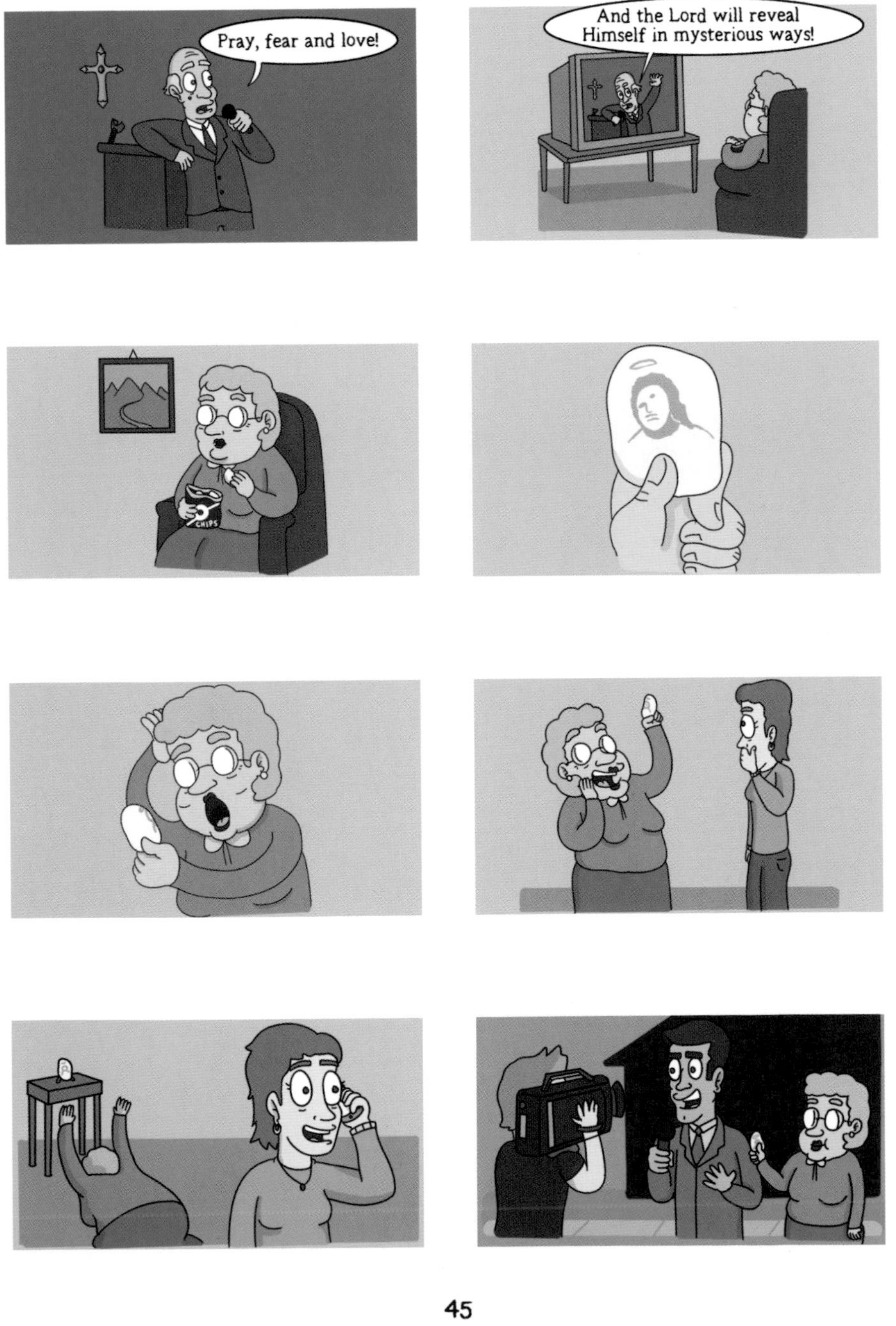
Pray, fear and love!
And the Lord will reveal Himself in mysterious ways!
CHIPS

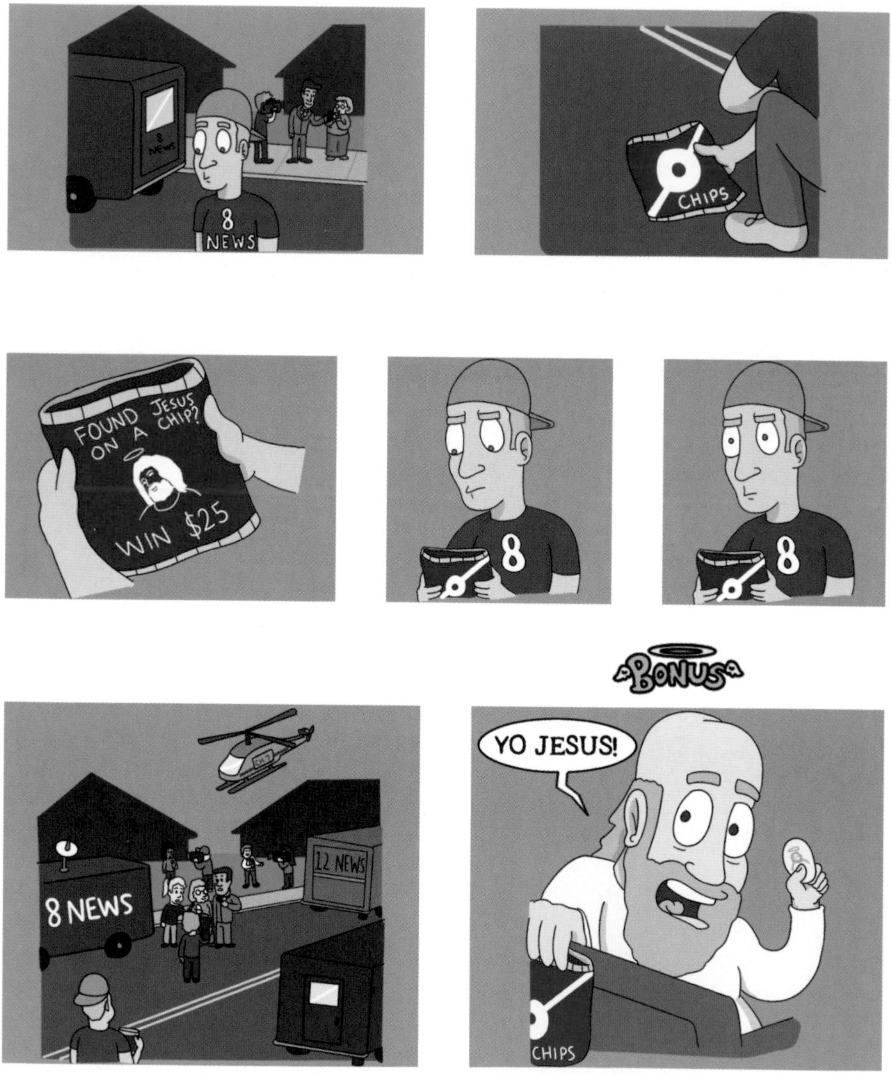
8 NEWS
8 NEWS
CHIPS
FOUND JESUS ON A CHIP?
WIN $25
8
8
8 NEWS
12 NEWS
BONUS
YO JESUS!
CHIPS

Signs

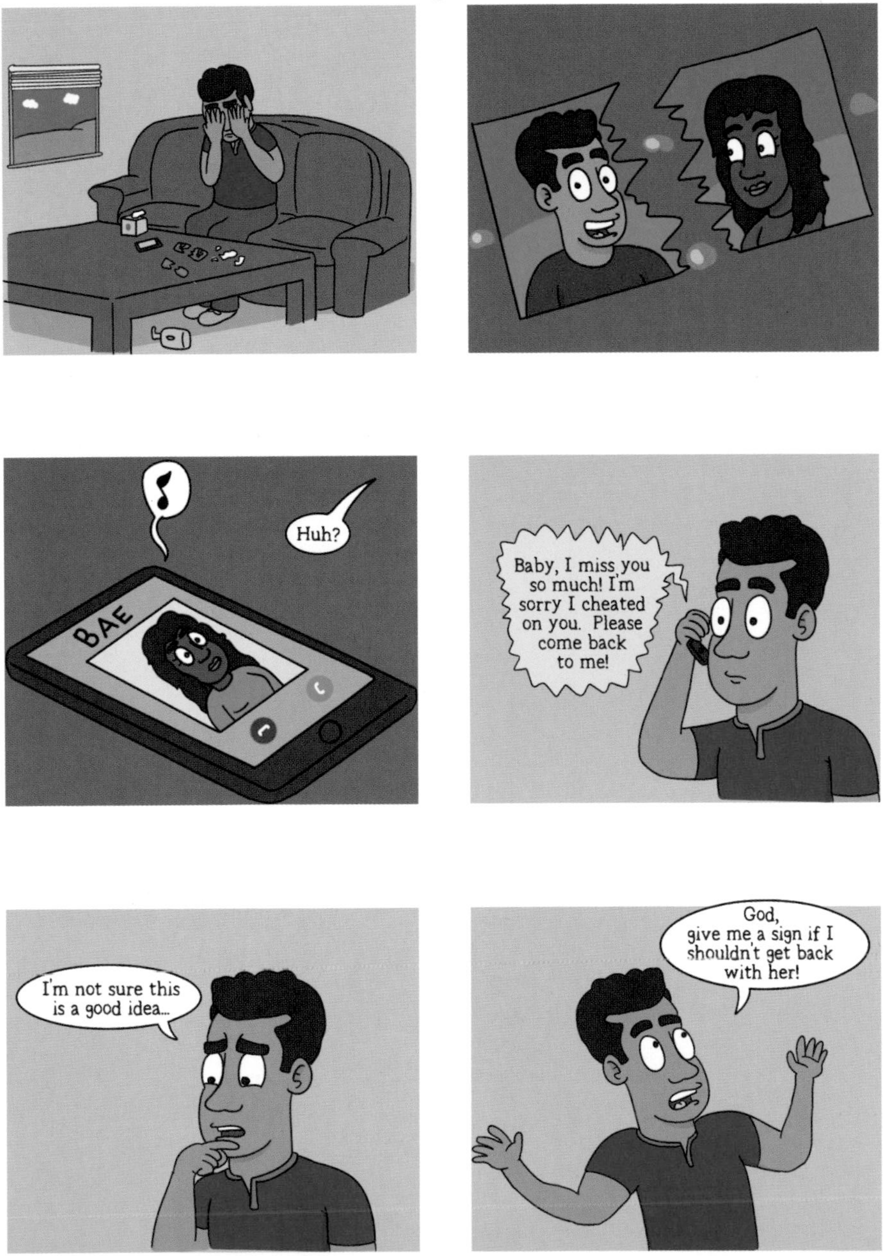

BAE
Huh?
Baby, I miss you so much! I'm sorry I cheated on you. Please come back to me!
I'm not sure this is a good idea...
God, give me a sign if I shouldn't get back with her!

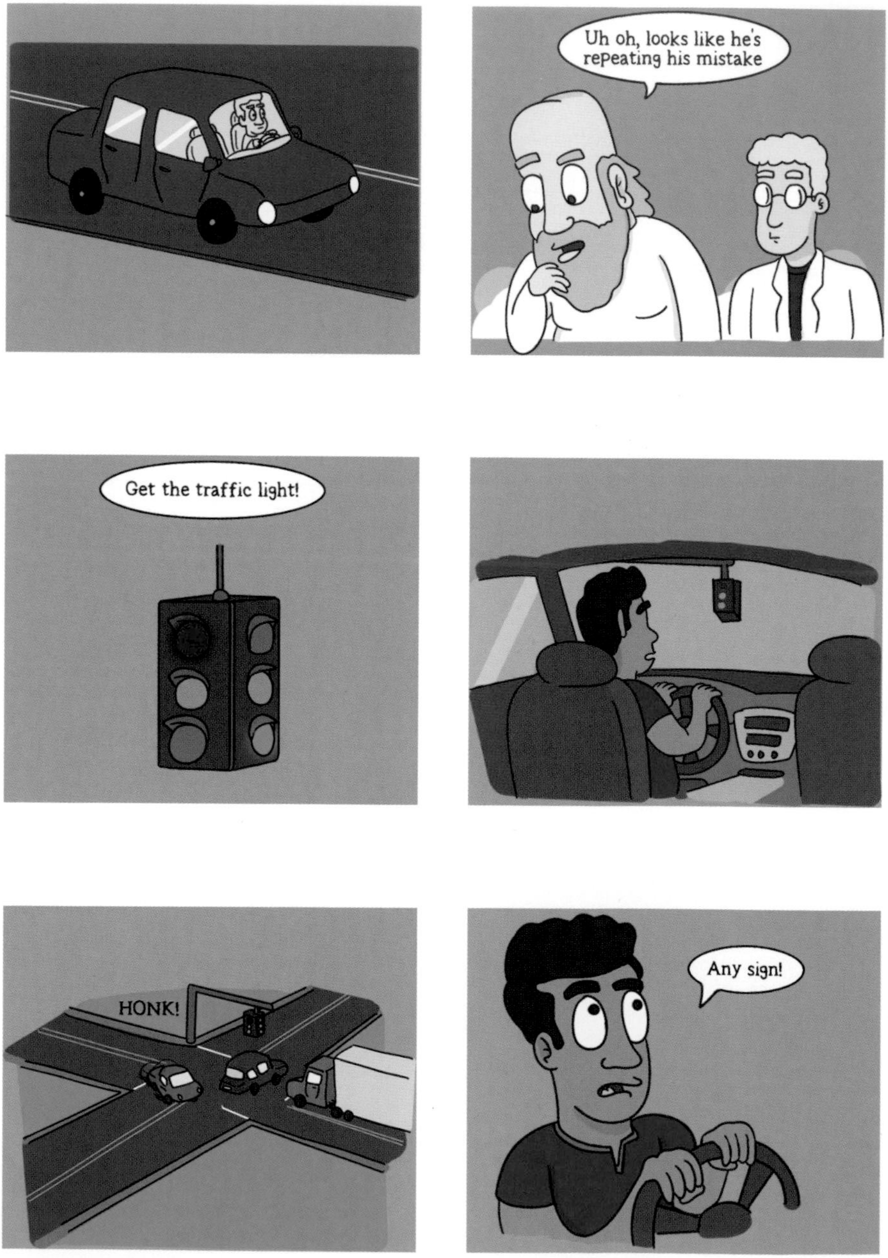
Uh oh, looks like he's repeating his mistake
Get the traffic light!
HONK!
Any sign!

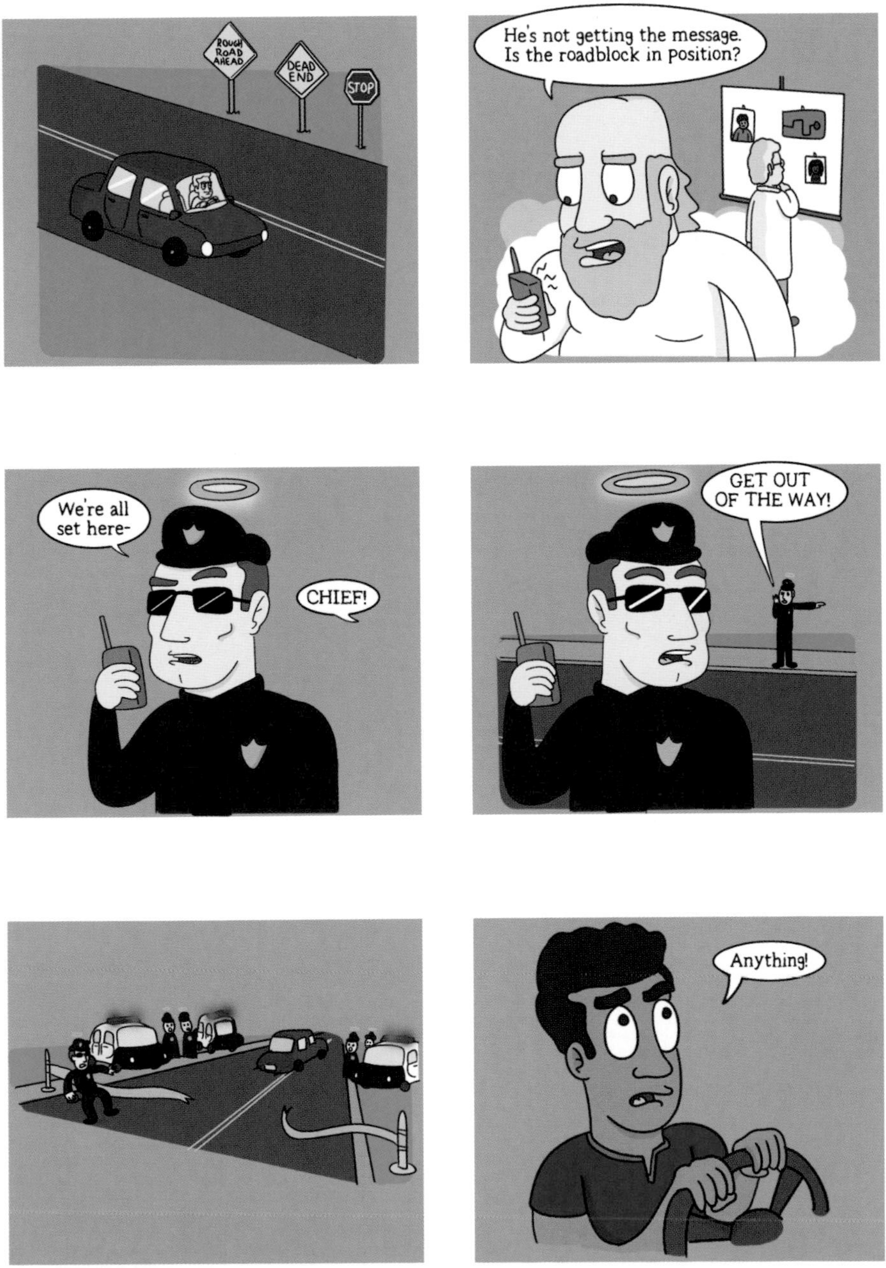
ROUGH ROAD AHEAD
DEAD END
STOP
He's not getting the message. Is the roadblock in position?
We're all set here-
CHIEF!
GET OUT OF THE WAY!
Anything!

SKRRRT
SLAM
!
Alright... no more Mr. Nice Guy! Time to pull out the Big Guns
Sir, with all due respect-
It's all or nothing

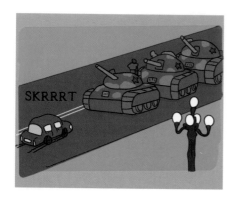

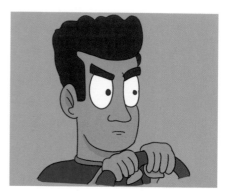

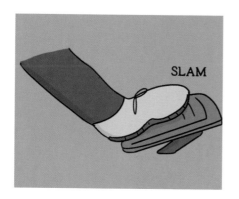

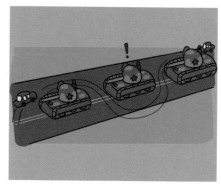

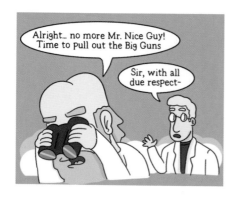

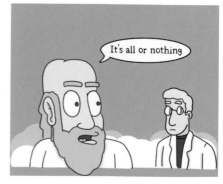

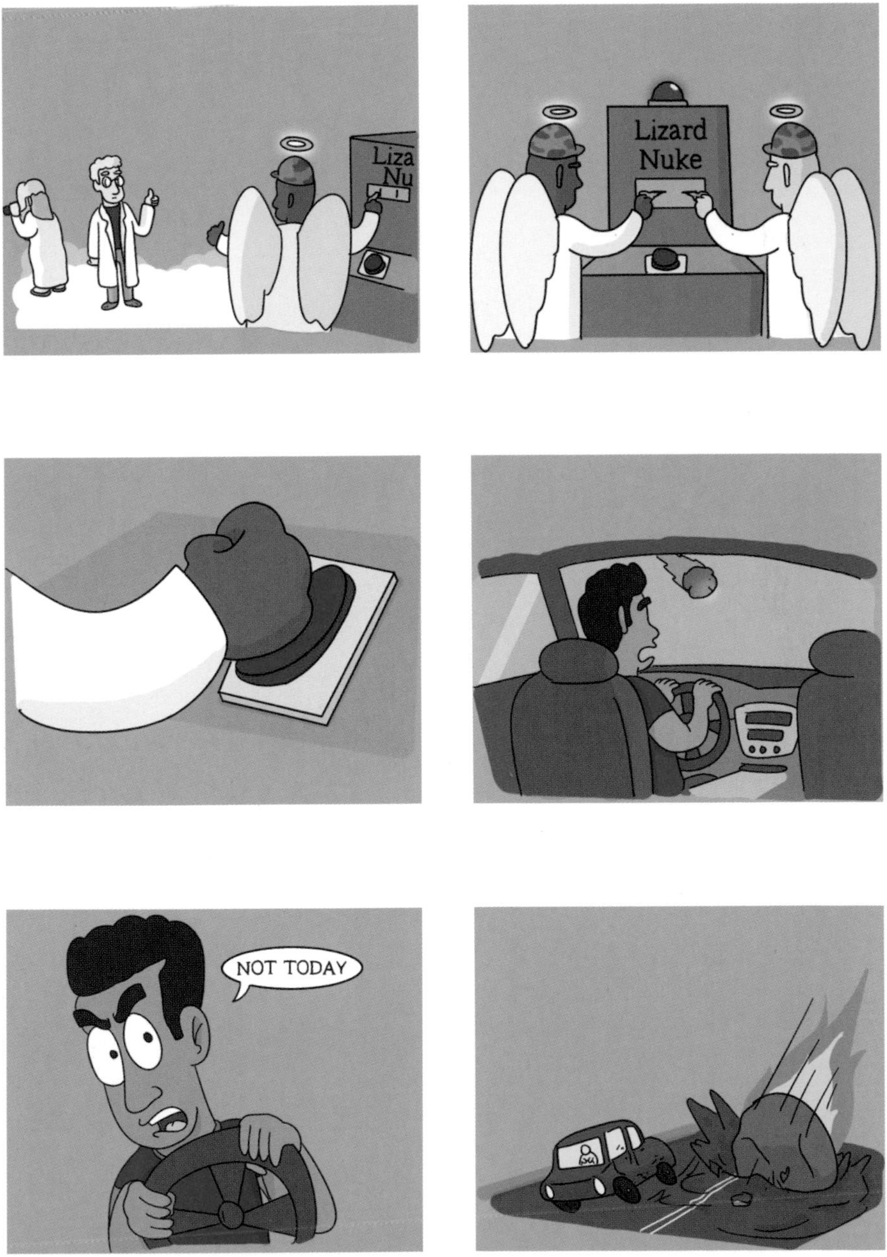
Liza
Nu
Lizard
Nuke
NOT TODAY

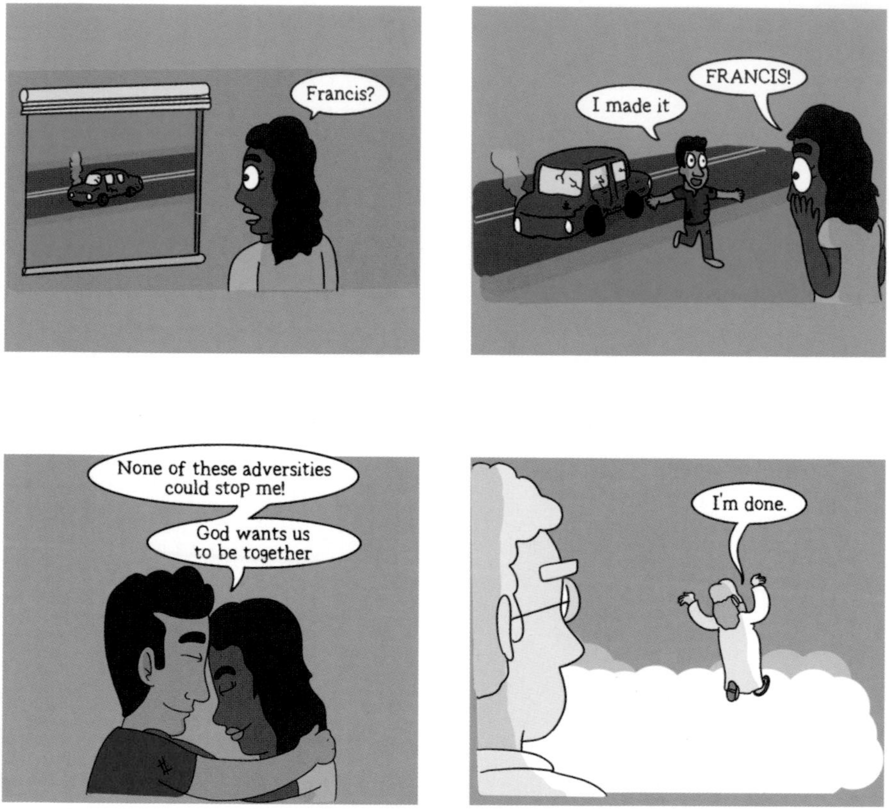
Francis?
FRANCIS!
I made it
None of these adversities could stop me!
God wants us to be together
I'm done.

BONUS

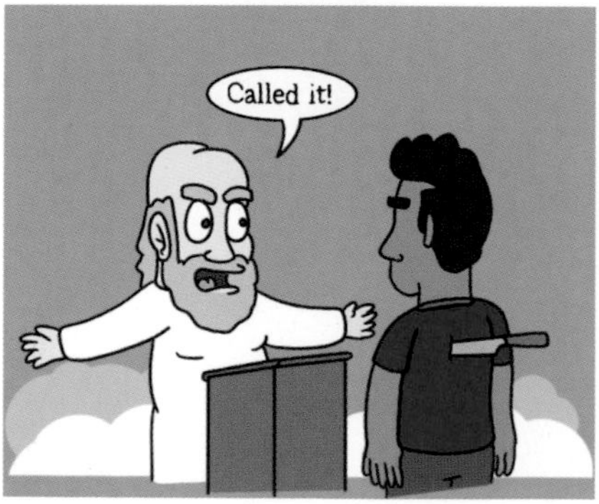
Called it!

The Tower

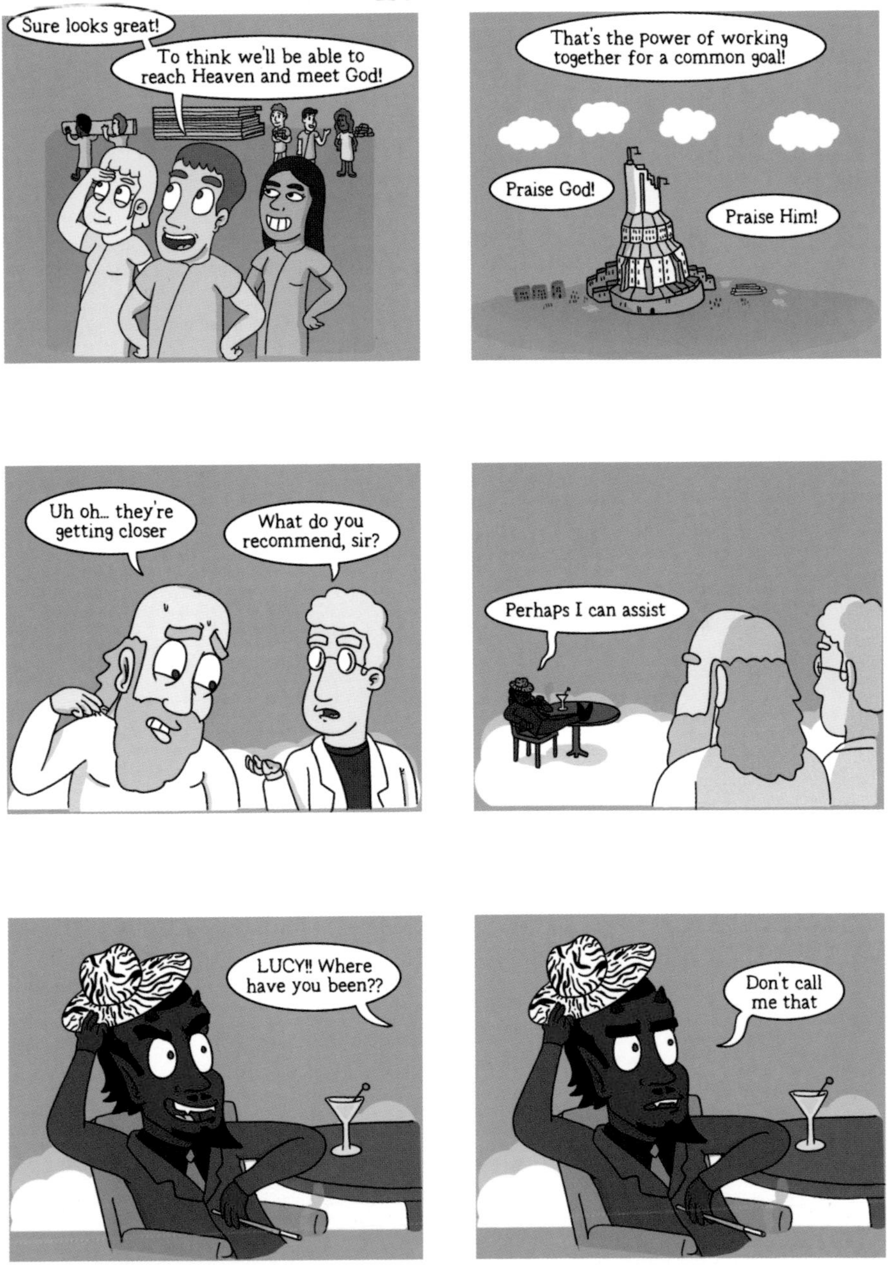

Sure looks great!
To think we'll be able to reach Heaven and meet God!
That's the power of working together for a common goal!
Praise God!
Praise Him!
Uh oh... they're getting closer
What do you recommend, sir?
Perhaps I can assist
LUCY!! Where have you been??
Don't call me that

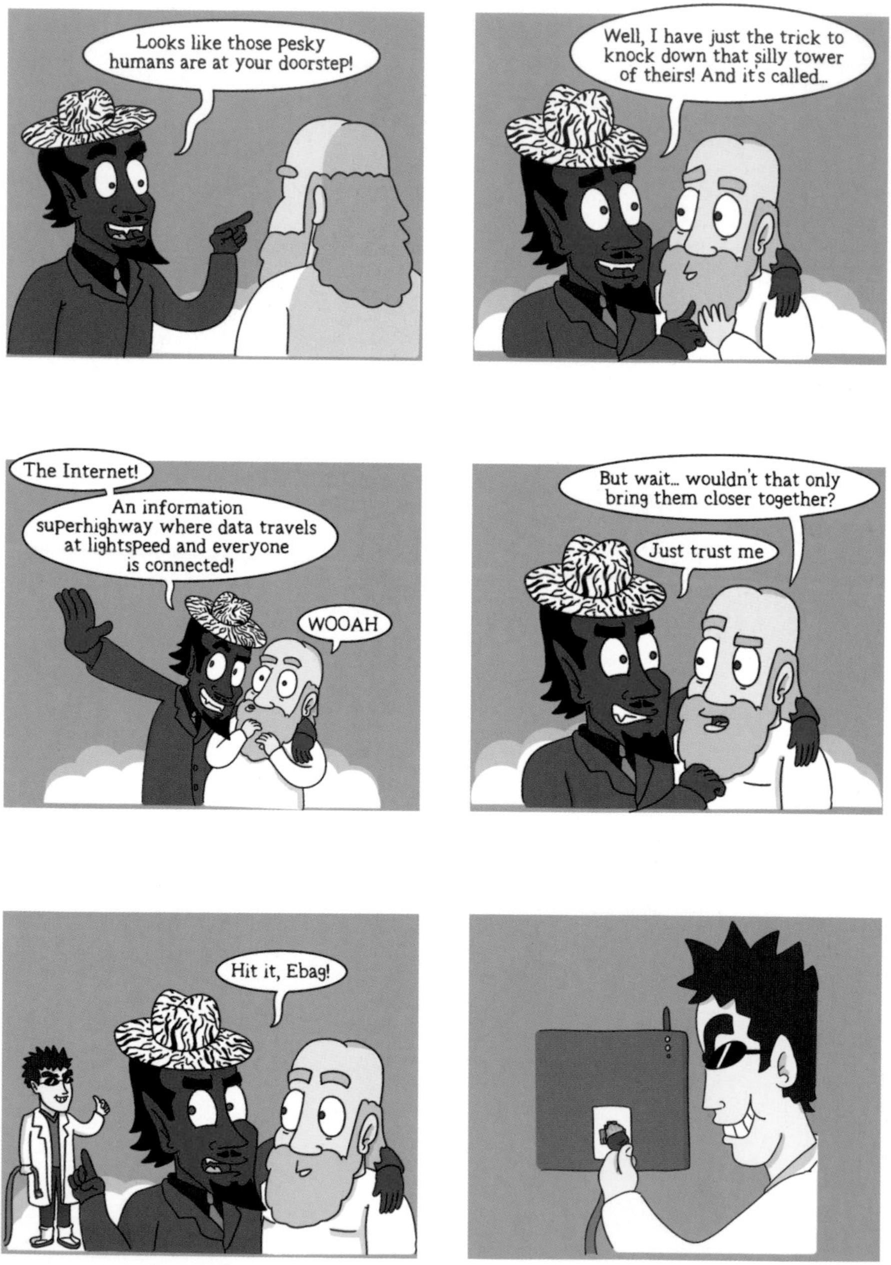
Looks like those pesky humans are at your doorstep!
Well, I have just the trick to knock down that silly tower of theirs! And it's called...
The Internet!
An information superhighway where data travels at lightspeed and everyone is connected!
WOOAH
But wait... wouldn't that only bring them closer together?
Just trust me
Hit it, Ebag!

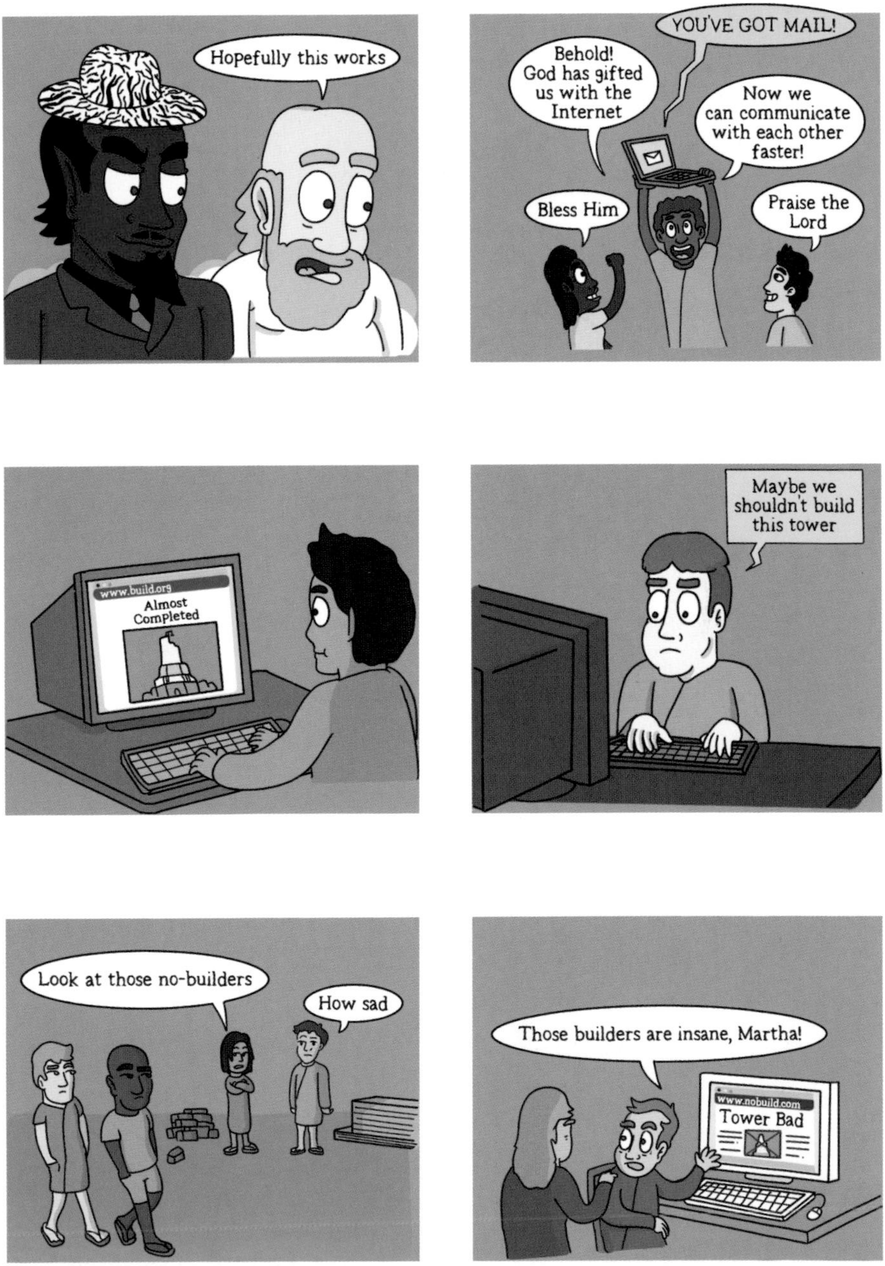
Hopefully this works
Behold! God has gifted us with the Internet
YOU'VE GOT MAIL!
Now we can communicate with each other faster!
Bless Him
Praise the Lord
www.build.org
Almost Completed
Maybe we shouldn't build this tower
Look at those no-builders
How sad
Those builders are insane, Martha!
www.nobuild.com
Tower Bad

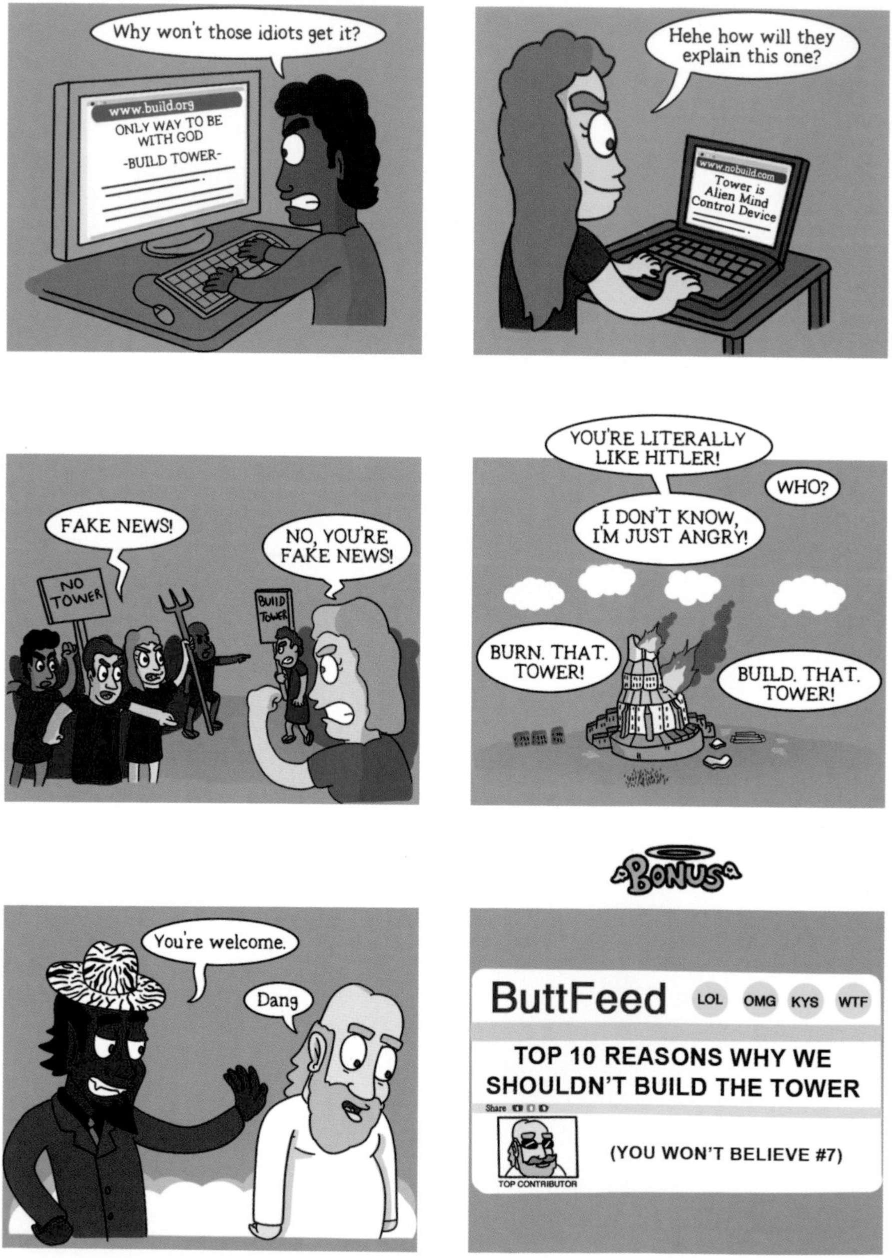
Why won't those idiots get it?
www.build.org
ONLY WAY TO BE WITH GOD
-BUILD TOWER-
Hehe how will they explain this one?
www.nobuild.com
Tower is Alien Mind Control Device
FAKE NEWS!
NO TOWER
NO, YOU'RE FAKE NEWS!
BUILD TOWER
YOU'RE LITERALLY LIKE HITLER!
WHO?
I DON'T KNOW, I'M JUST ANGRY!
BURN. THAT. TOWER!
BUILD. THAT. TOWER!
You're welcome.
Dang
BONUS
ButtFeed
LOL
OMG
KYS
WTF
TOP 10 REASONS WHY WE SHOULDN'T BUILD THE TOWER
Share
(YOU WON'T BELIEVE #7)
TOP CONTRIBUTOR

Noah's Ark: The Prequel

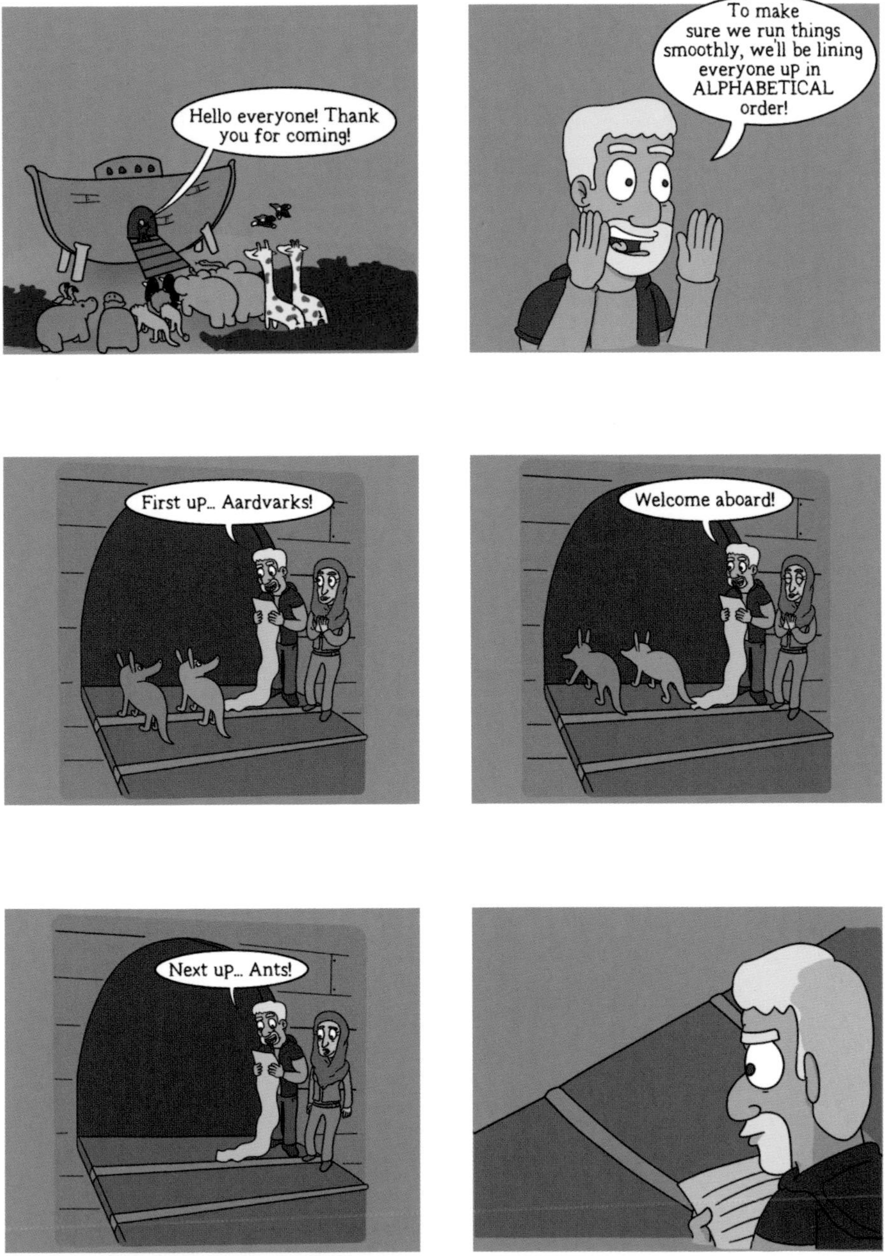
Hello everyone! Thank you for coming!
To make sure we run things smoothly, we'll be lining everyone up in ALPHABETICAL order!
First up... Aardvarks!
Welcome aboard!
Next up... Ants!

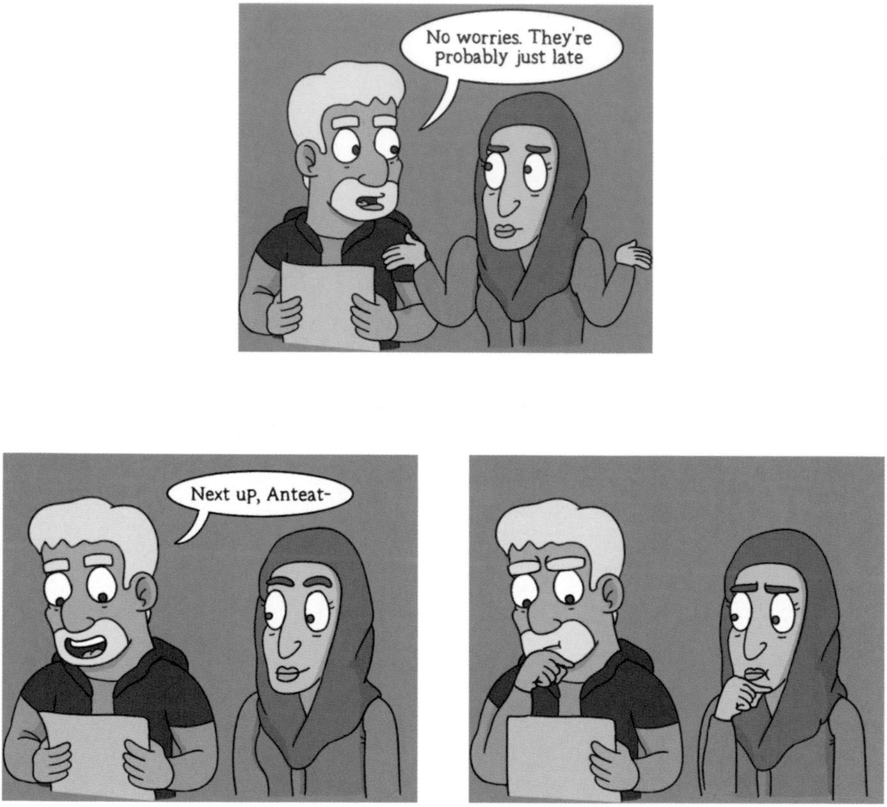
No worries. They're probably just late
Next up, Anteat-

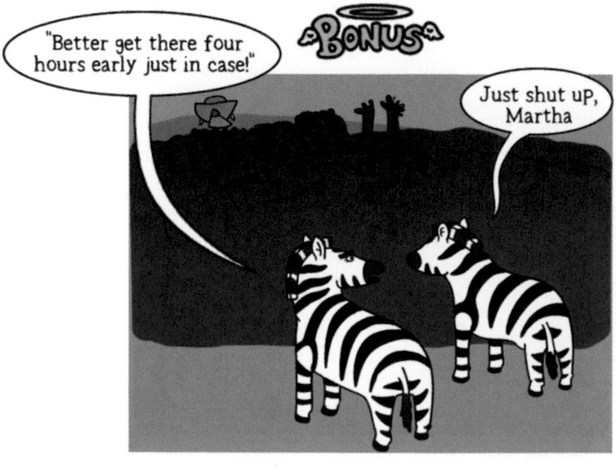
BONUS
"Better get there four hours early just in case!"
Just shut up, Martha

God Bless America!

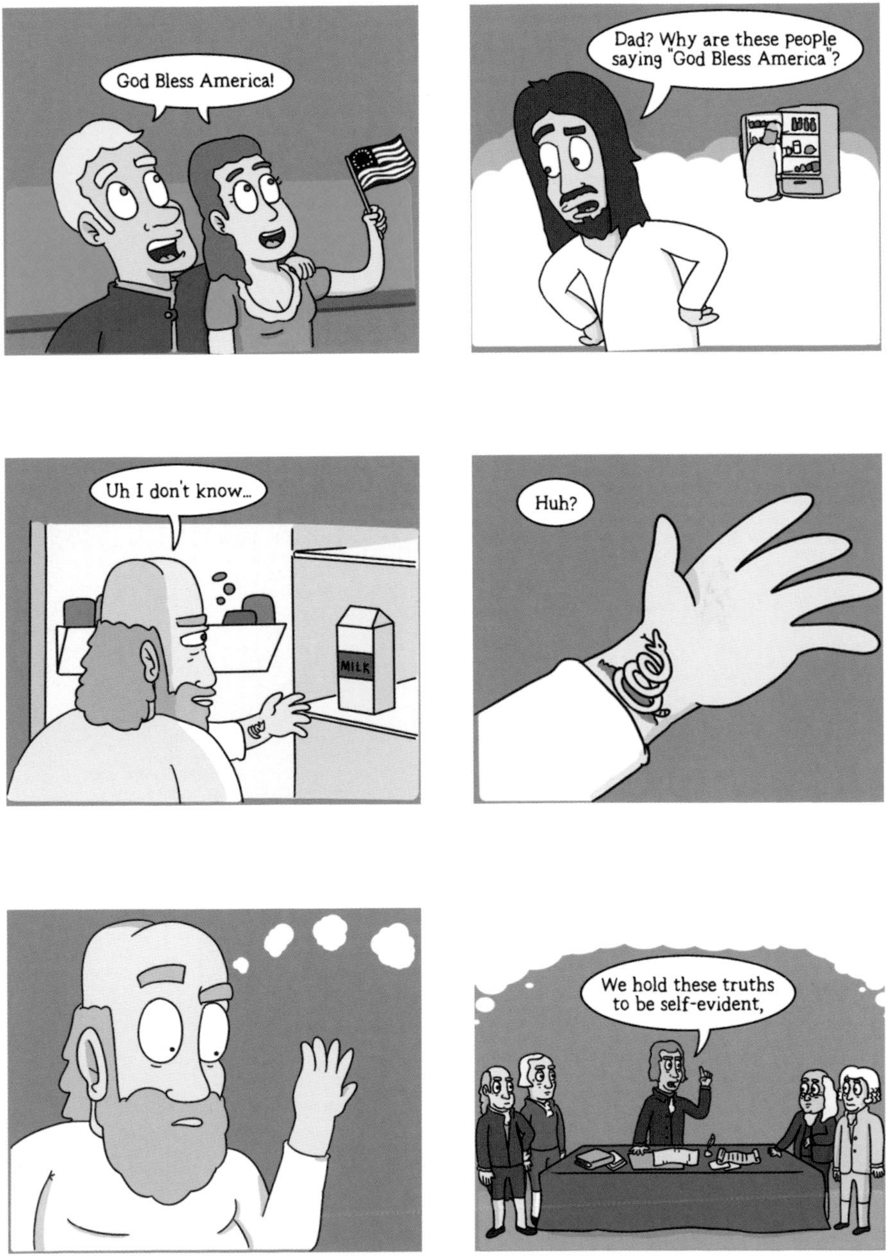
God Bless America!
Dad? Why are these people saying "God Bless America"?
Uh I don't know...
MILK
Huh?
We hold these truths to be self-evident,

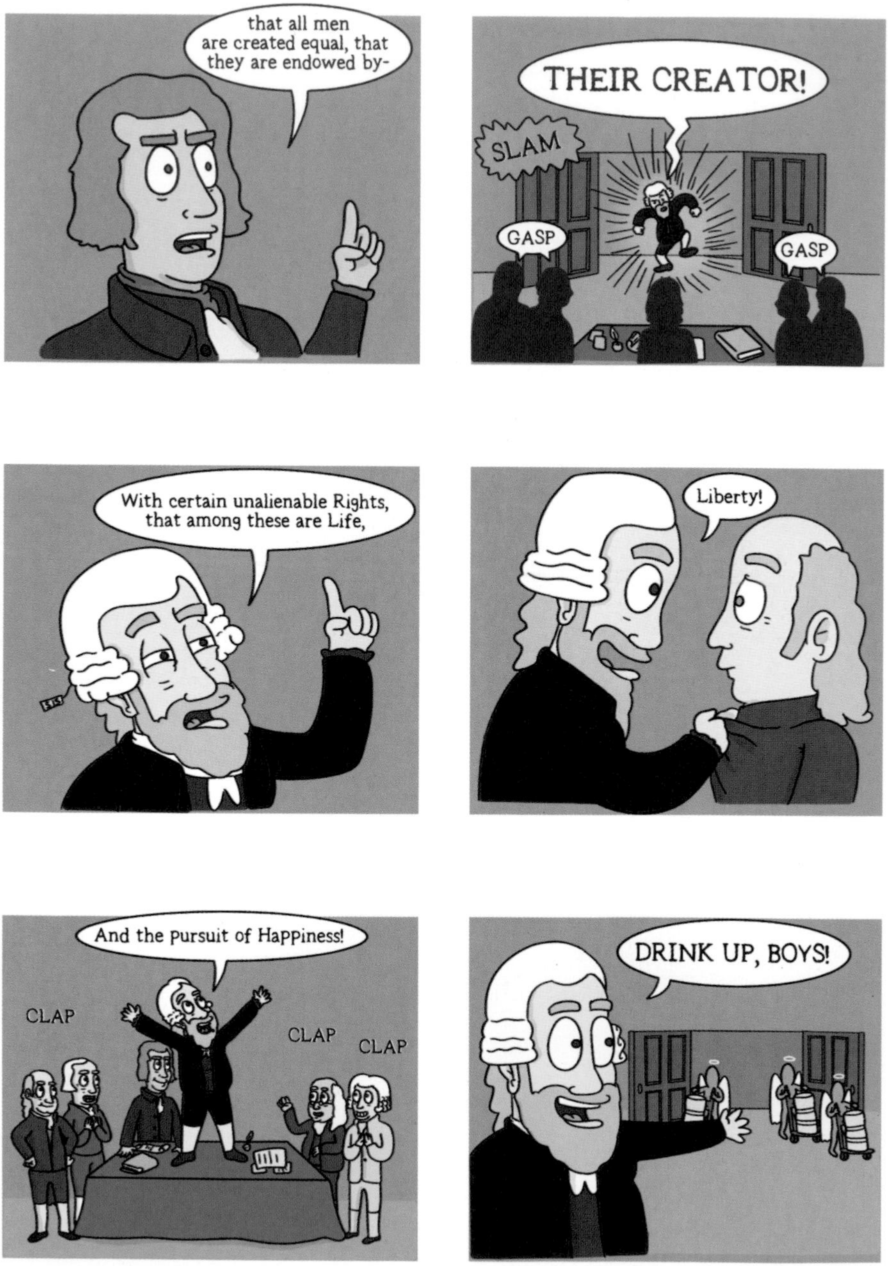
that all men are created equal, that they are endowed by-
THEIR CREATOR!
SLAM
GASP
GASP
With certain unalienable Rights, that among these are Life,
Liberty!
And the pursuit of Happiness!
CLAP
CLAP
CLAP
DRINK UP, BOYS!

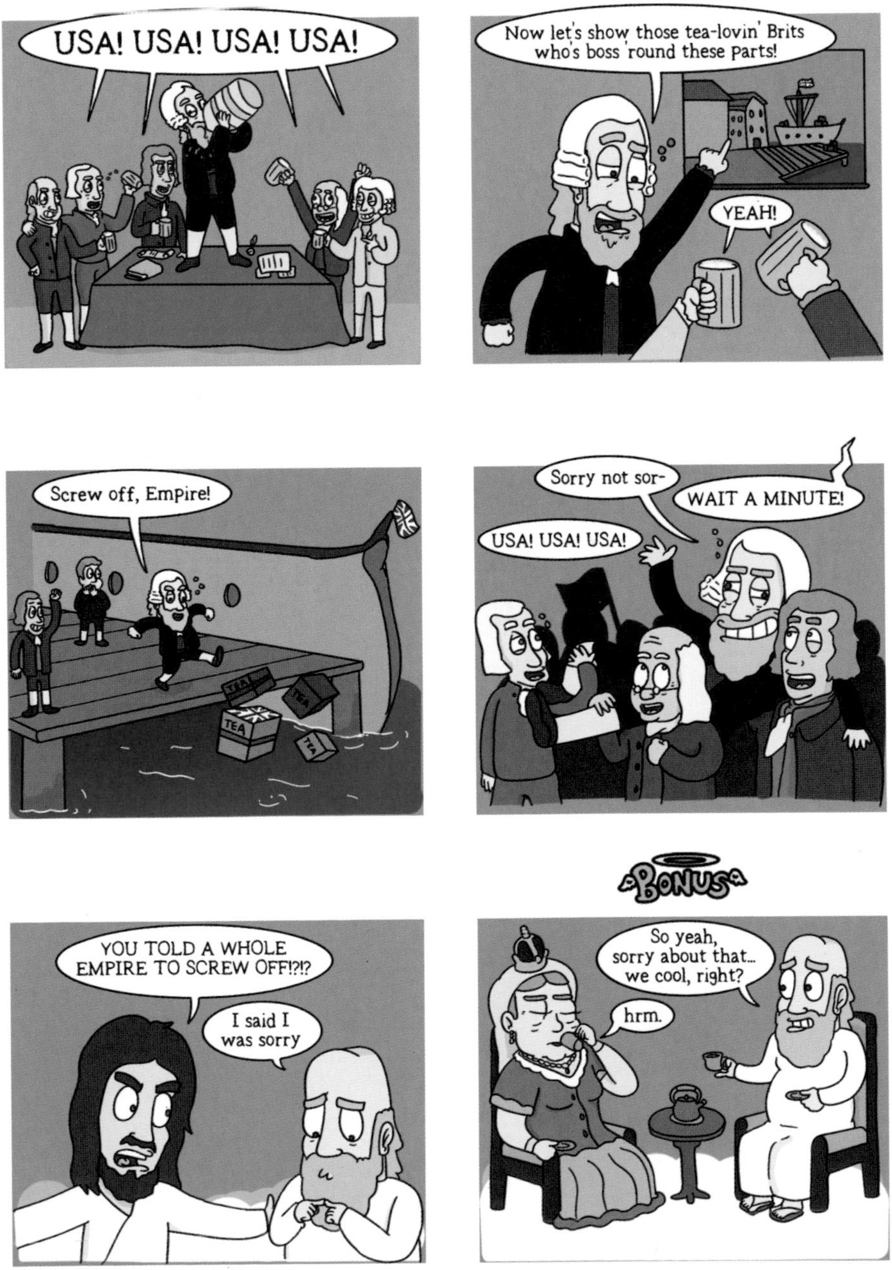
USA! USA! USA! USA!
Now let's show those tea-lovin' Brits who's boss 'round these parts!
YEAH!
Screw off, Empire!
Sorry not sor-
WAIT A MINUTE!
USA! USA! USA!
YOU TOLD A WHOLE EMPIRE TO SCREW OFF!?!?
I said I was sorry
BONUS
So yeah, sorry about that... we cool, right?
hrm.

Watch

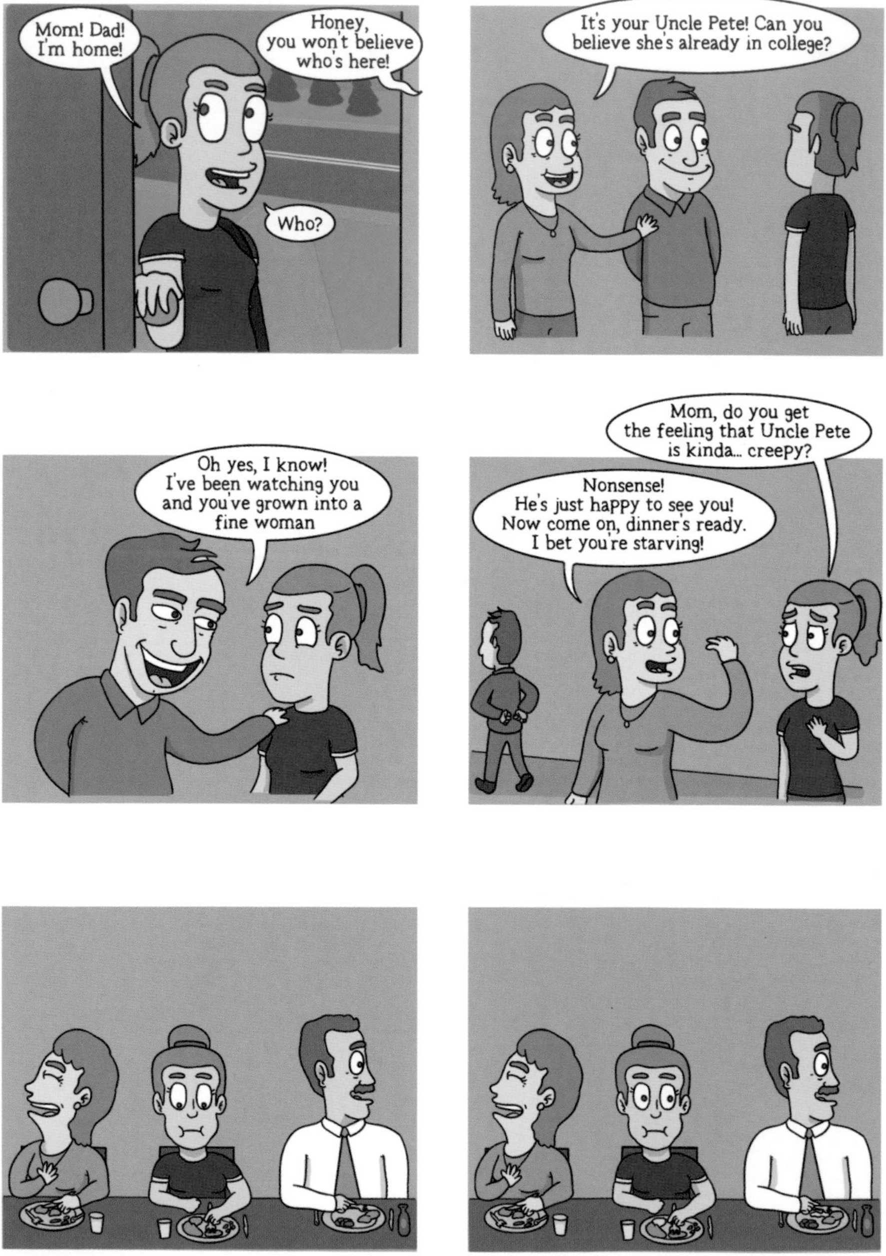
Mom! Dad! I'm home!
Honey, you won't believe who's here!
Who?
It's your Uncle Pete! Can you believe she's already in college?
Oh yes, I know! I've been watching you and you've grown into a fine woman
Mom, do you get the feeling that Uncle Pete is kinda... creepy?
Nonsense! He's just happy to see you! Now come on, dinner's ready. I bet you're starving!

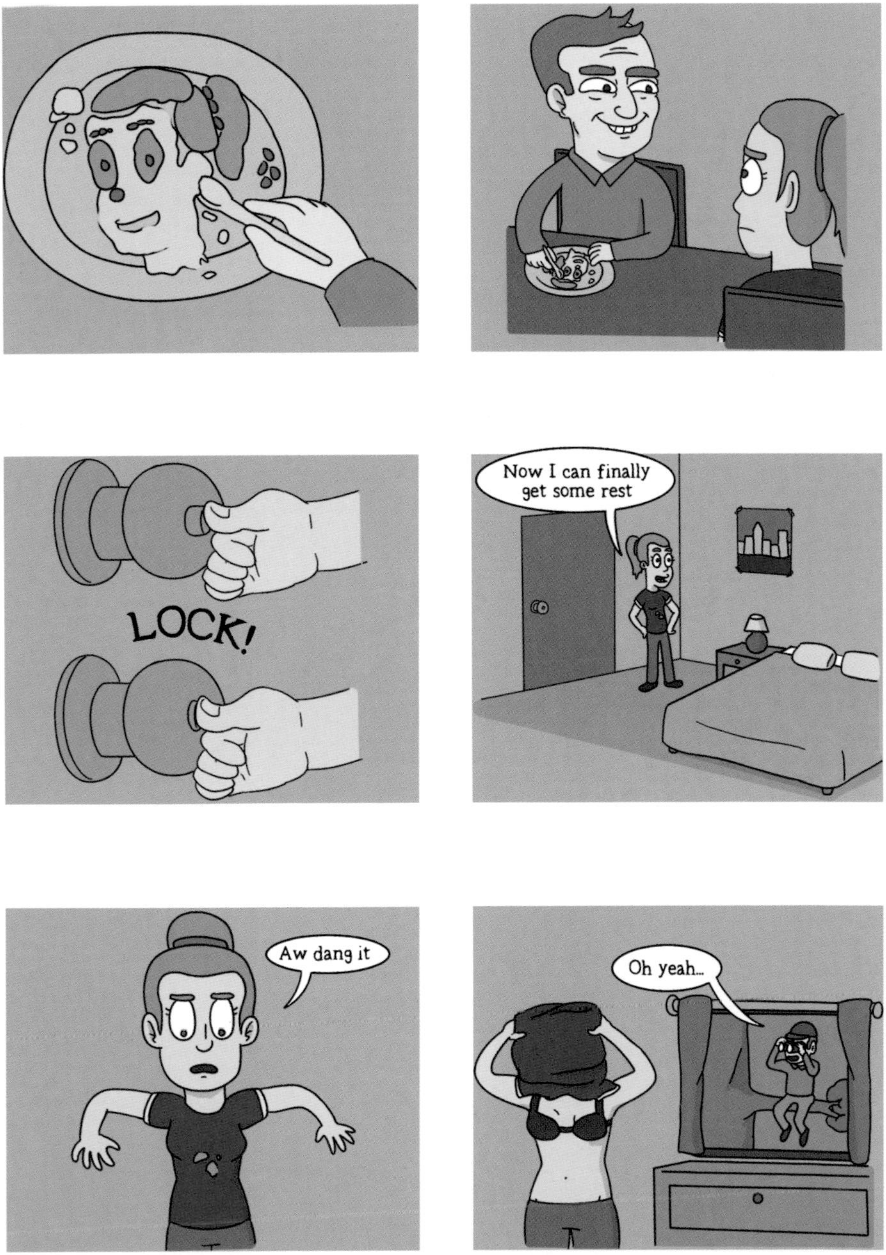
LOCK!
Now I can finally get some rest
Aw dang it
Oh yeah...

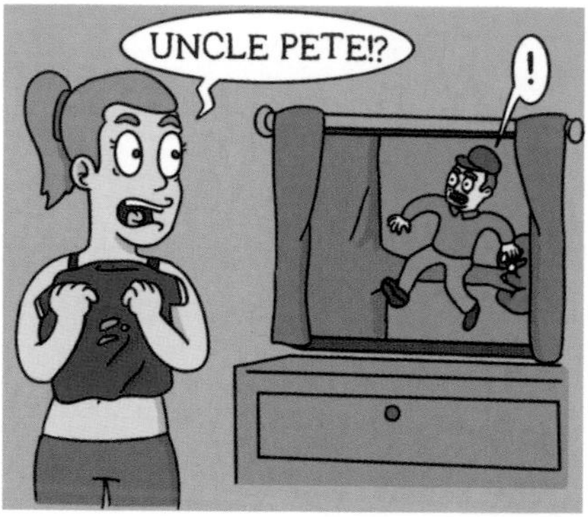
UNCLE PETE!?
!

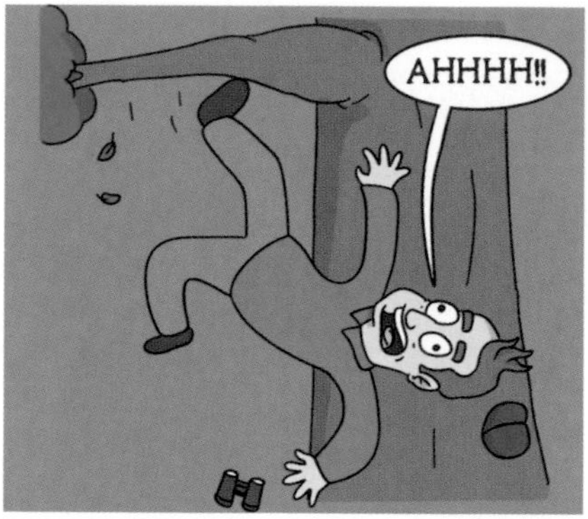
AHHHH!!

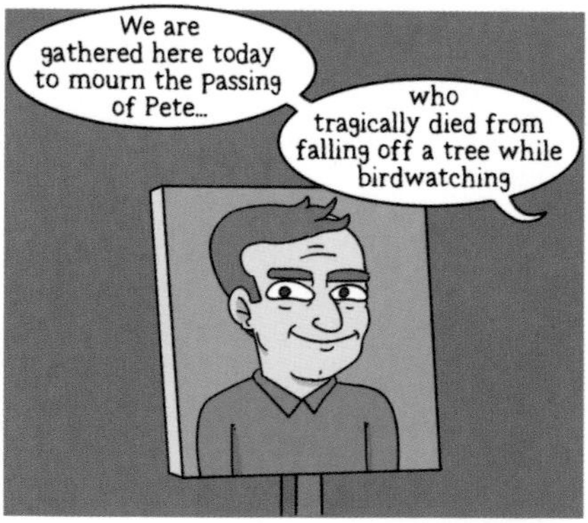
We are gathered here today to mourn the passing of Pete...
who tragically died from falling off a tree while birdwatching

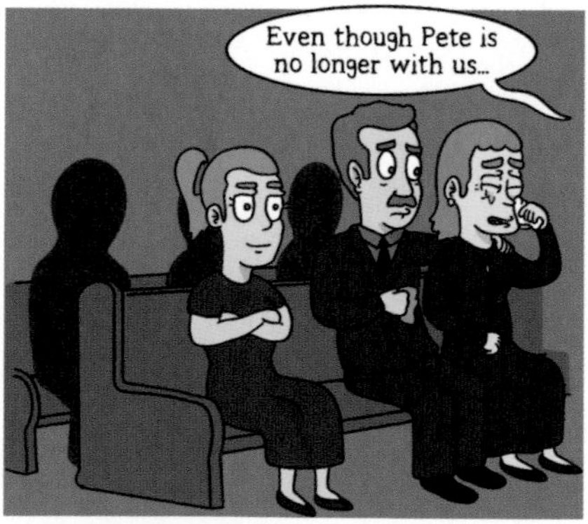
Even though Pete is no longer with us...

Rest assured, he's still watching us from Heaven
ARE YOU KIDDING ME!!

BONUS
What is he doing here?
I guess he repented or something?
I know, I know. We need to fix that loophole
DID HE!?

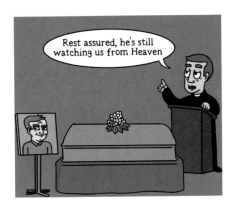

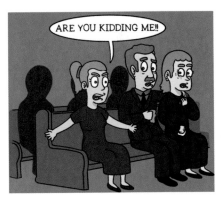

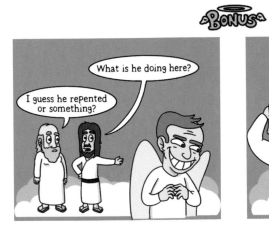

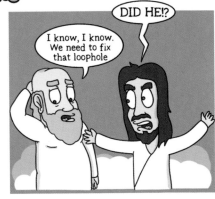

Summoned

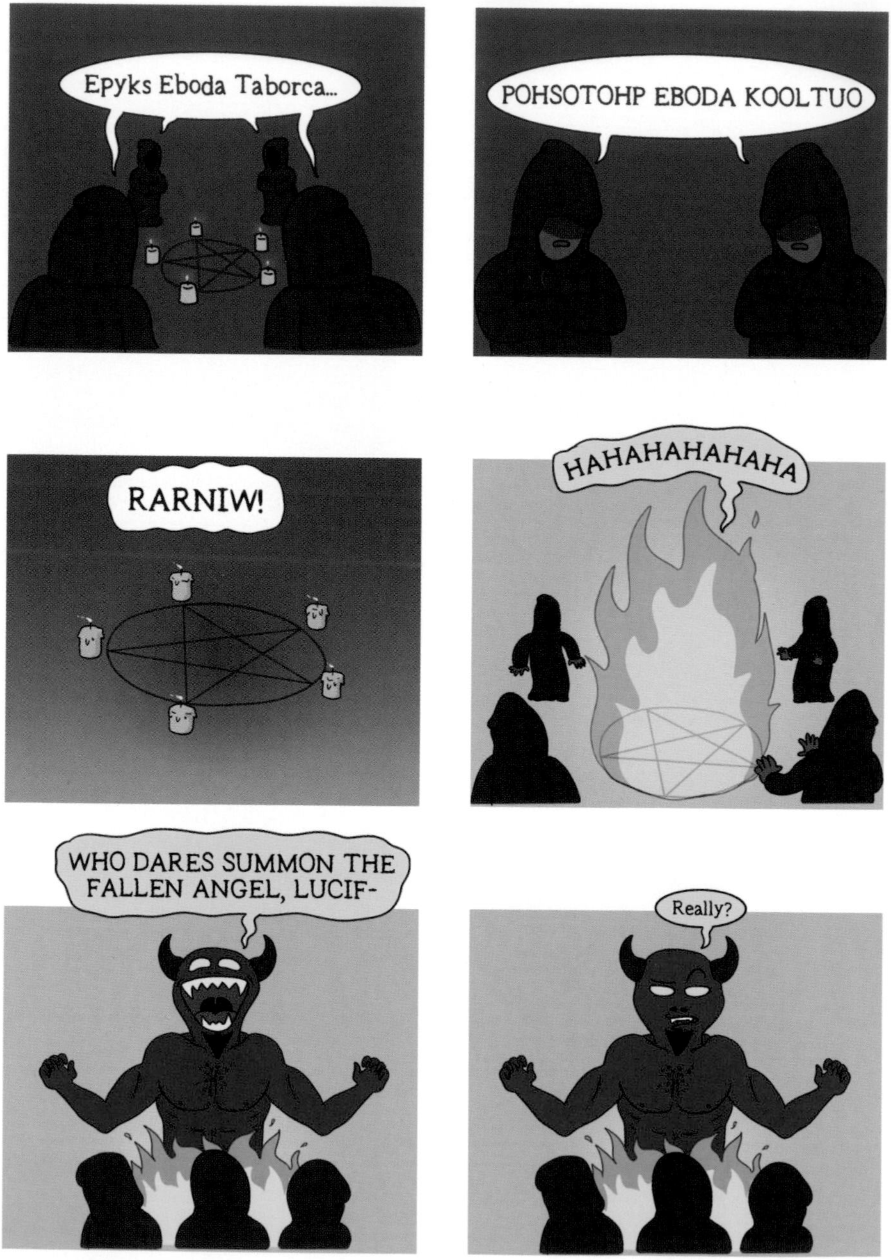
Epyks Eboda Taborca...
POHSOTOHP EBODA KOOLTUO
RARNIW!
HAHAHAHAHAHA
WHO DARES SUMMON THE FALLEN ANGEL, LUCIF-
Really?

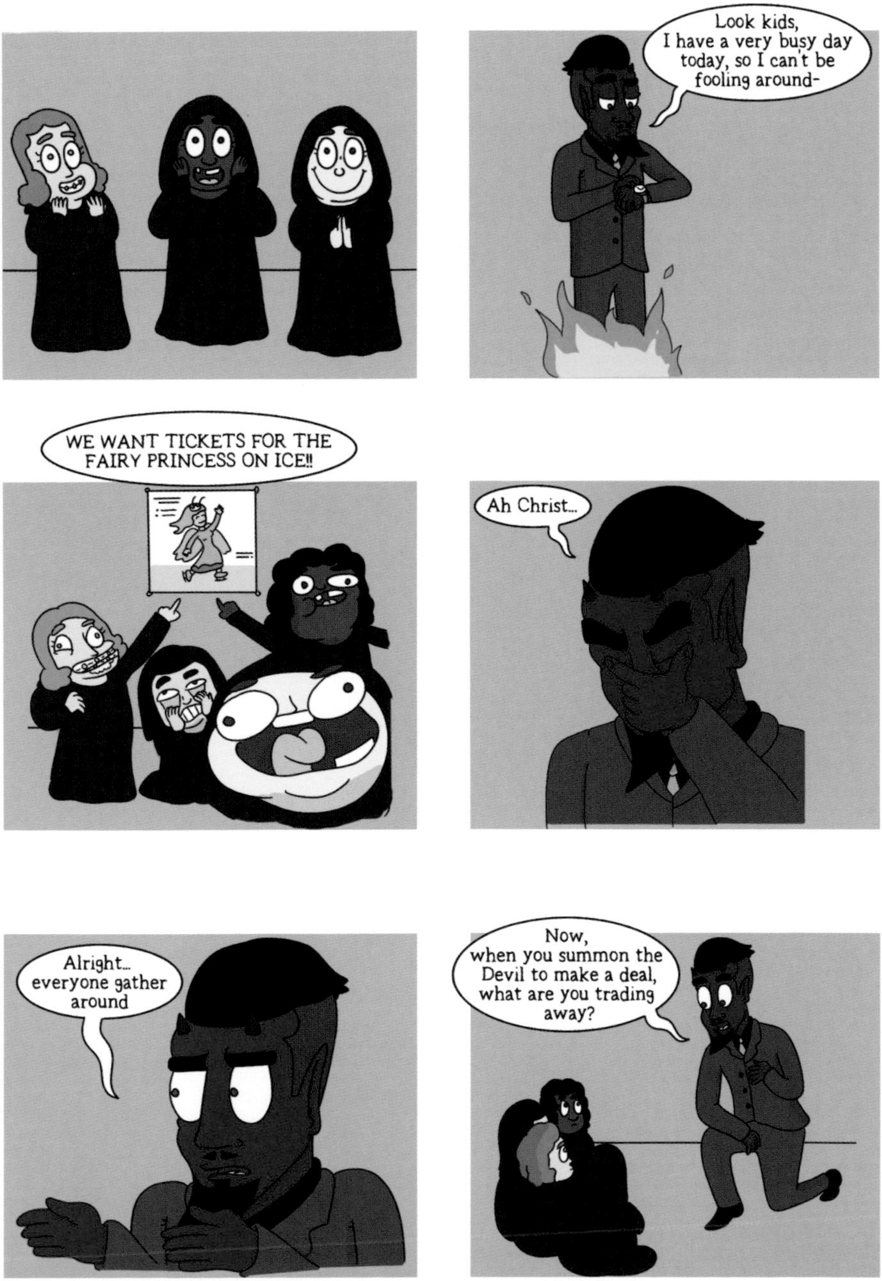
Look kids,
I have a very busy day
today, so I can't be
fooling around-
WE WANT TICKETS FOR THE
FAIRY PRINCESS ON ICE!!
Ah Christ...
Alright...
everyone gather
around
Now,
when you summon the
Devil to make a deal,
what are you trading
away?

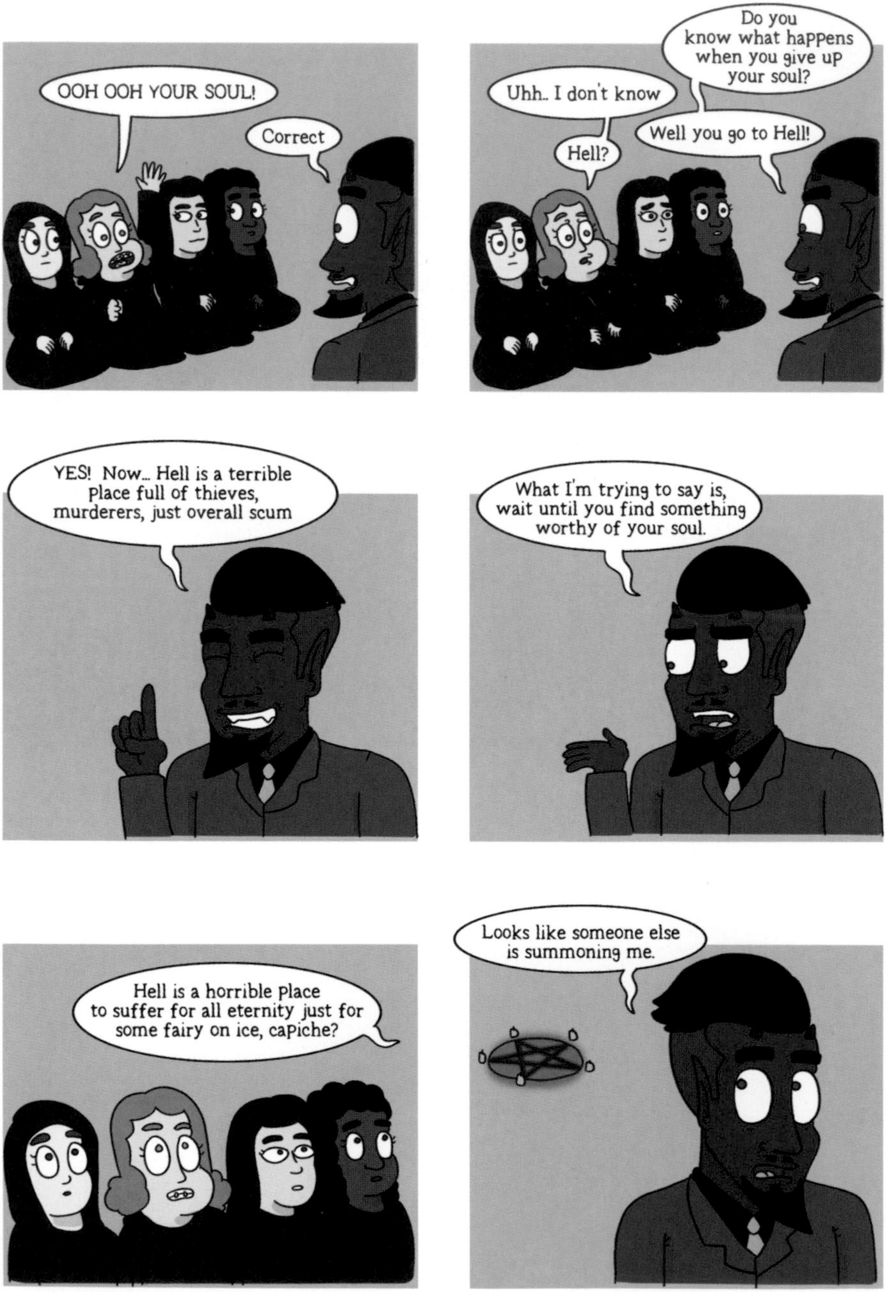
OOH OOH YOUR SOUL!
Correct
Do you know what happens when you give up your soul?
Uhh.. I don't know
Hell?
Well you go to Hell!
YES! Now... Hell is a terrible place full of thieves, murderers, just overall scum
What I'm trying to say is, wait until you find something worthy of your soul.
Hell is a horrible place to suffer for all eternity just for some fairy on ice, capiche?
Looks like someone else is summoning me.

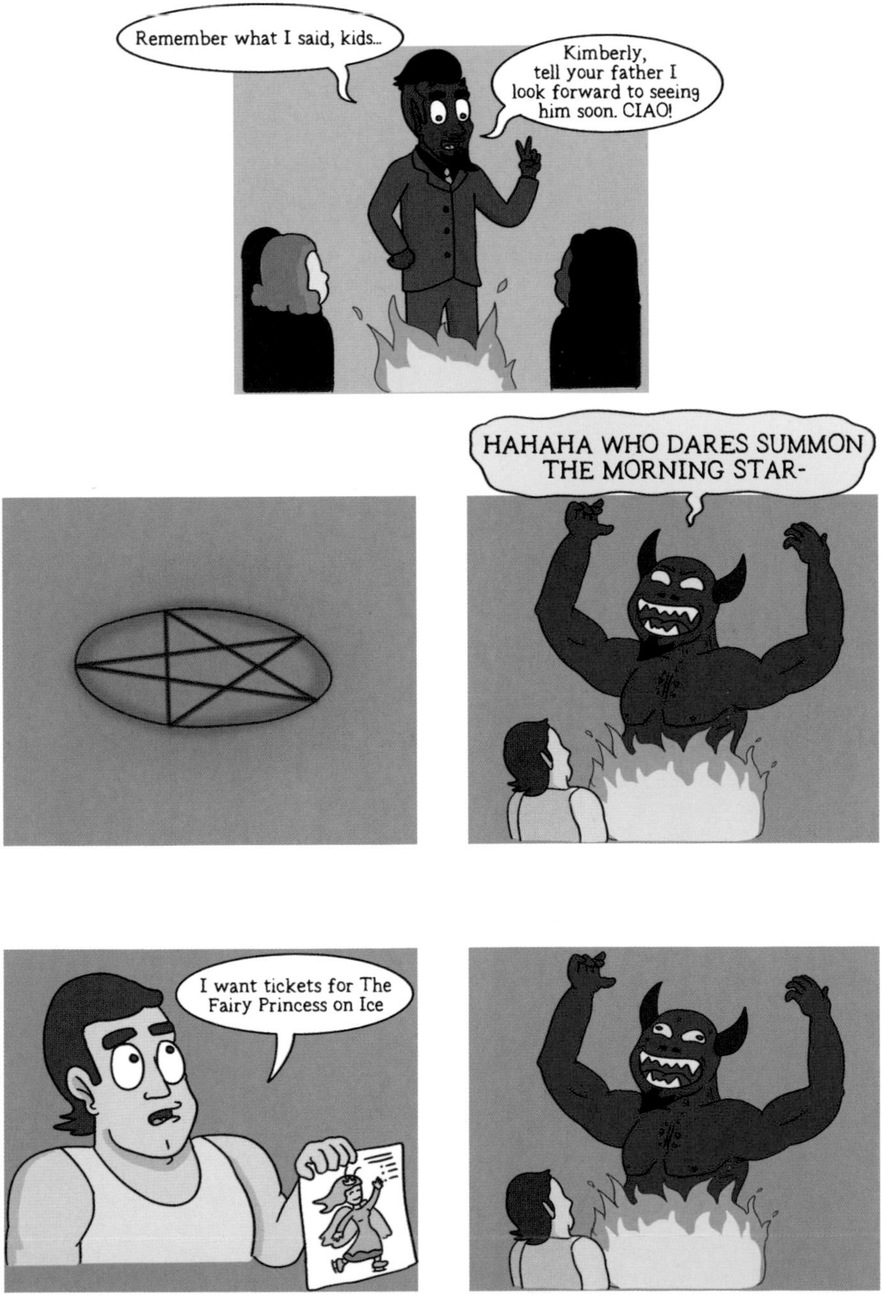
Remember what I said, kids...
Kimberly, tell your father I look forward to seeing him soon. CIAO!
HAHAHA WHO DARES SUMMON THE MORNING STAR-
I want tickets for The Fairy Princess on Ice

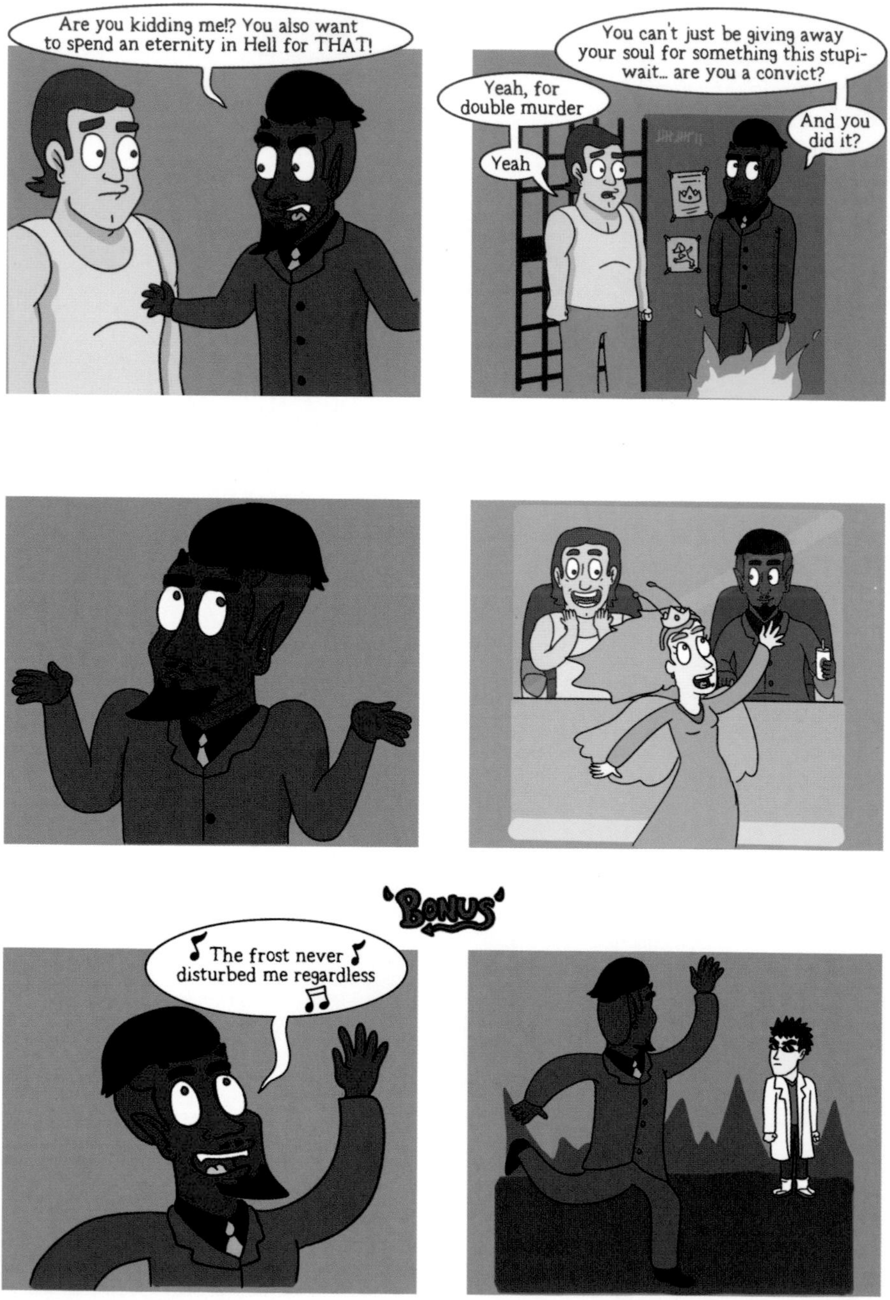
Are you kidding me!? You also want to spend an eternity in Hell for THAT!
You can't just be giving away your soul for something this stupi- wait... are you a convict?
Yeah, for double murder
And you did it?
Yeah
BONUS
The frost never disturbed me regardless

Noah's Ark: Dodos

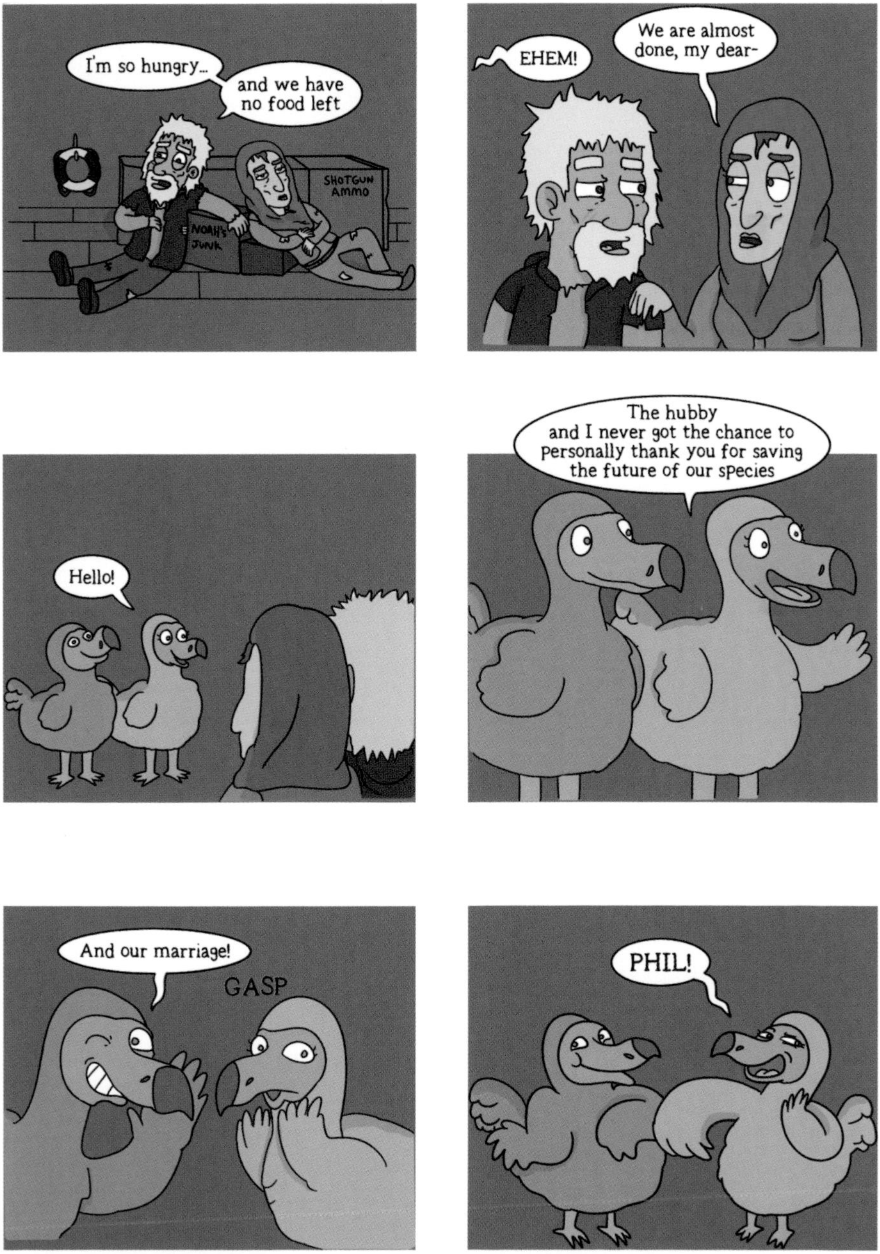
I'm so hungry...
and we have no food left
SHOTGUN AMMO
NOAH'S JUNK
EHEM!
We are almost done, my dear-
Hello!
The hubby and I never got the chance to personally thank you for saving the future of our species
And our marriage!
GASP
PHIL!

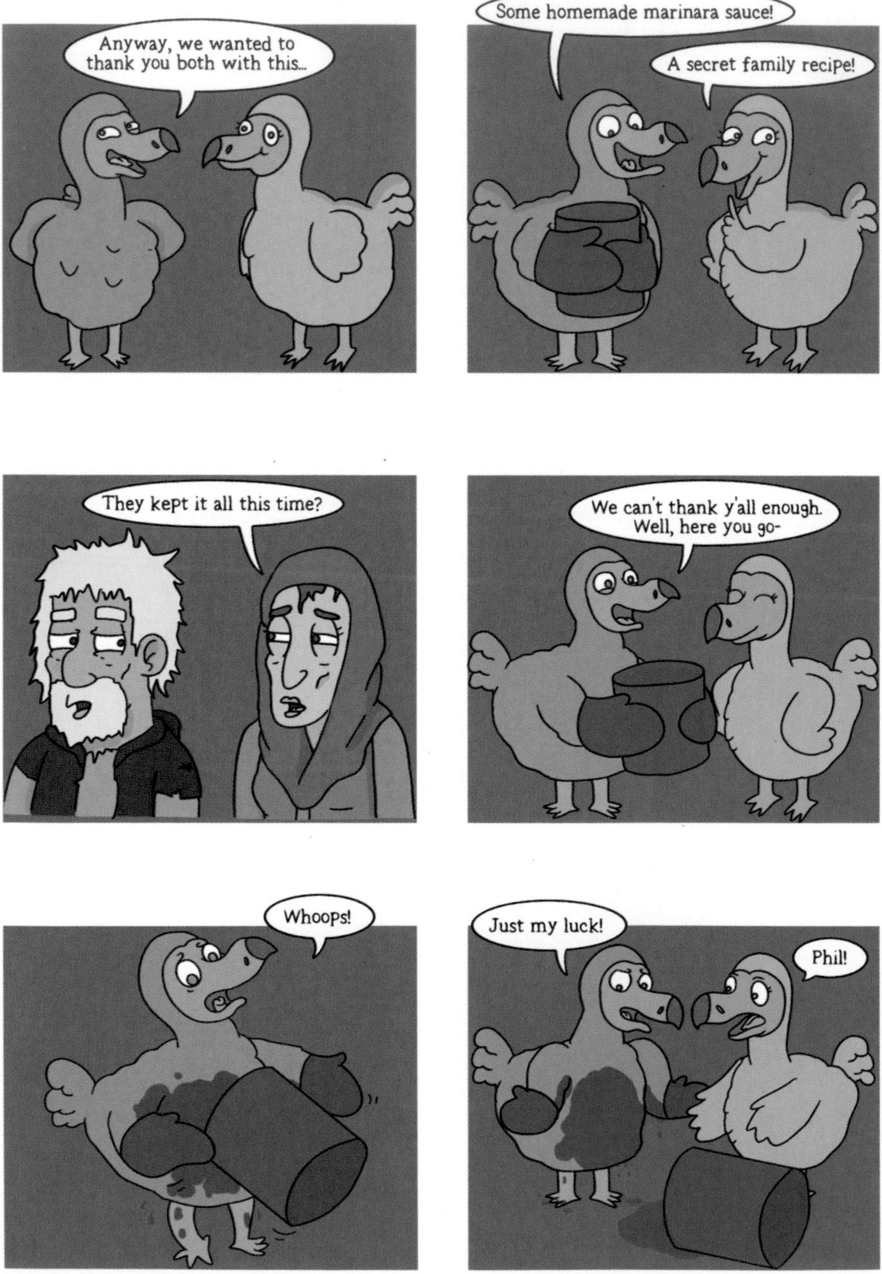
Anyway, we wanted to thank you both with this...
Some homemade marinara sauce!
A secret family recipe!
They kept it all this time?
We can't thank y'all enough. Well, here you go-
Whoops!
Just my luck!
Phil!

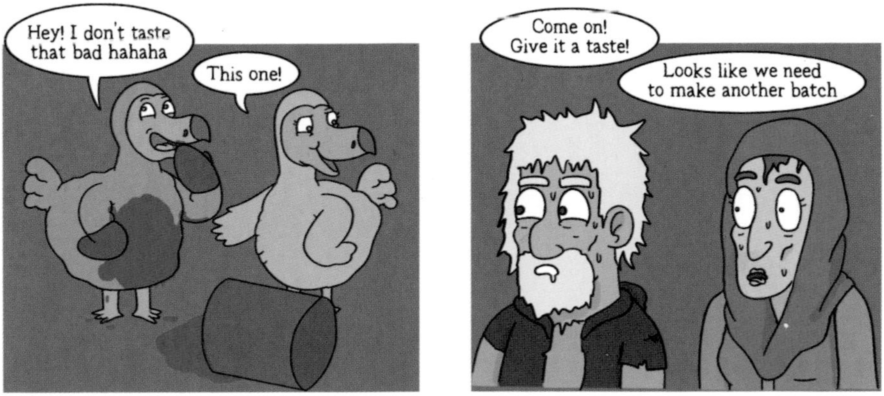
Hey! I don't taste that bad hahaha
This one!
Come on! Give it a taste!
Looks like we need to make another batch

BONUS

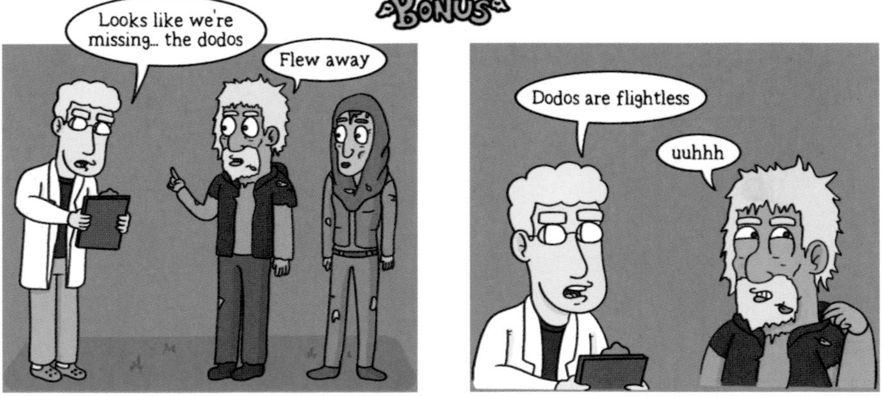
Looks like we're missing... the dodos
Flew away
Dodos are flightless
uuhhh

BONUS BONUS

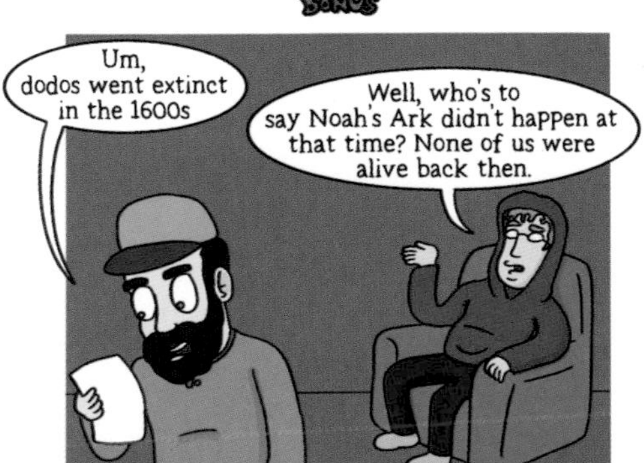
Um, dodos went extinct in the 1600s
Well, who's to say Noah's Ark didn't happen at that time? None of us were alive back then.

Praise the Sun

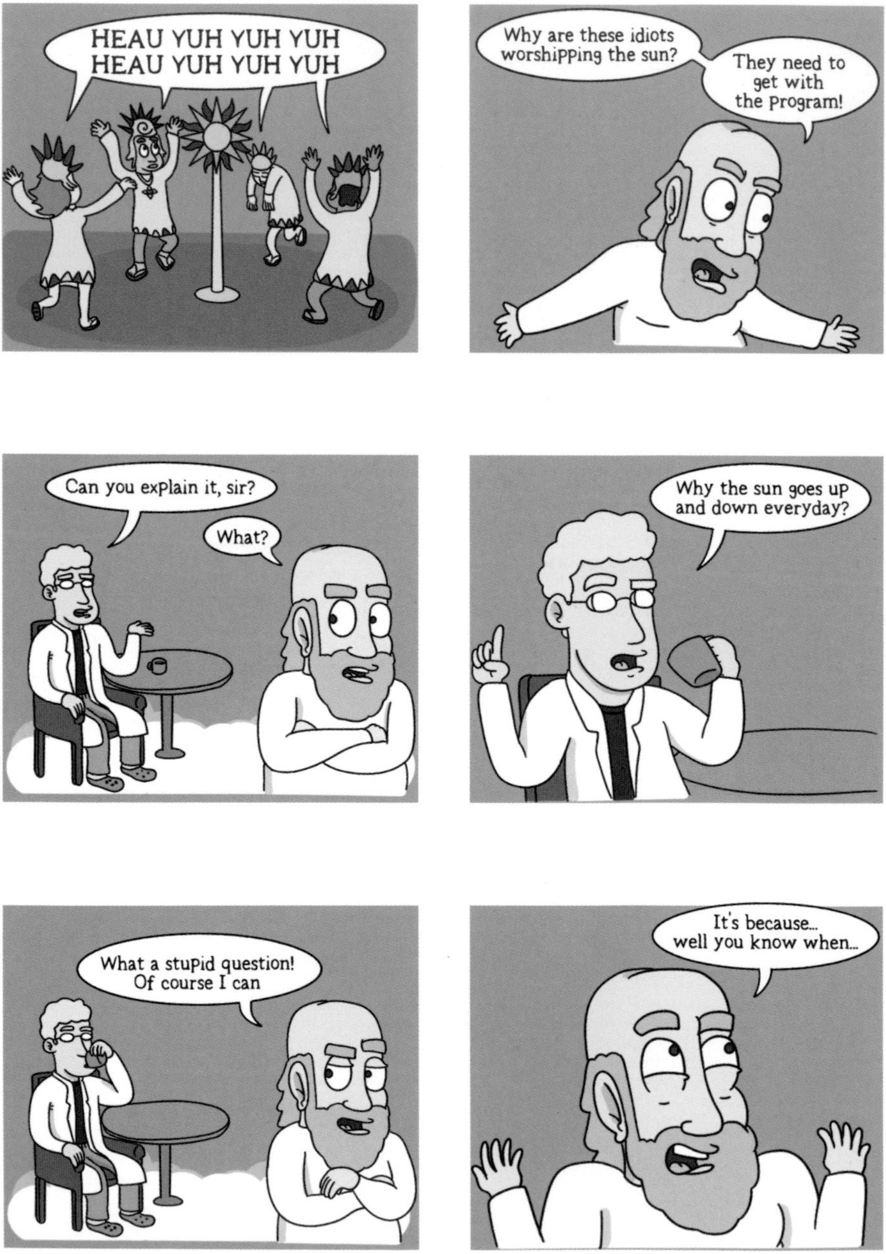

HEAU YUH YUH YUH
HEAU YUH YUH YUH
Why are these idiots worshipping the sun?
They need to get with the program!
Can you explain it, sir?
What?
Why the sun goes up and down everyday?
What a stupid question! Of course I can
It's because... well you know when...

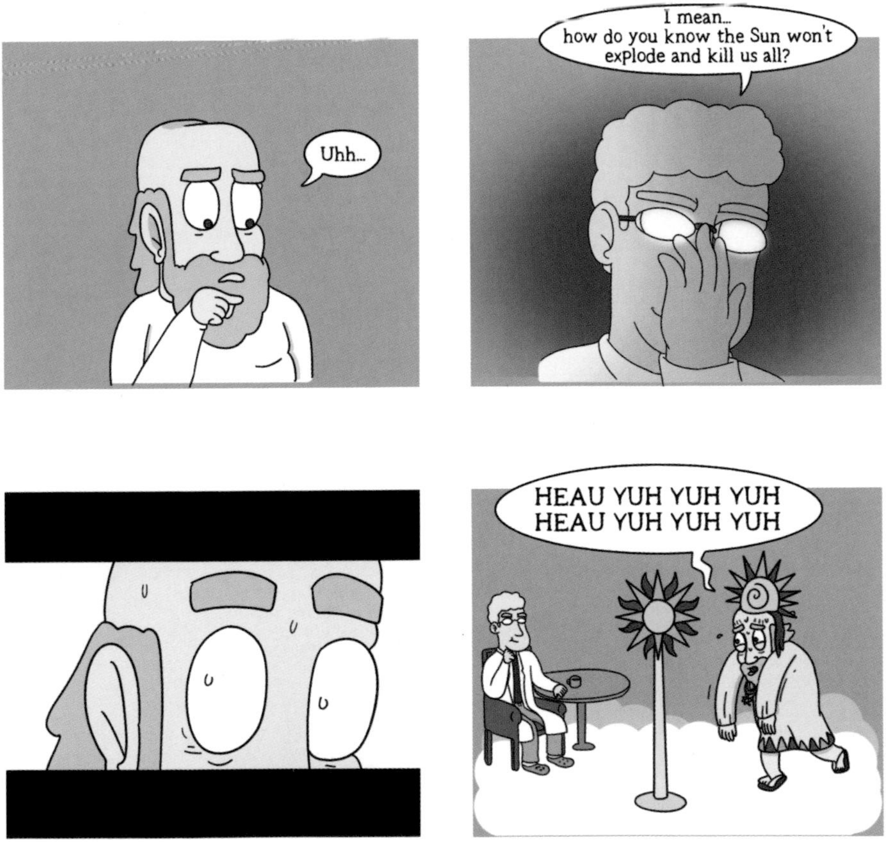
Uhh...
I mean...
how do you know the Sun won't
explode and kill us all?
HEAU YUH YUH YUH
HEAU YUH YUH YUH

BONUS

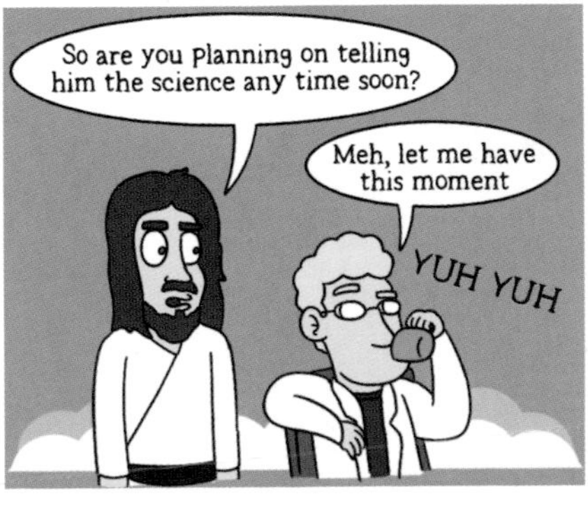
So are you planning on telling
him the science any time soon?
Meh, let me have
this moment
YUH YUH

The Surgery

Pass me the forceps, STAT!
Yes, doctor!
Mr. and Mrs. Thompson...
The surgery was a success, so your son is going to be OK!
THANK YOU GOD!!
Oh thank God!
Heh, all in a day's work
However, there was a complication and we had to remove a kidney

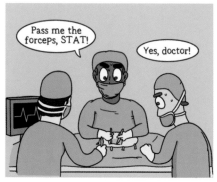

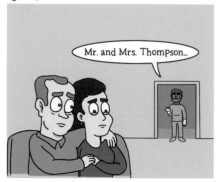

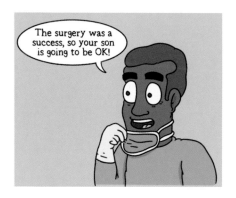

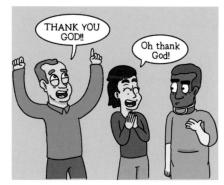

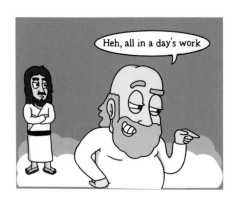

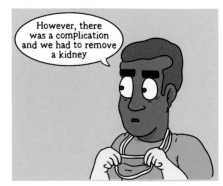

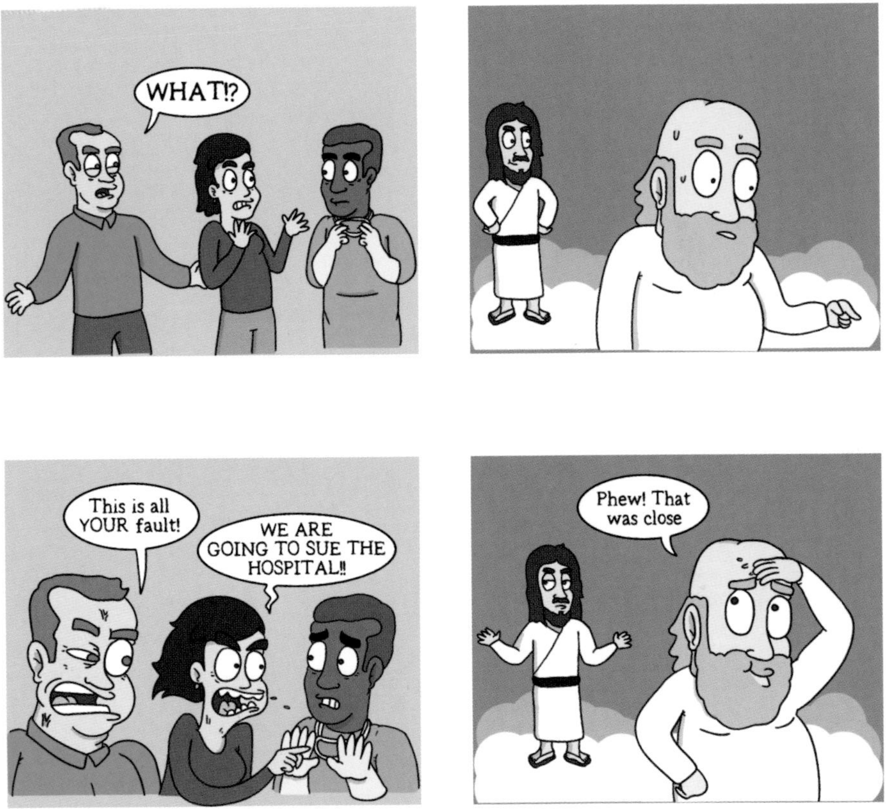
WHAT!?
This is all YOUR fault!
WE ARE GOING TO SUE THE HOSPITAL!!
Phew! That was close

BONUS

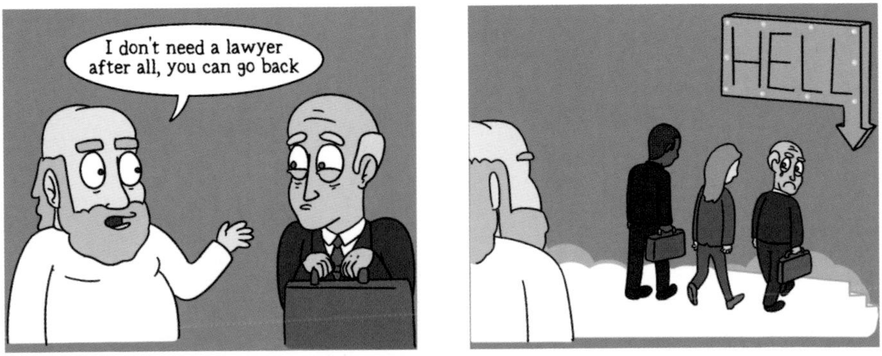
I don't need a lawyer after all, you can go back
HELL

Free

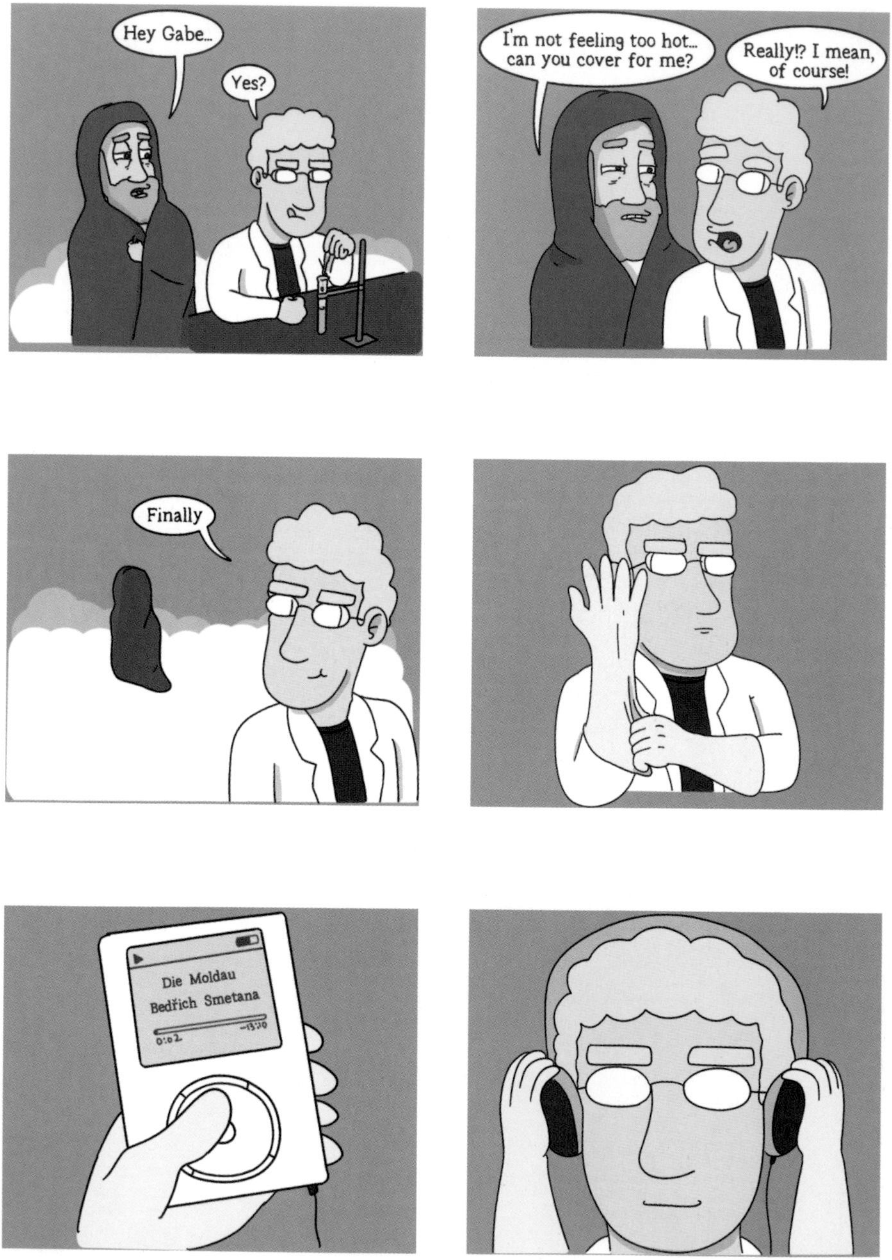
Hey Gabe...
Yes?
I'm not feeling too hot... can you cover for me?
Really!? I mean, of course!
Finally
Die Moldau
Bedřich Smetana

CRACK

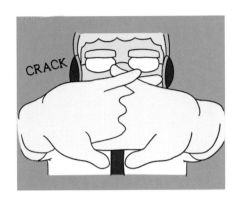

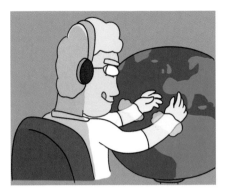

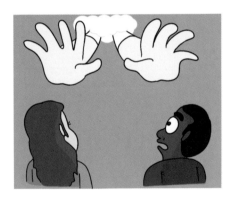

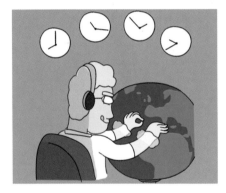

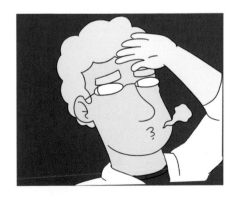

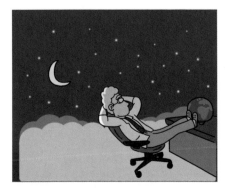

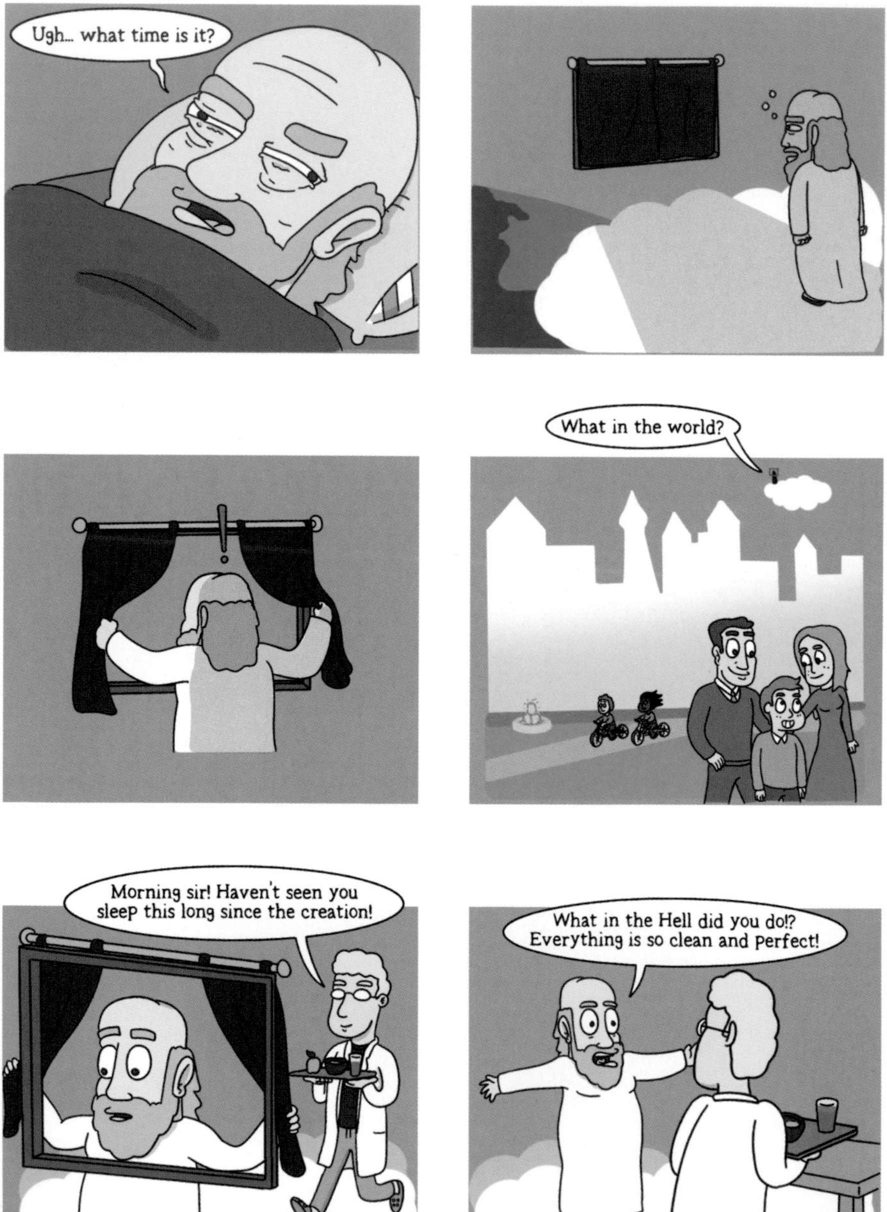
Ugh... what time is it?
What in the world?
Morning sir! Haven't seen you sleep this long since the creation!
What in the Hell did you do!? Everything is so clean and perfect!

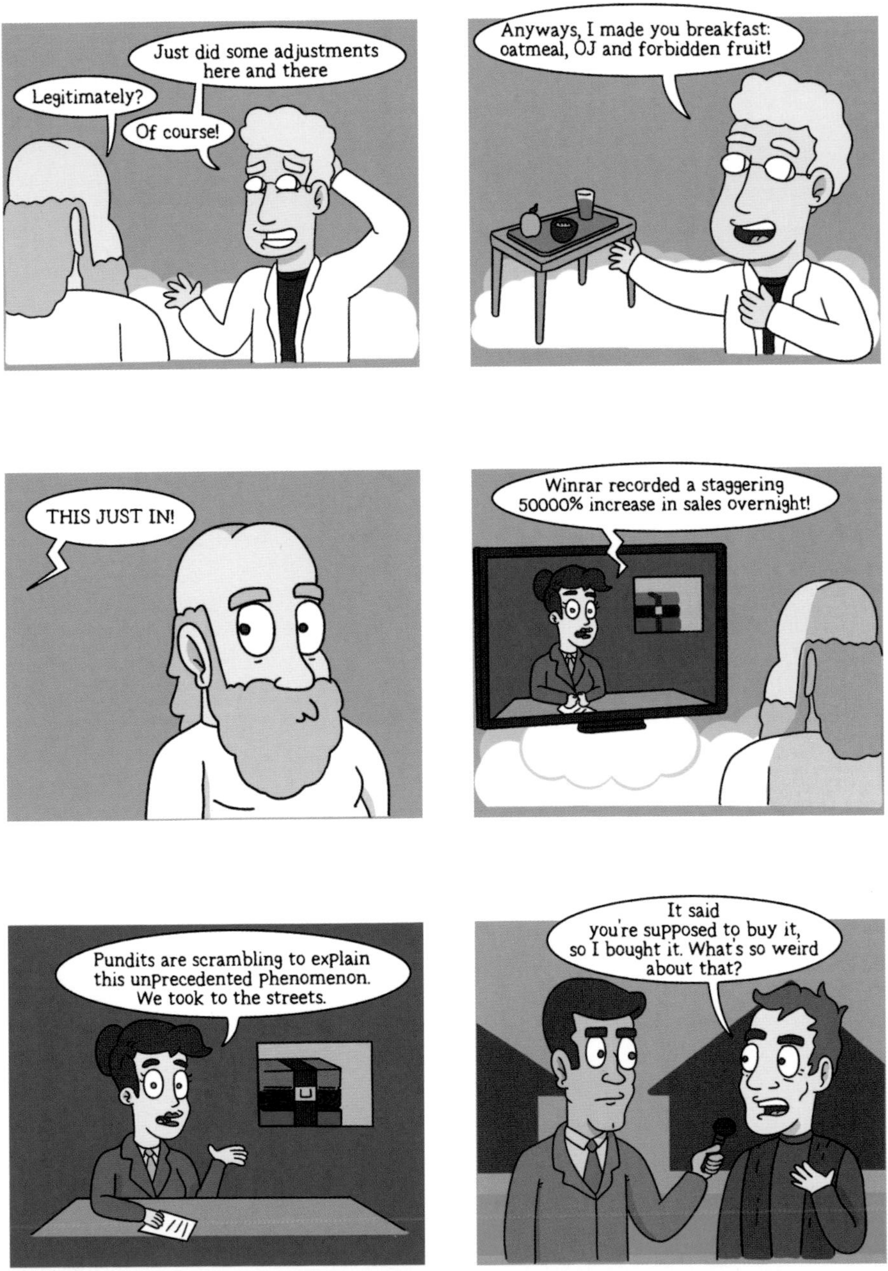
Just did some adjustments here and there
Legitimately?
Of course!
Anyways, I made you breakfast: oatmeal, OJ and forbidden fruit!
THIS JUST IN!
Winrar recorded a staggering 50000% increase in sales overnight!
Pundits are scrambling to explain this unprecedented phenomenon. We took to the streets.
It said you're supposed to buy it, so I bought it. What's so weird about that?

Now that's just peculiar
People have more disposable income, that's all!

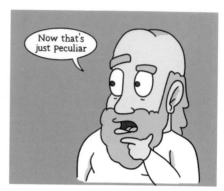

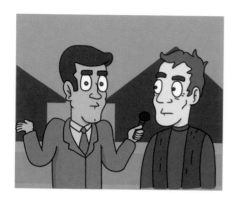

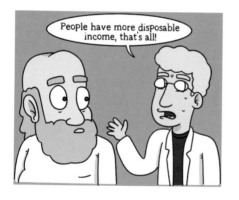

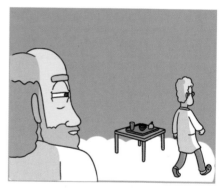

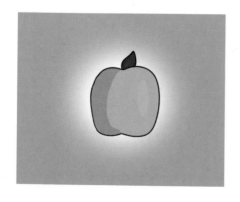

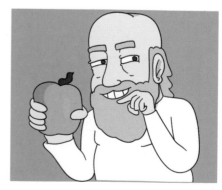

Will

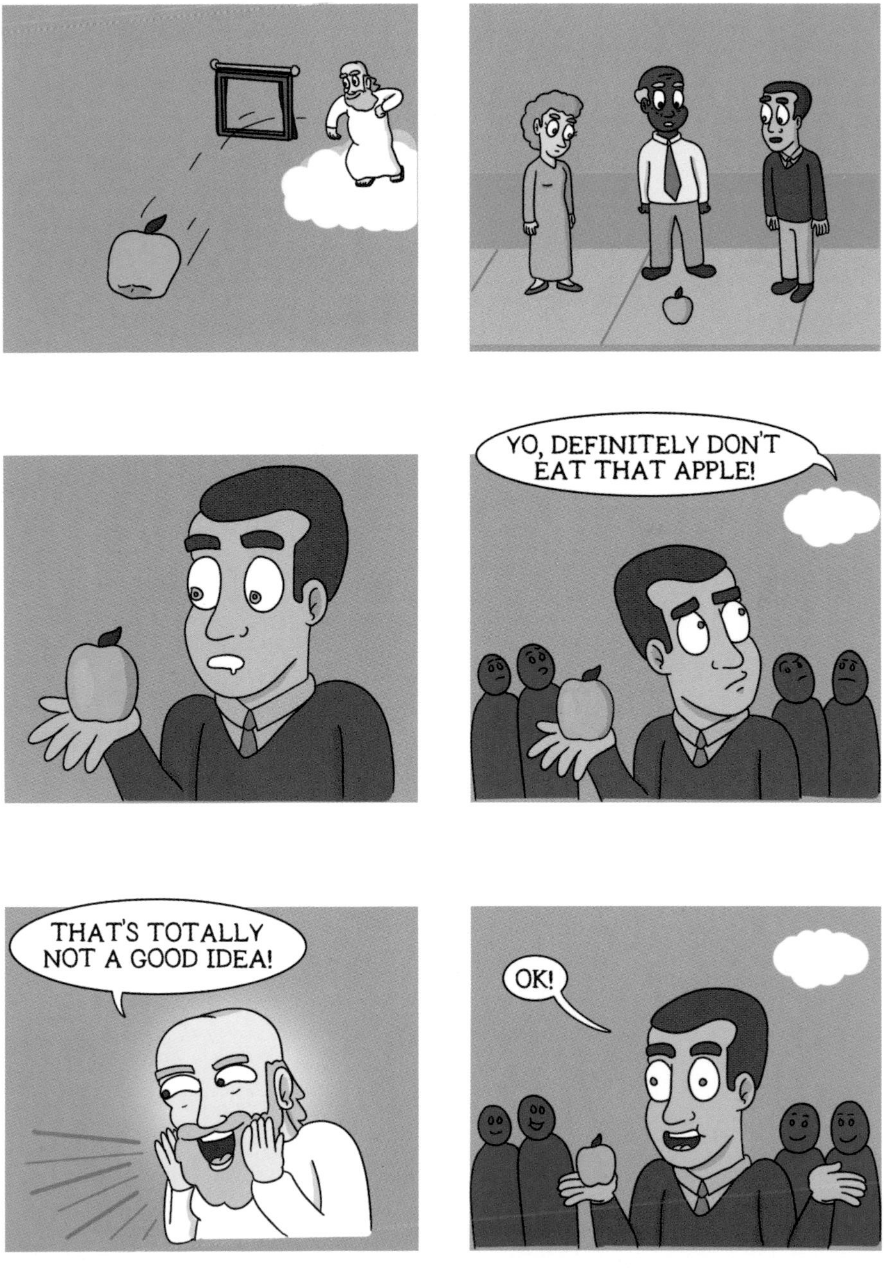
YO, DEFINITELY DON'T EAT THAT APPLE!
THAT'S TOTALLY NOT A GOOD IDEA!
OK!

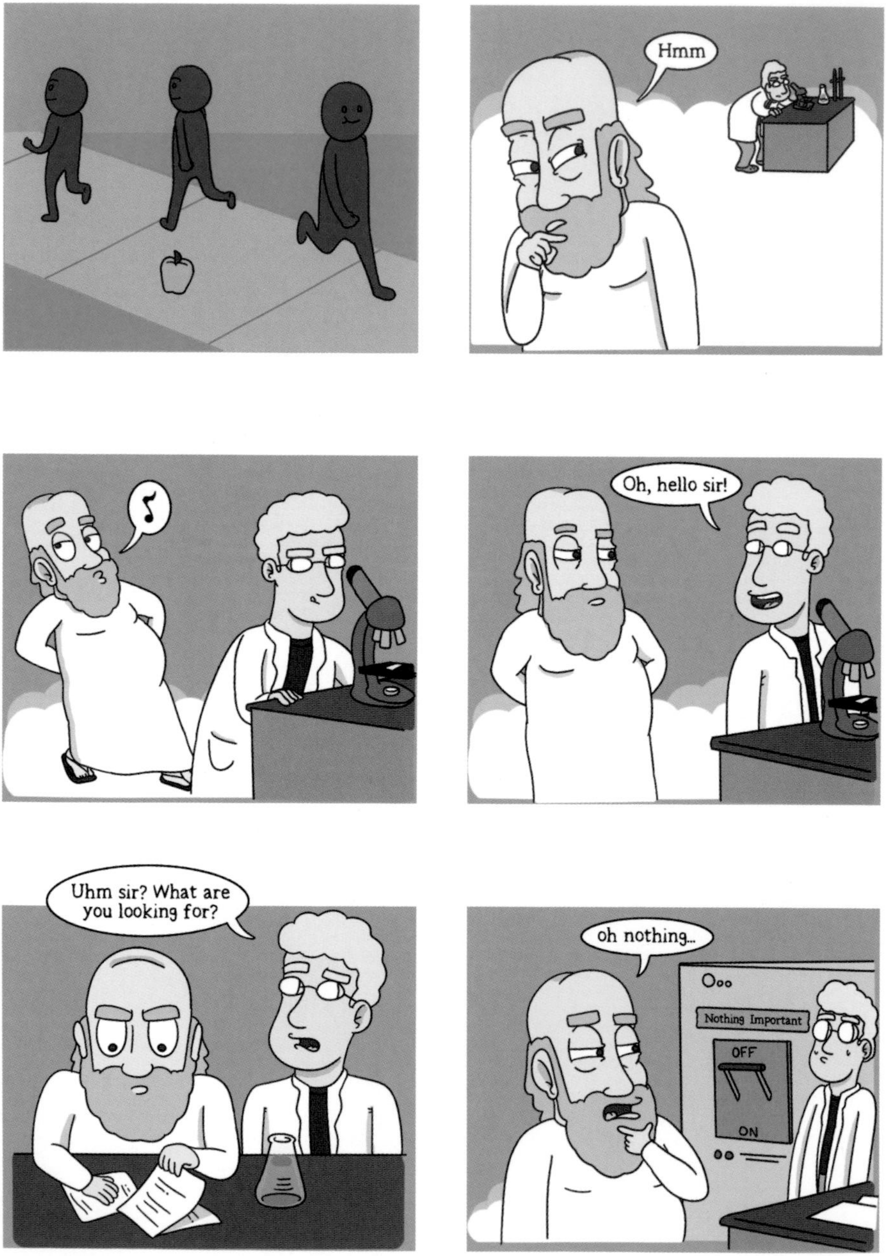
Hmm
Oh, hello sir!
Uhm sir? What are you looking for?
oh nothing...
Ooo
Nothing Important
OFF
ON

Just checking the lab- AHA!
I knew it!
IMPORTANT
FREE WILL
OFF
ON
I'm sorry, that was just temporary until I got things in order!
Sorry, dem's the rules
Ooo
FREE WILL
OFF
ON
Ooo
FREE WILL
OFF
ON

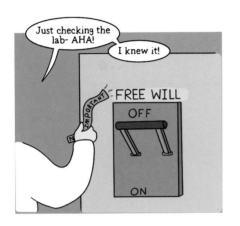

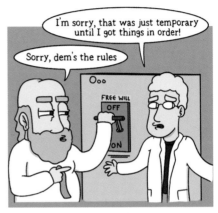

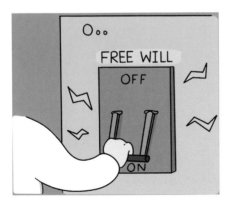

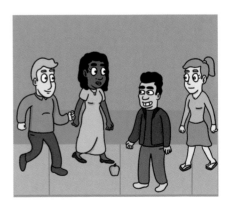

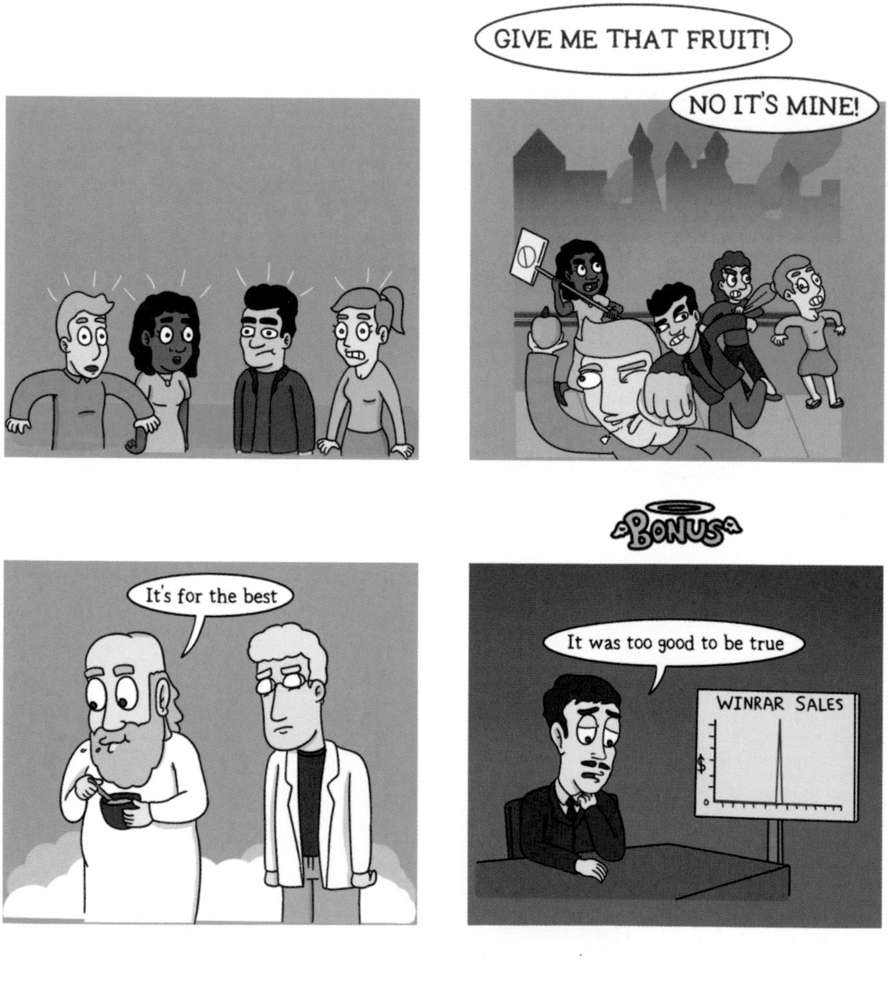
GIVE ME THAT FRUIT!
NO IT'S MINE!
It's for the best
BONUS
It was too good to be true
WINRAR SALES
$
0

#Blessed

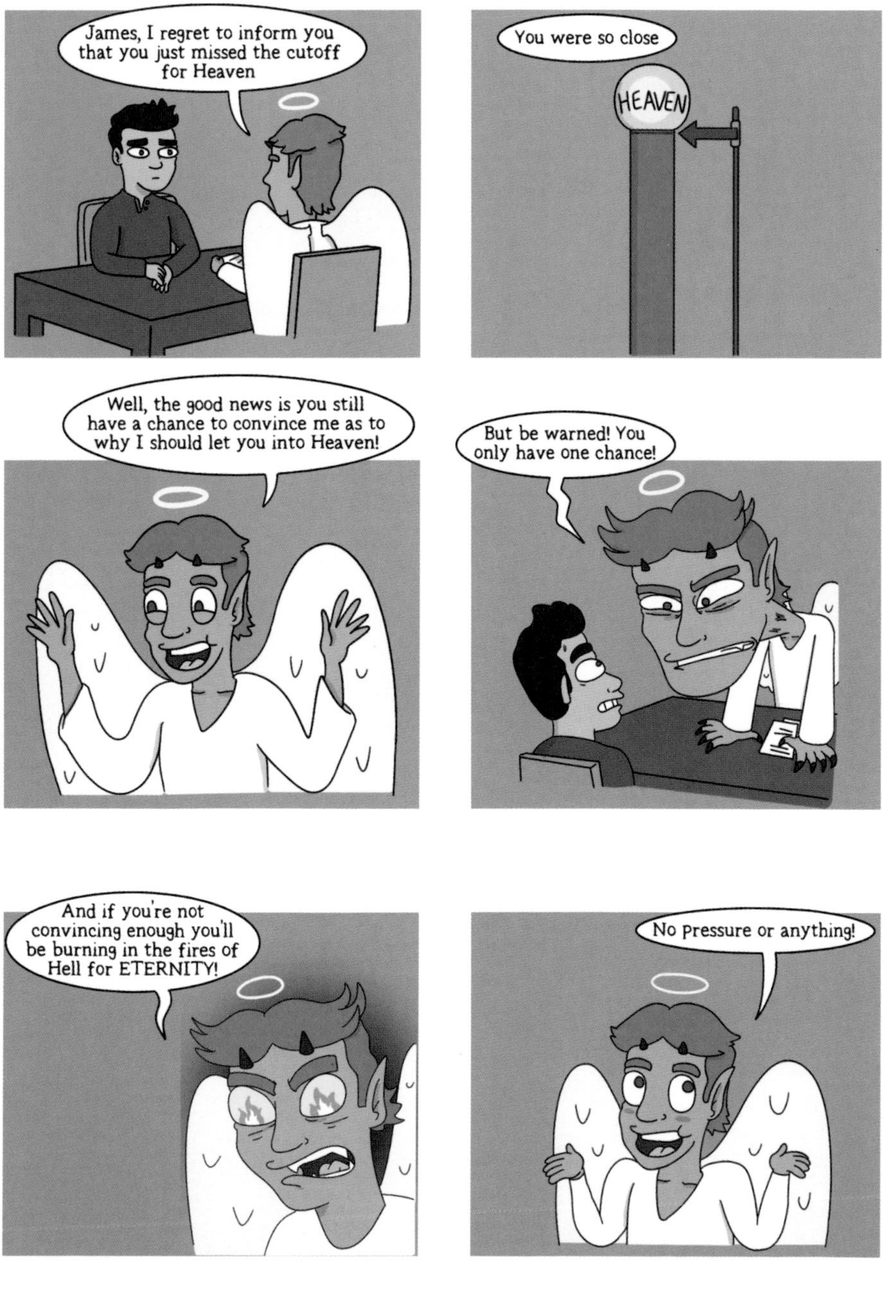
James, I regret to inform you that you just missed the cutoff for Heaven
You were so close
HEAVEN
Well, the good news is you still have a chance to convince me as to why I should let you into Heaven!
But be warned! You only have one chance!
And if you're not convincing enough you'll be burning in the fires of Hell for ETERNITY!
No pressure or anything!

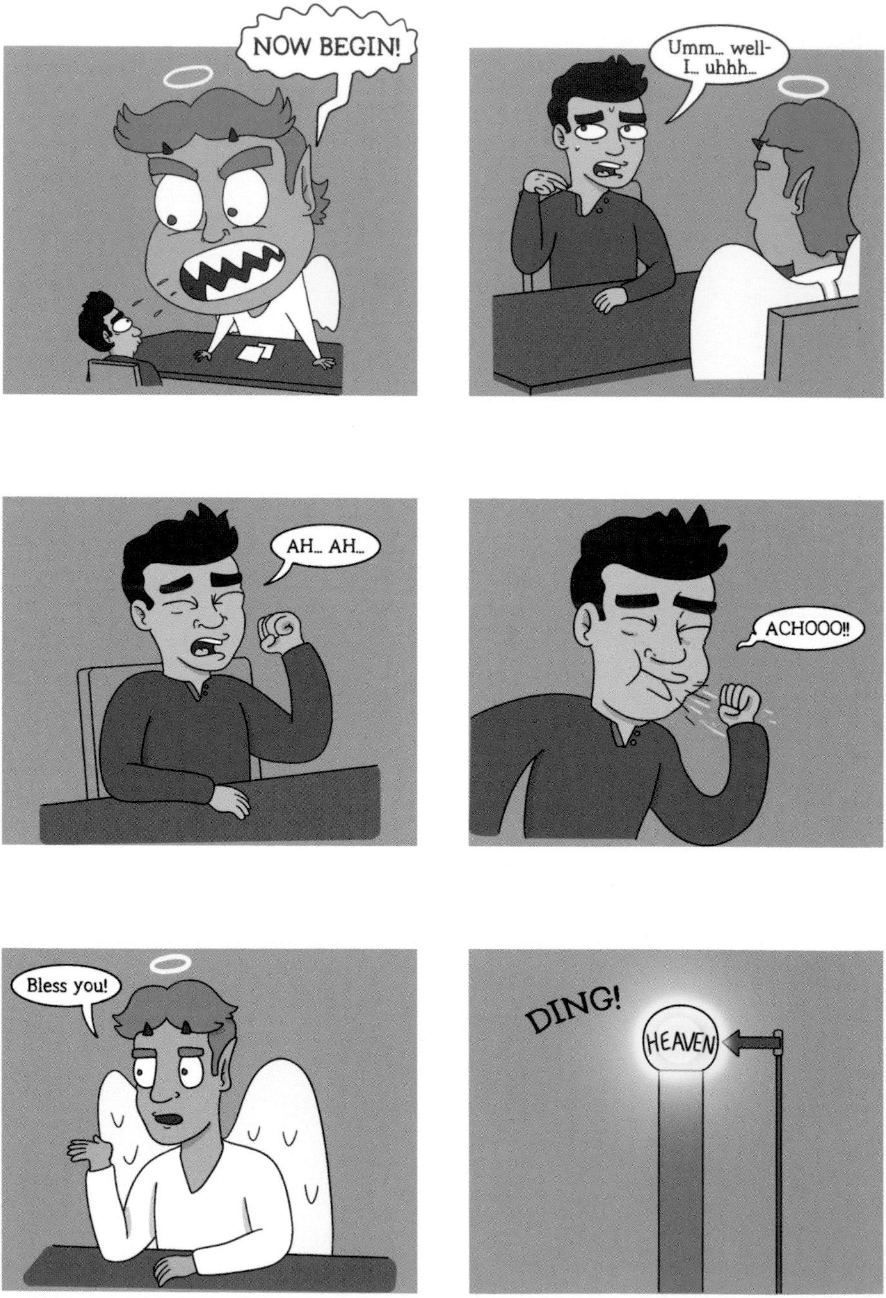
NOW BEGIN!
Umm... well-
I... uhhh...
AH... AH...
ACHOOO!!
Bless you!
DING!
HEAVEN

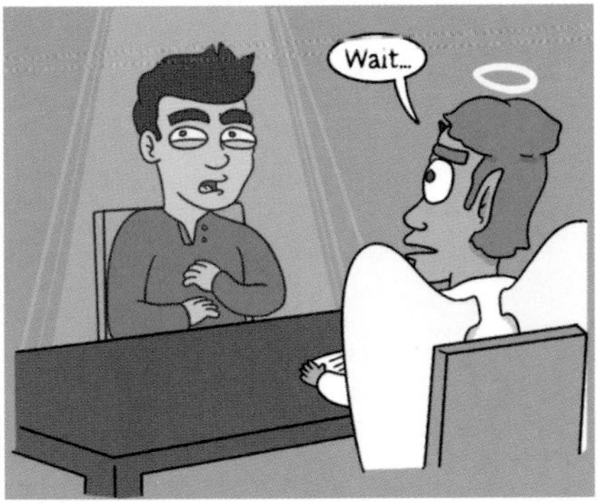
Wait...

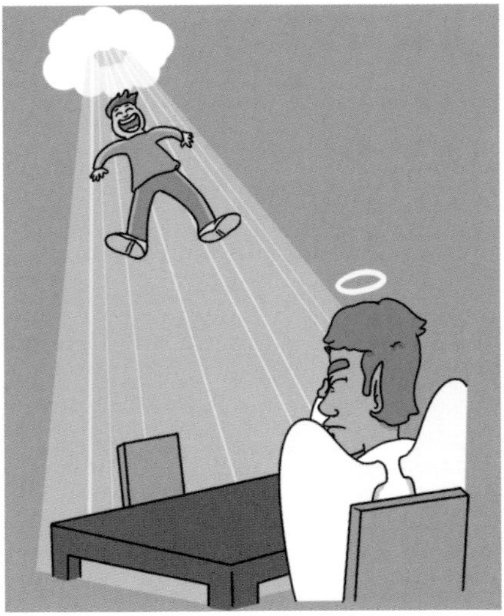

BONUS

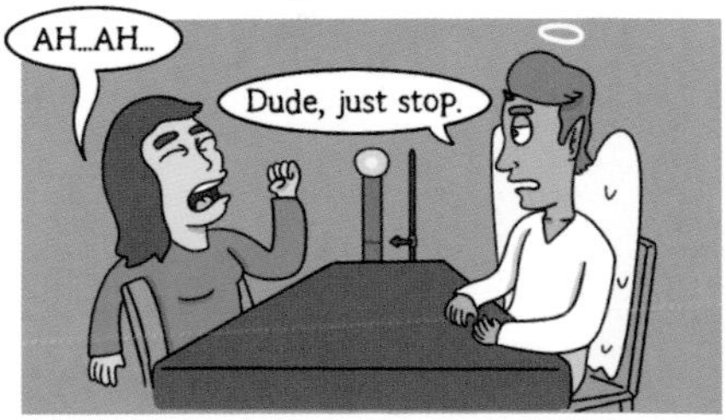
AH...AH...
Dude, just stop.

Climate Change

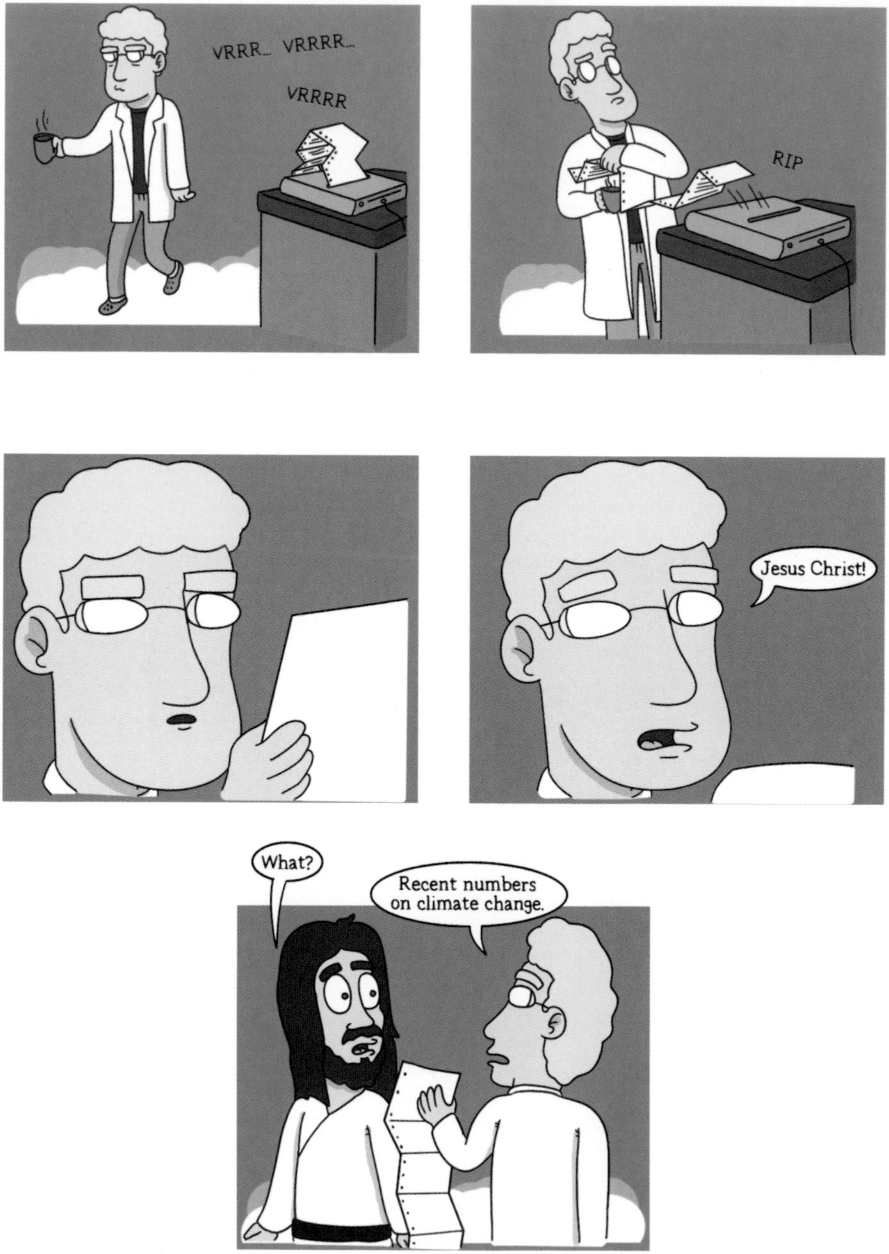
VRRR... VRRRR...
VRRRR
RIP
Jesus Christ!
What?
Recent numbers on climate change.

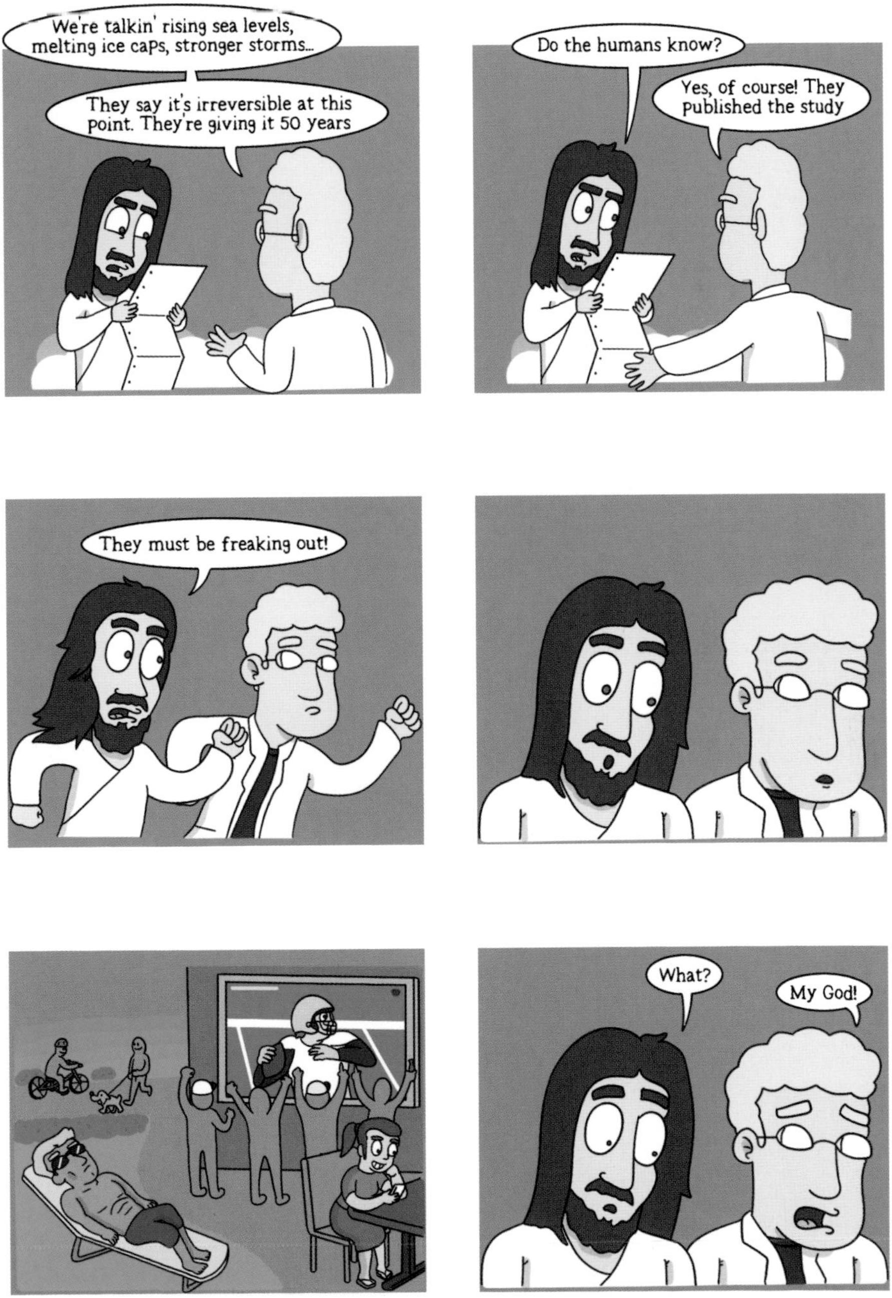
We're talkin' rising sea levels, melting ice caps, stronger storms...
They say it's irreversible at this point. They're giving it 50 years
Do the humans know?
Yes, of course! They published the study
They must be freaking out!
What?
My God!

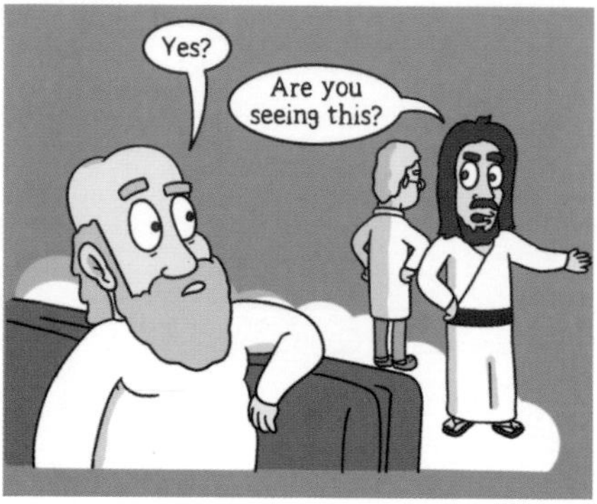
Yes?
Are you seeing this?

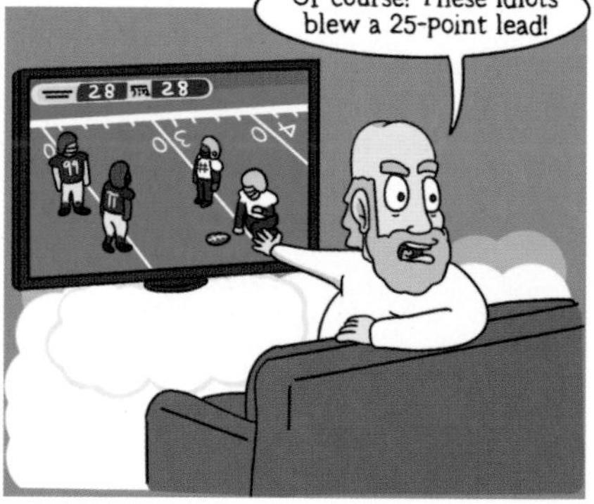
Of course! These idiots blew a 25-point lead!
28 28

BONUS

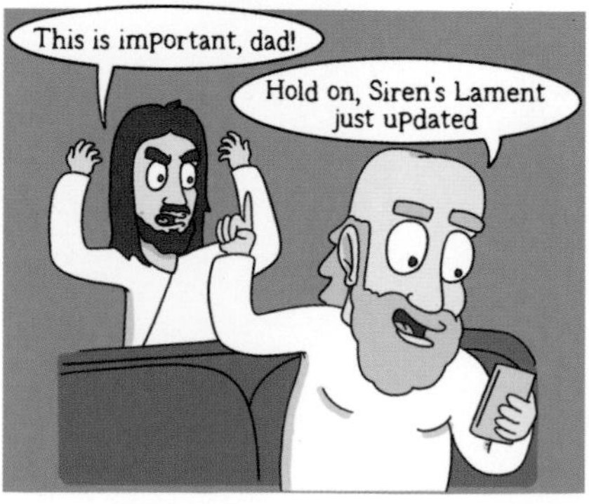
This is important, dad!
Hold on, Siren's Lament just updated

Truth

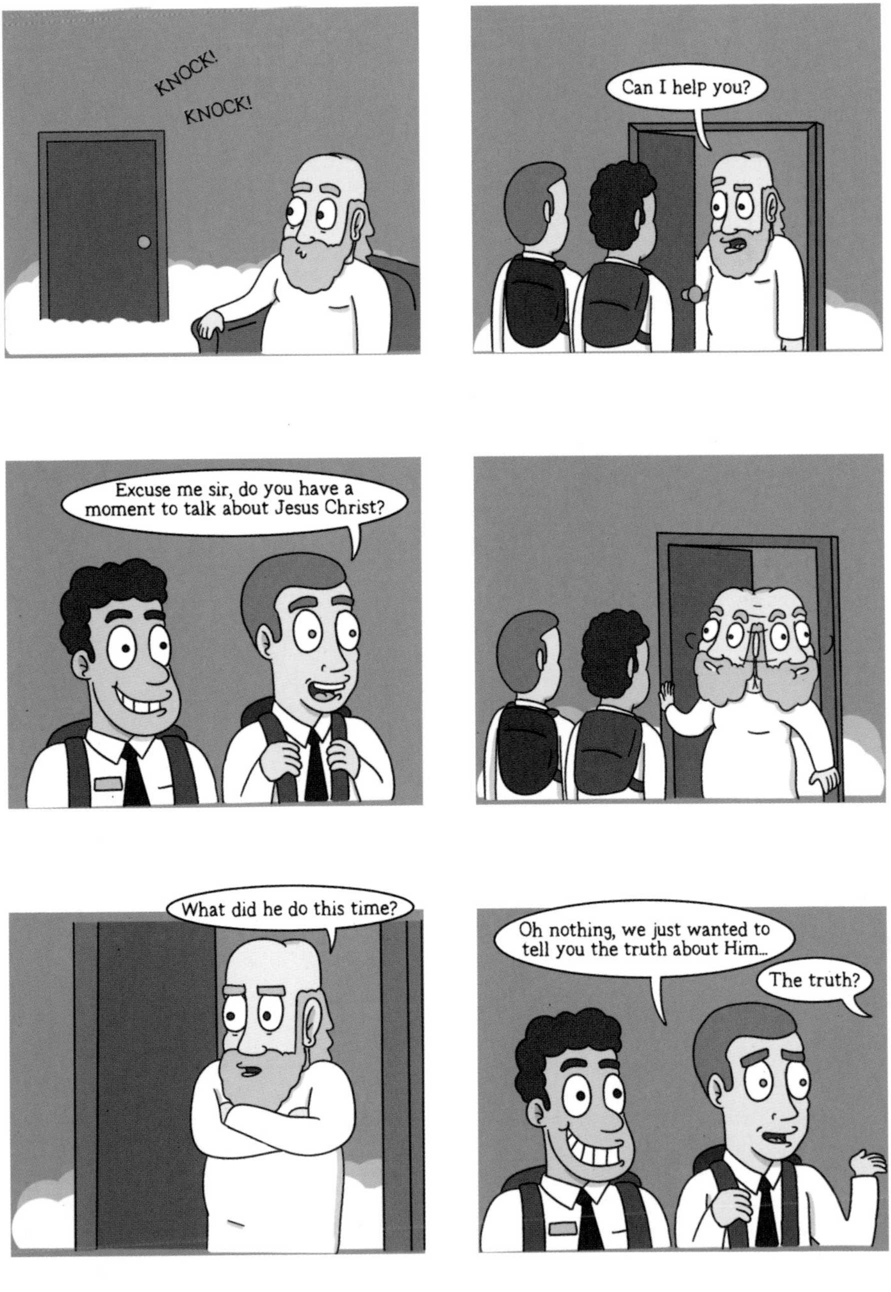
KNOCK!
KNOCK!
Can I help you?
Excuse me sir, do you have a moment to talk about Jesus Christ?
What did he do this time?
Oh nothing, we just wanted to tell you the truth about Him...
The truth?

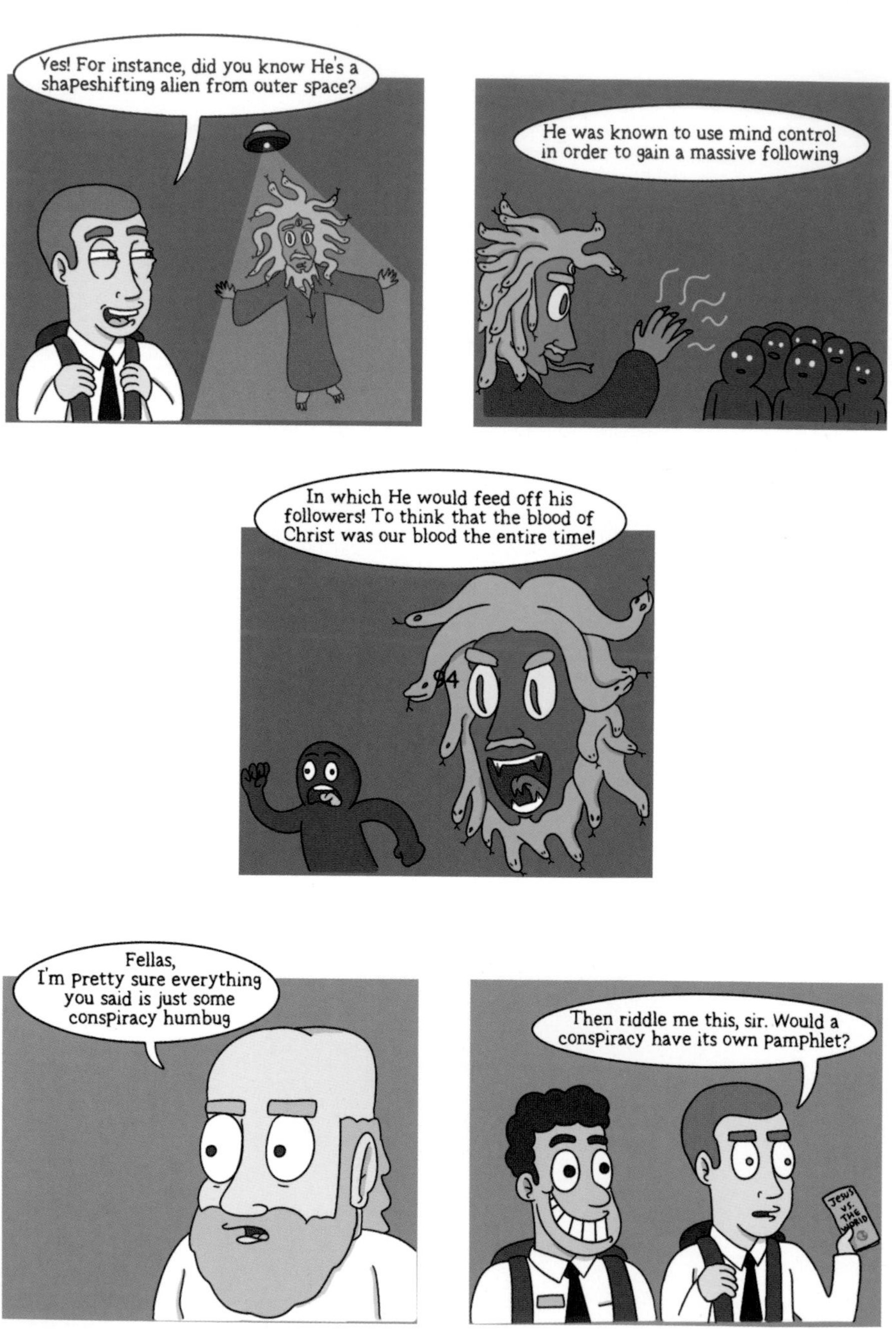
Yes! For instance, did you know He's a shapeshifting alien from outer space?
He was known to use mind control in order to gain a massive following
In which He would feed off his followers! To think that the blood of Christ was our blood the entire time!
Fellas, I'm pretty sure everything you said is just some conspiracy humbug
Then riddle me this, sir. Would a conspiracy have its own pamphlet?
JESUS VS. THE WORLD

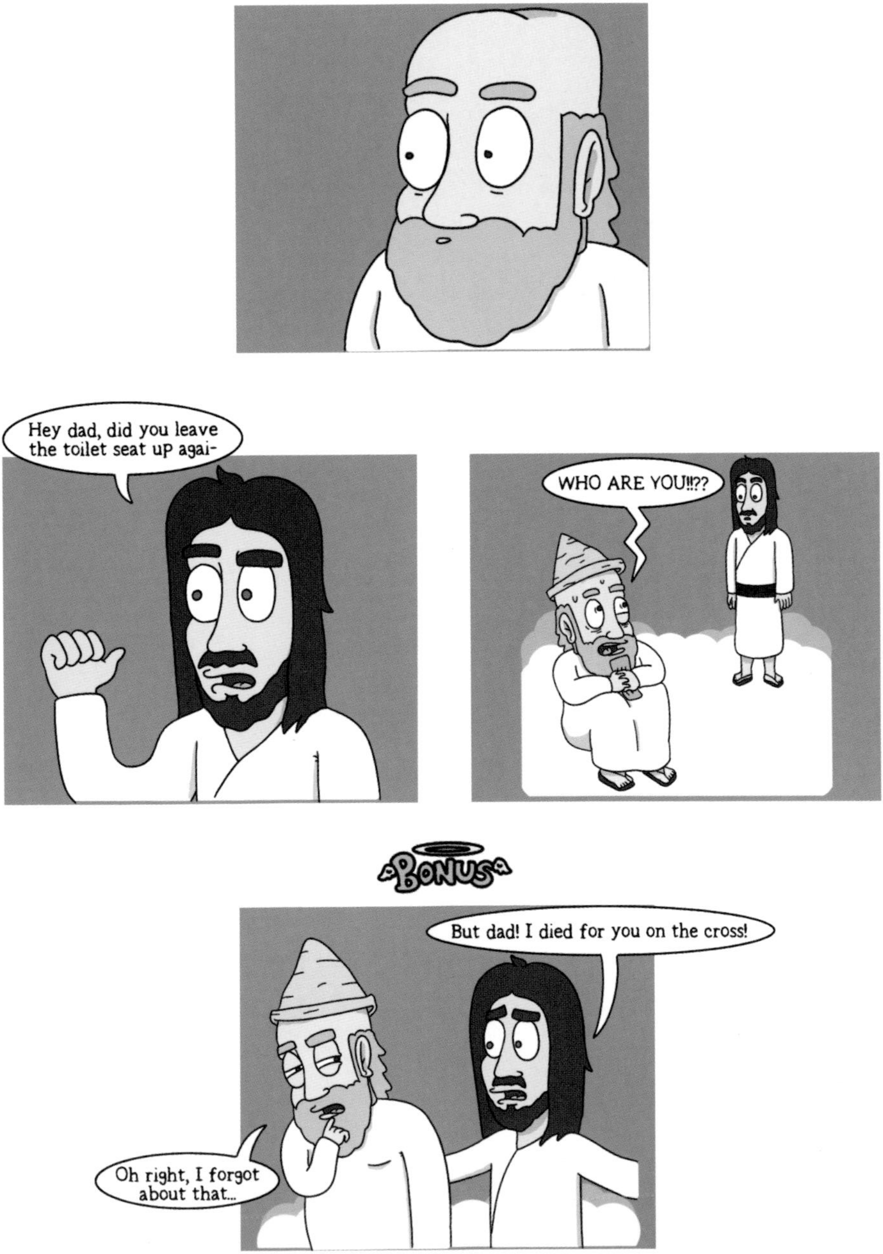
Hey dad, did you leave the toilet seat up agai-
WHO ARE YOU!!??
BONUS
But dad! I died for you on the cross!
Oh right, I forgot about that...

Noah's Ark: Pandas

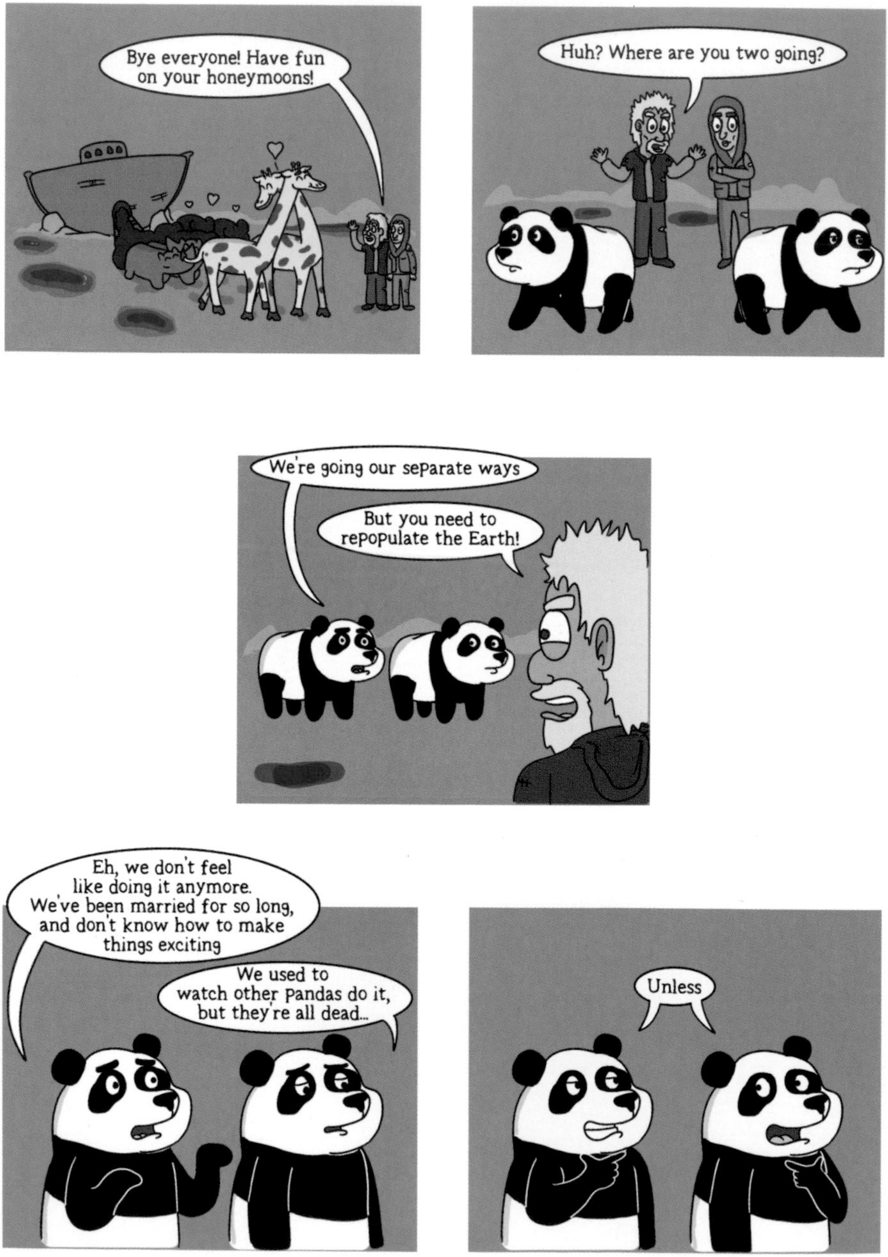

Bye everyone! Have fun on your honeymoons!
Huh? Where are you two going?
We're going our separate ways
But you need to repopulate the Earth!
Eh, we don't feel like doing it anymore. We've been married for so long, and don't know how to make things exciting
We used to watch other pandas do it, but they're all dead...
Unless

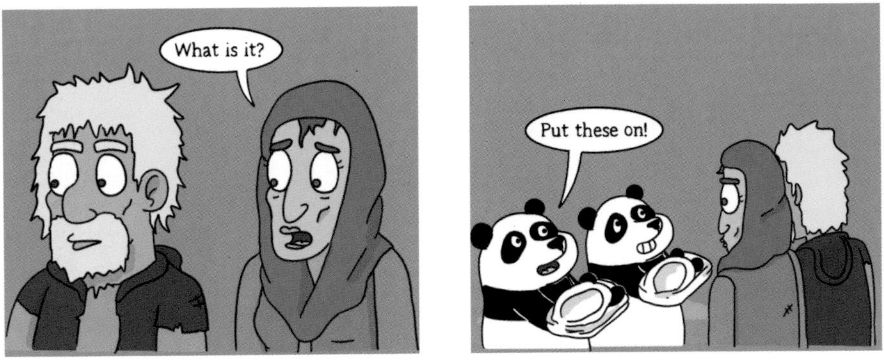
What is it?
Put these on!

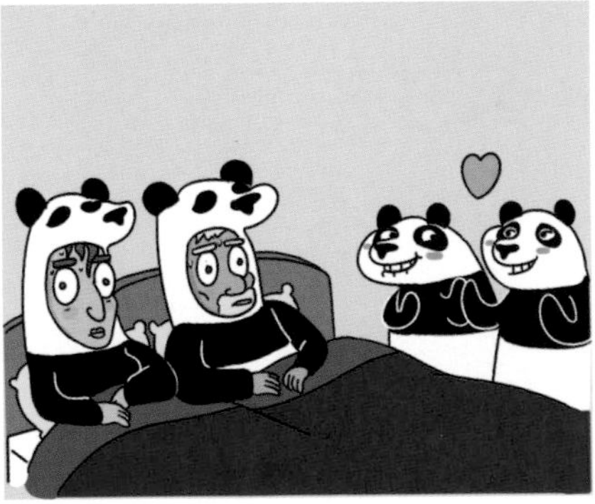

BONUS

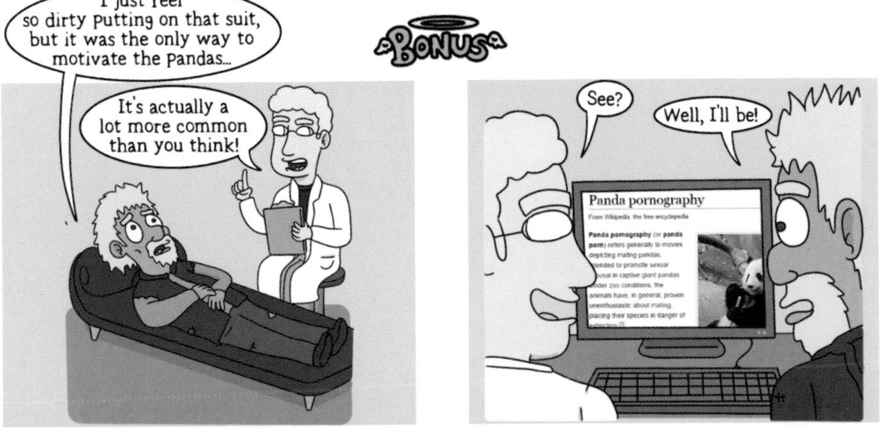
I just feel so dirty putting on that suit, but it was the only way to motivate the pandas...
It's actually a lot more common than you think!
See?
Well, I'll be!
Panda pornography
From Wikipedia, the free encyclopedia
Panda pornography (or panda porn) refers generally to movies depicting mating pandas,
to promote sexual
in captive giant pandas.
zoo conditions, the
animals have, in general, proven
unenthusiastic about mating,
placing their species in danger of

Alternate Universes

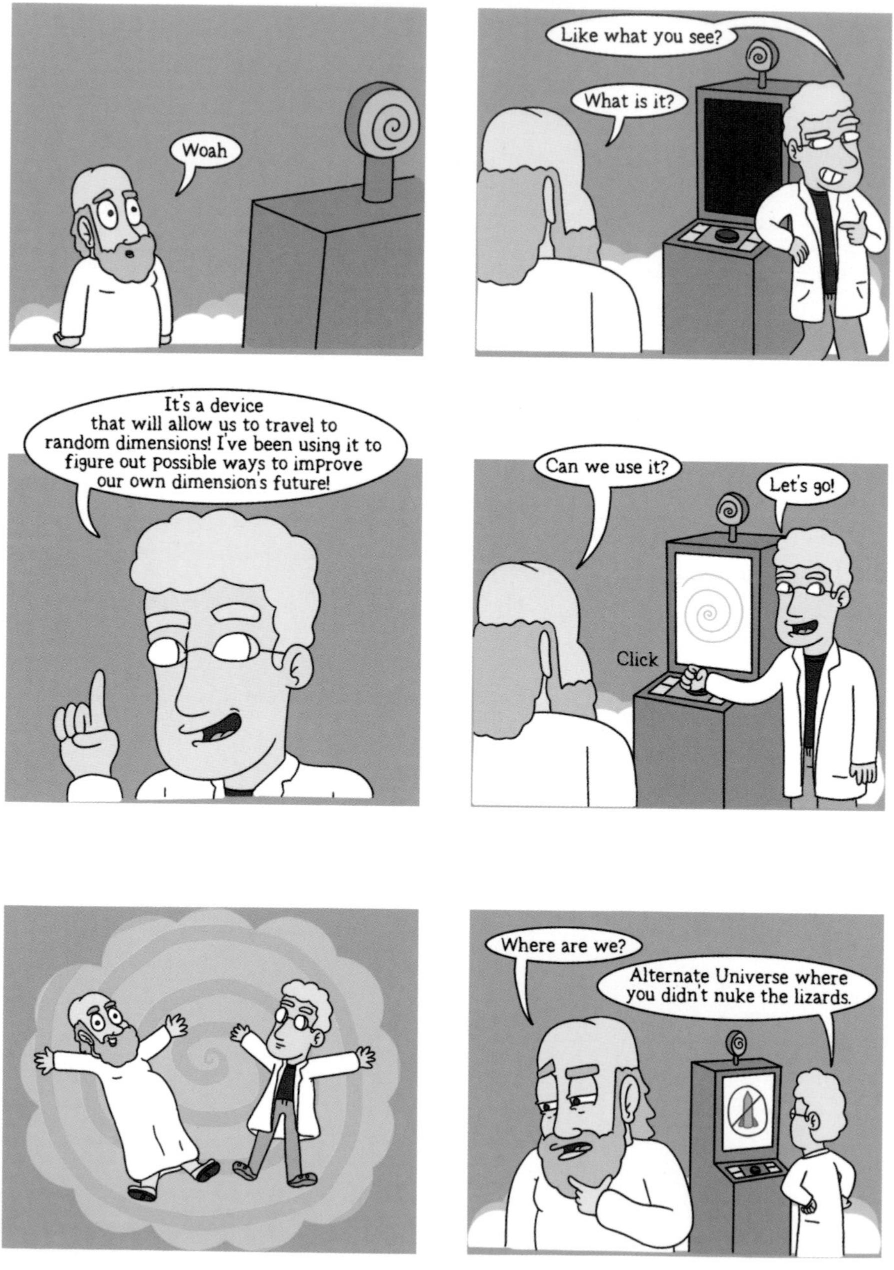
Woah
Like what you see?
What is it?
It's a device that will allow us to travel to random dimensions! I've been using it to figure out possible ways to improve our own dimension's future!
Can we use it?
Let's go!
Click
Where are we?
Alternate Universe where you didn't nuke the lizards.

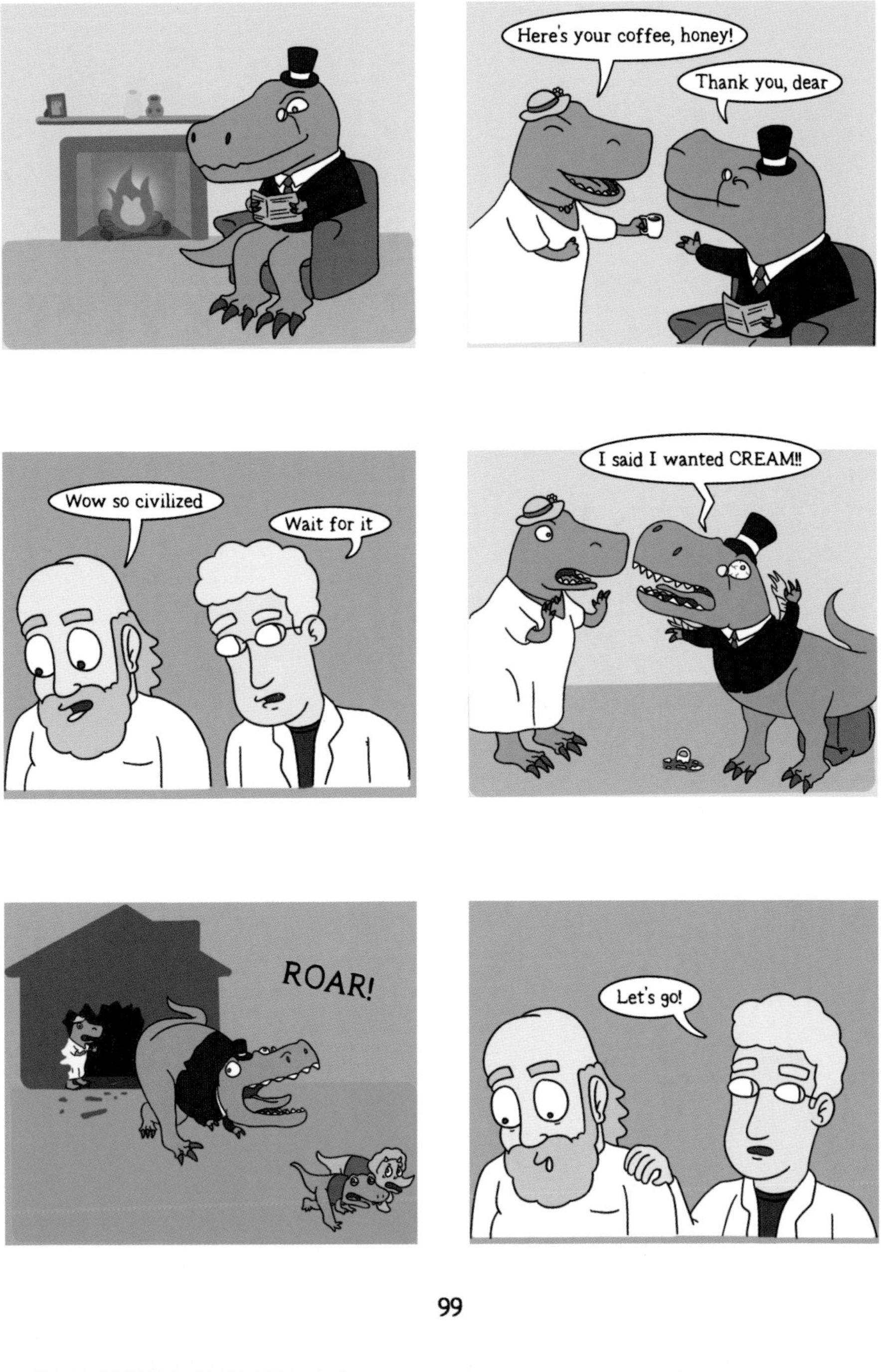
Here's your coffee, honey!
Thank you, dear
Wow so civilized
Wait for it
I said I wanted CREAM!!
ROAR!
Let's go!

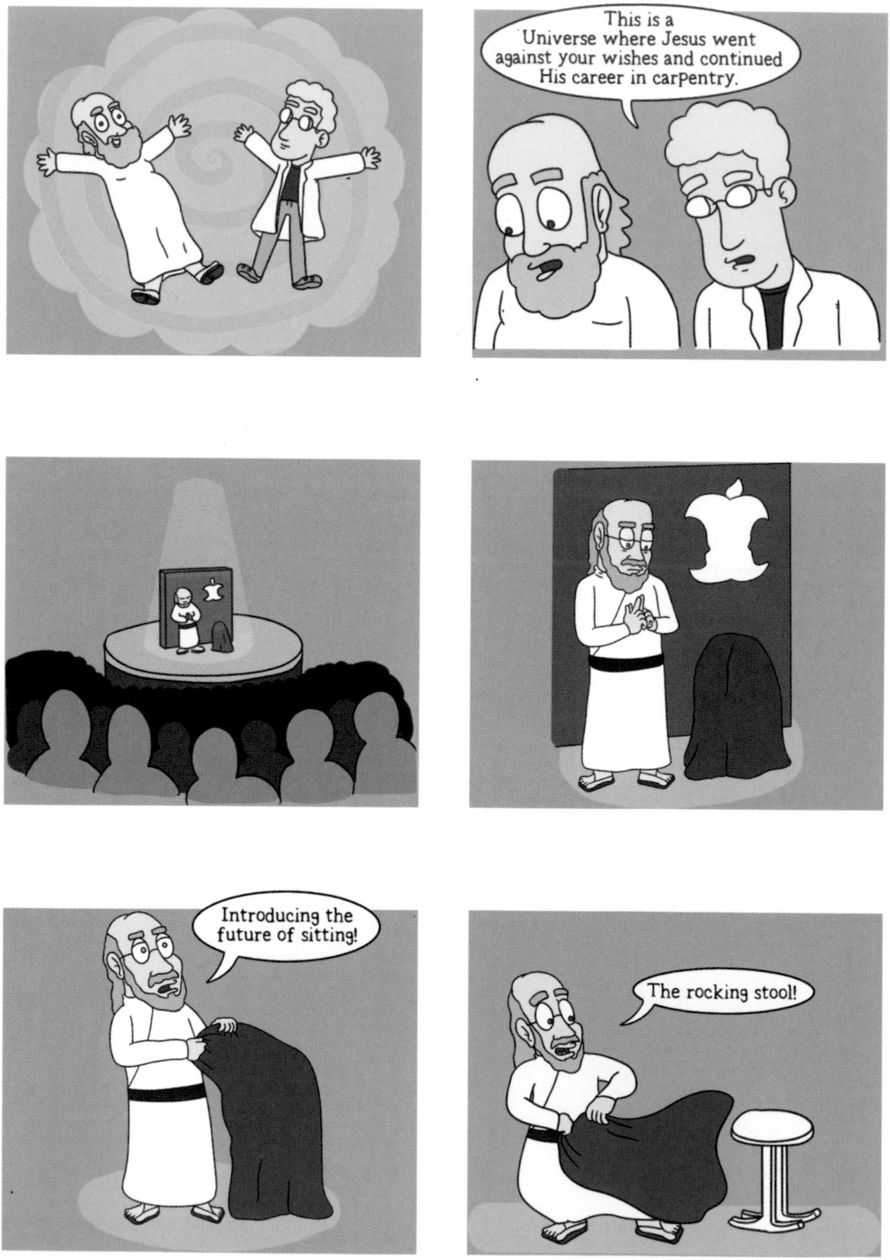
This is a Universe where Jesus went against your wishes and continued His career in carpentry.
Introducing the future of sitting!
The rocking stool!

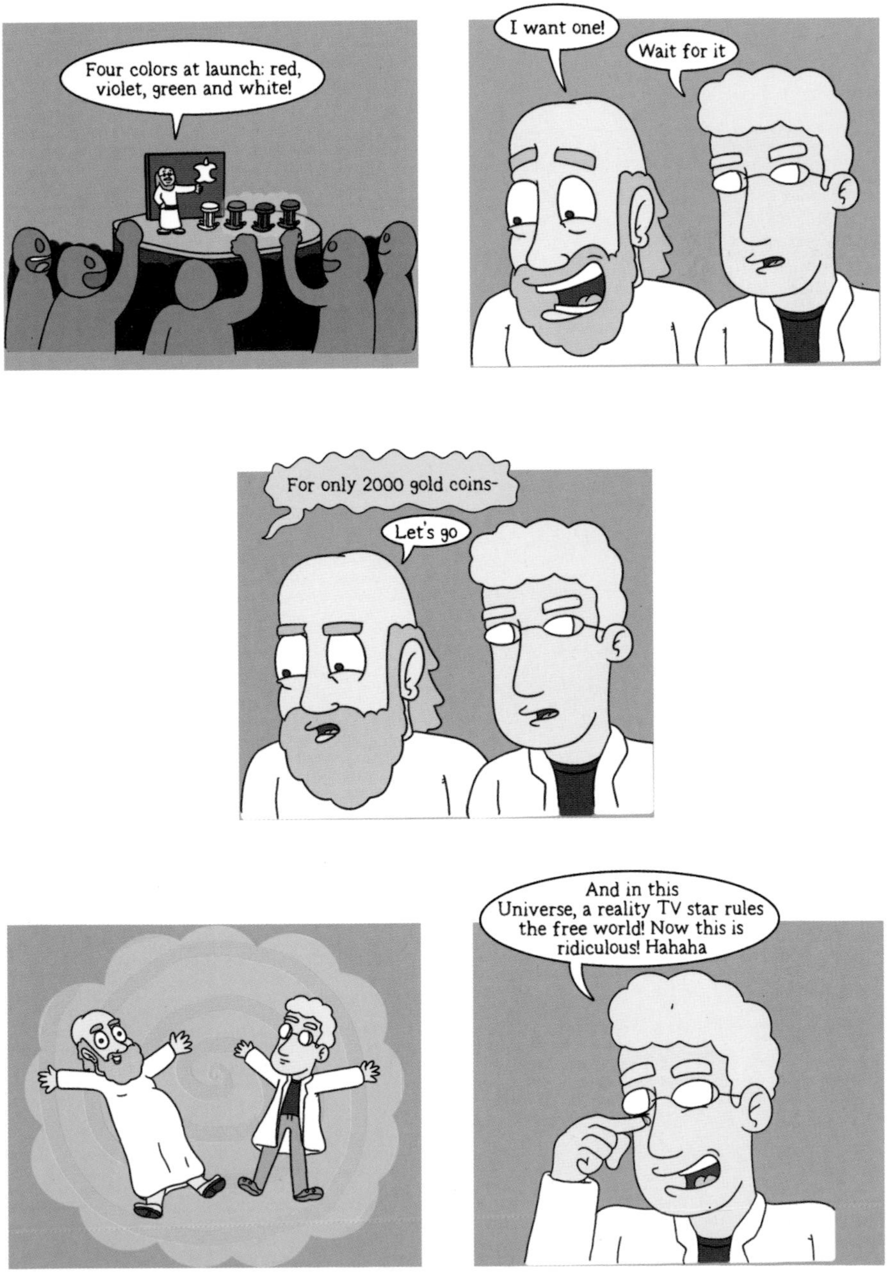

Four colors at launch: red, violet, green and white!
I want one!
Wait for it
For only 2000 gold coins-
Let's go
And in this Universe, a reality TV star rules the free world! Now this is ridiculous! Hahaha

Wait a minute, this
is our Universe...

BONUS

Um, dad?
I think that's the
wrong reality TV star
President Kardashian

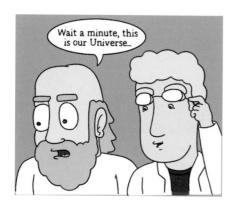

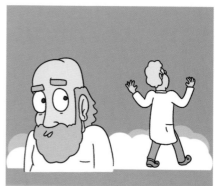

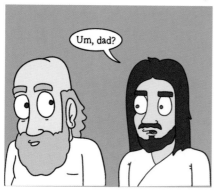

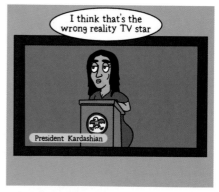

Typo

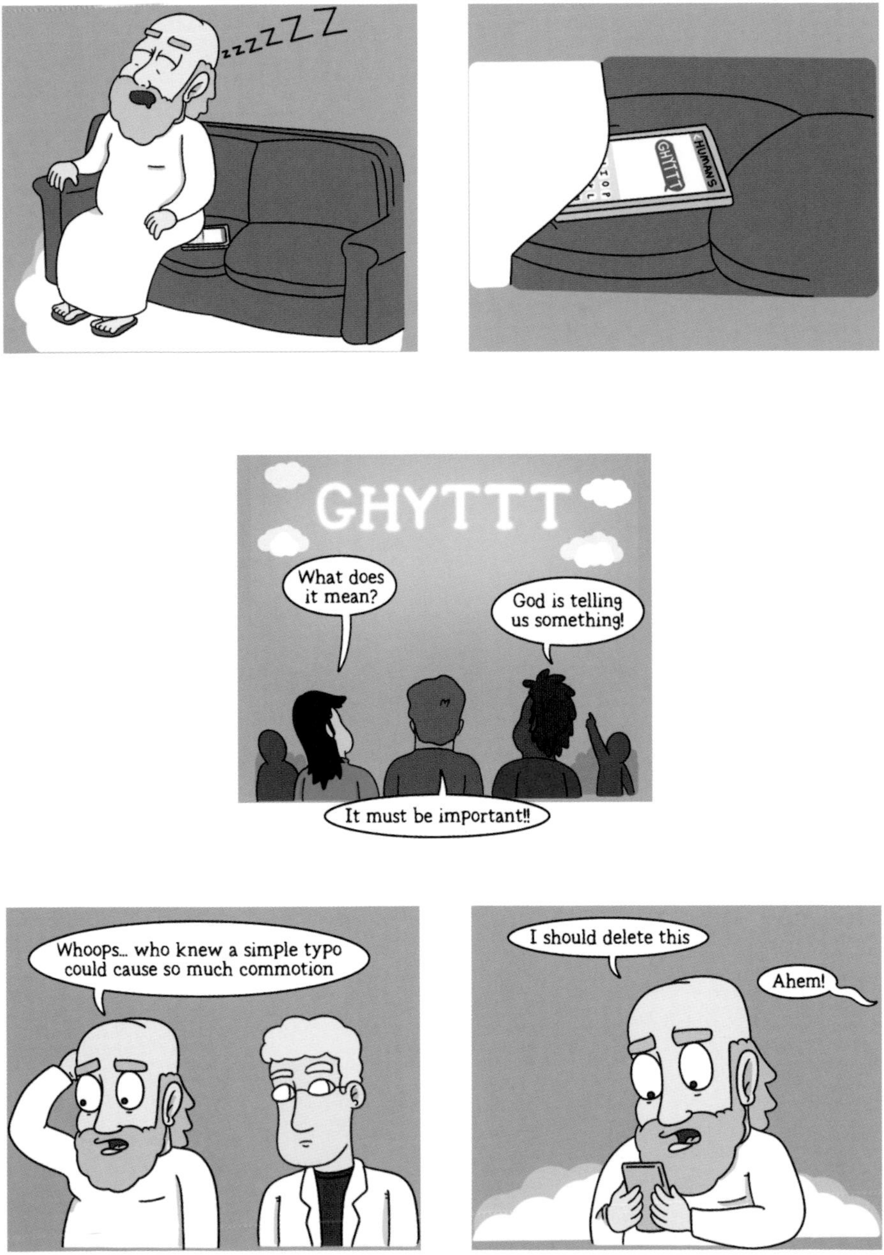
zzzZZZ
GHYTTT
What does it mean?
God is telling us something!
It must be important!!
Whoops... who knew a simple typo could cause so much commotion
I should delete this
Ahem!

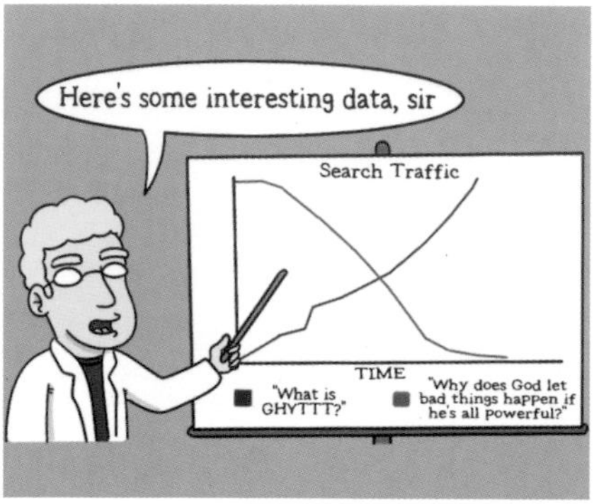
Here's some interesting data, sir
Search Traffic
TIME
"What is GHYTTT?"
"Why does God let bad things happen if he's all powerful?"

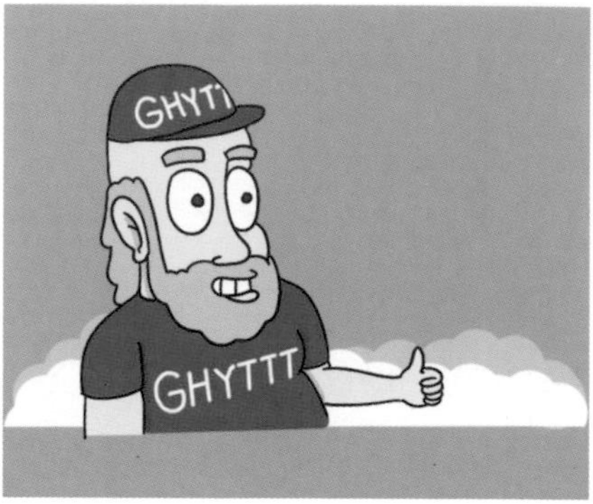
GHYTTT

BONUS

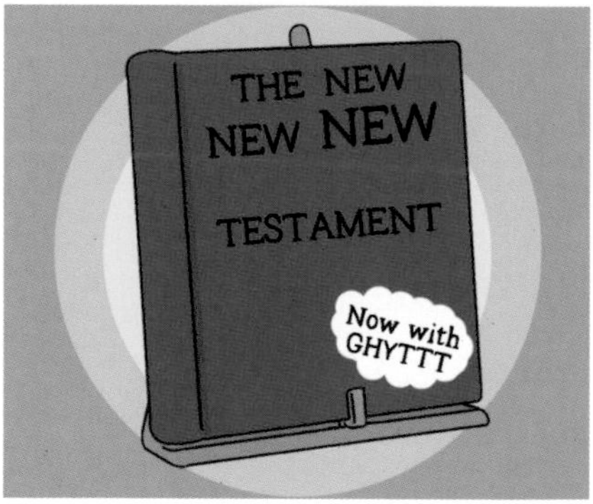
THE NEW NEW NEW TESTAMENT
Now with GHYTTT

BONUS BONUS

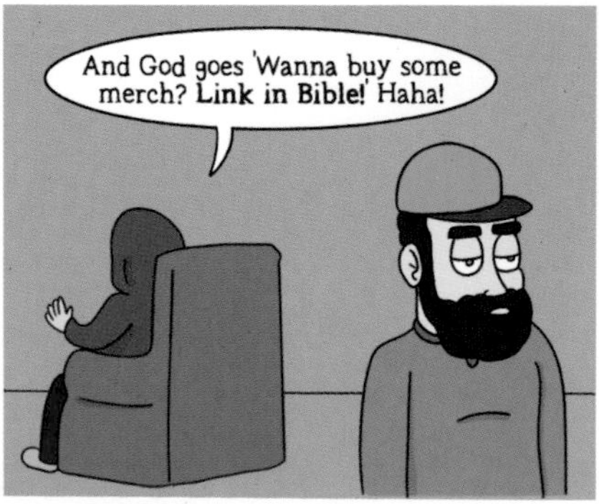
And God goes 'Wanna buy some merch? **Link in Bible!**' Haha!

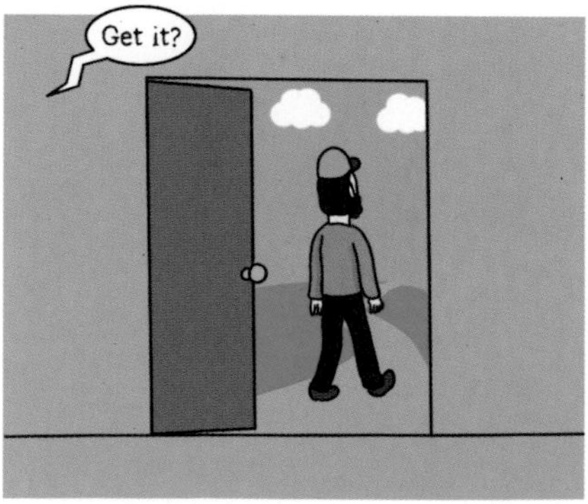
Get it?

Chad Gabe

What's wrong, Gabe?
Ugh, my eyesight is terrible. I couldn't even tell that I was in the wrong dimension last week!
Colony Collapse Disorder
Well, I can fix your vision like I did with the blind man on Earth!
Really?
Sure!
Vision be back!
I can see!
Ooh wow! Lookin' good, Gabe!

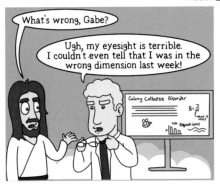

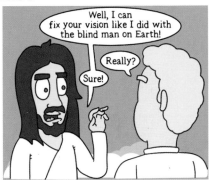

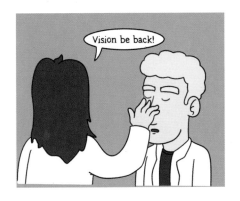

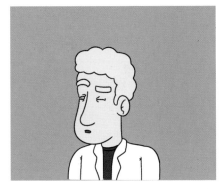

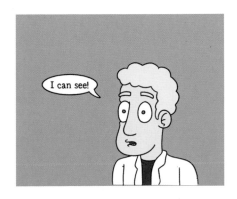

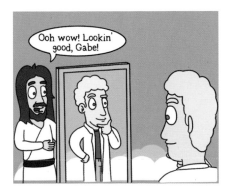

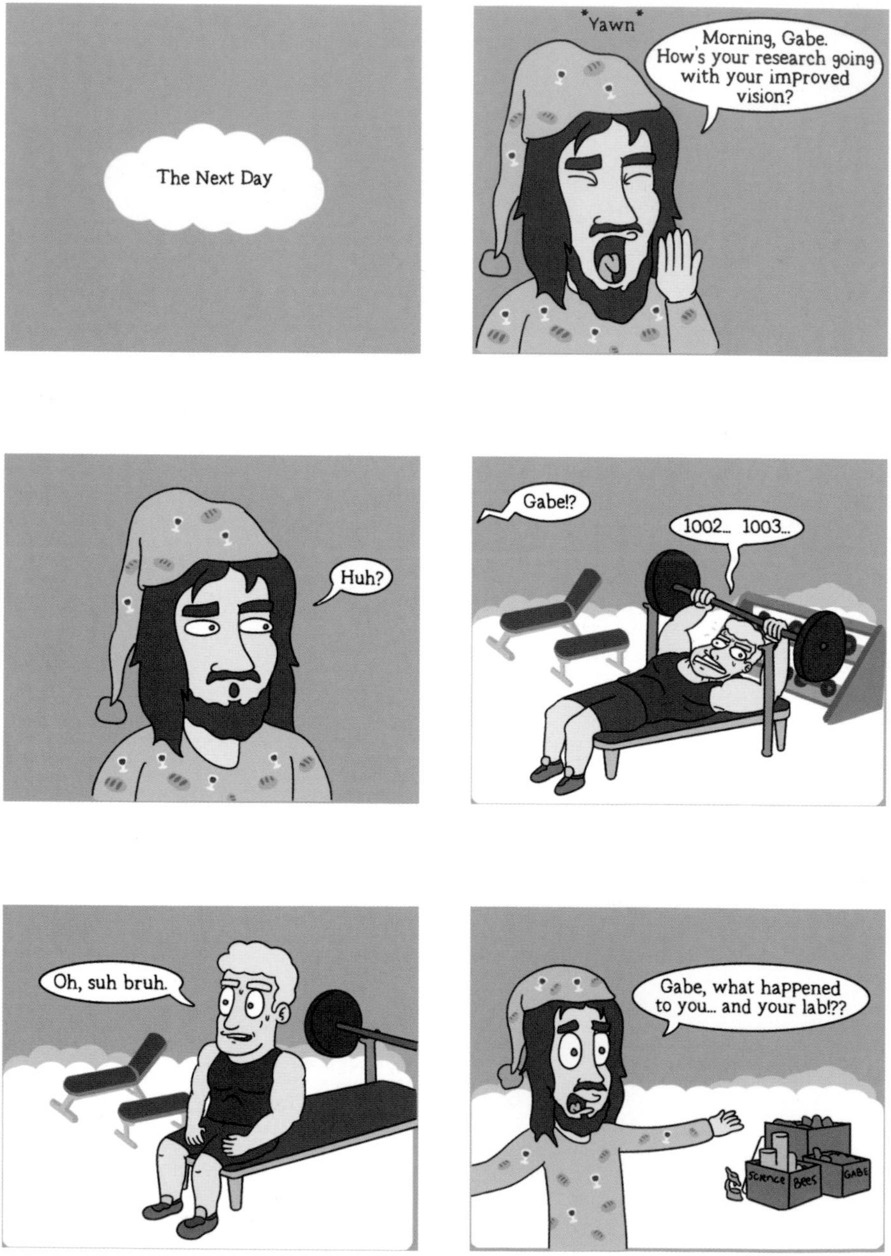
The Next Day
Yawn
Morning, Gabe. How's your research going with your improved vision?
Huh?
Gabe!?
1002... 1003...
Oh, suh bruh.
Gabe, what happened to you... and your lab!??
Science
Bees
GABE

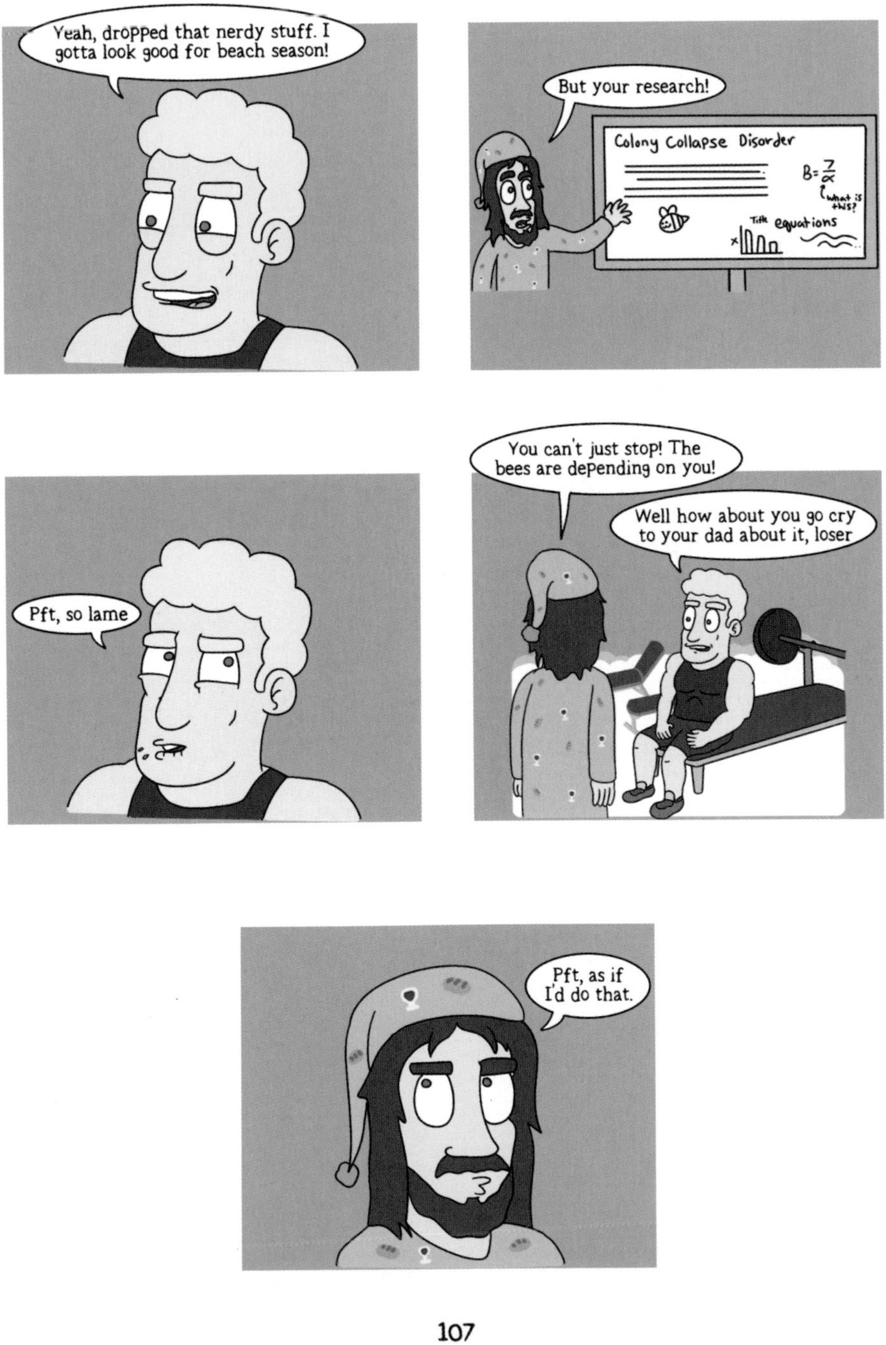
Yeah, dropped that nerdy stuff. I gotta look good for beach season!
But your research!
Colony Collapse Disorder
what is this?
equations
Pft, so lame
You can't just stop! The bees are depending on you!
Well how about you go cry to your dad about it, loser
Pft, as if I'd do that.

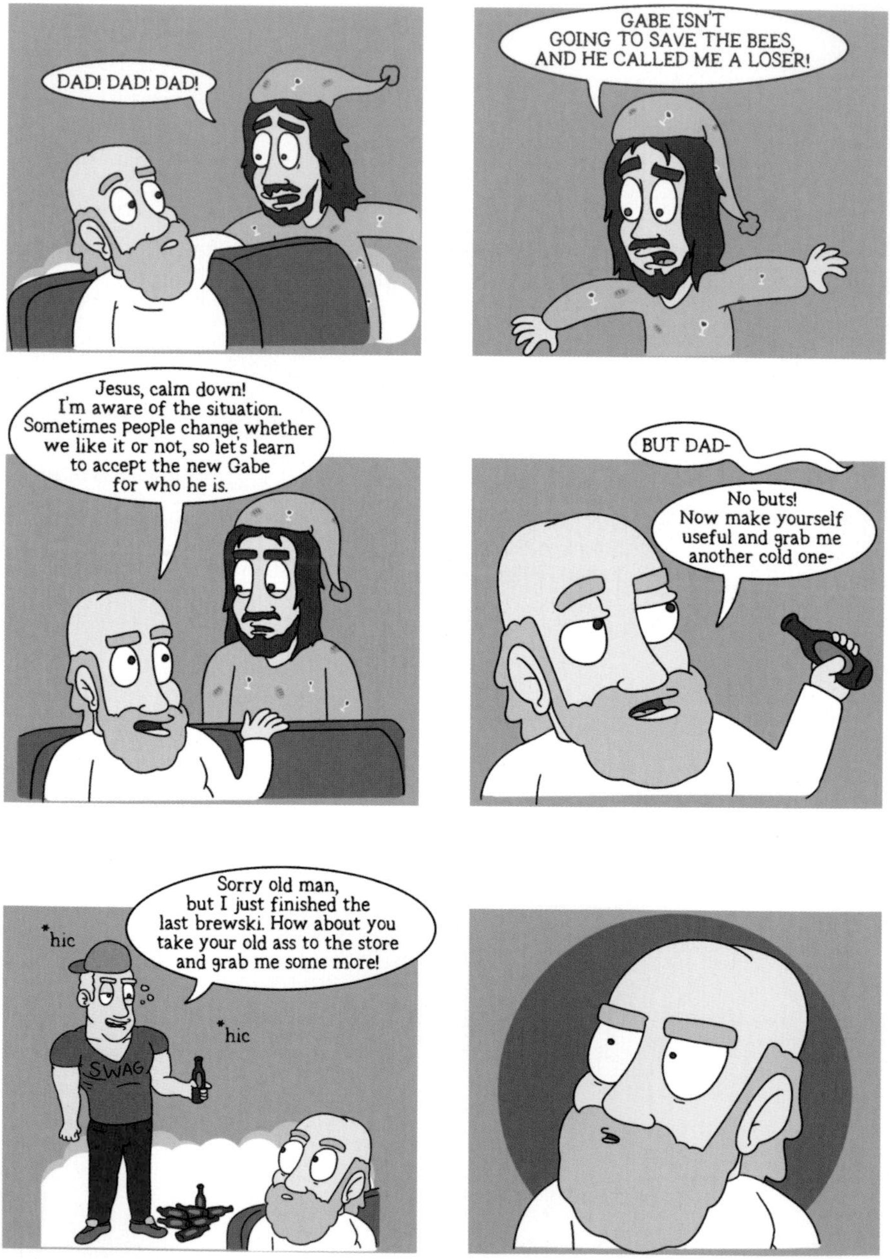
DAD! DAD! DAD!
GABE ISN'T GOING TO SAVE THE BEES, AND HE CALLED ME A LOSER!
Jesus, calm down! I'm aware of the situation. Sometimes people change whether we like it or not, so let's learn to accept the new Gabe for who he is.
BUT DAD-
No buts! Now make yourself useful and grab me another cold one-
*hic
Sorry old man, but I just finished the last brewski. How about you take your old ass to the store and grab me some more!
*hic
SWAG

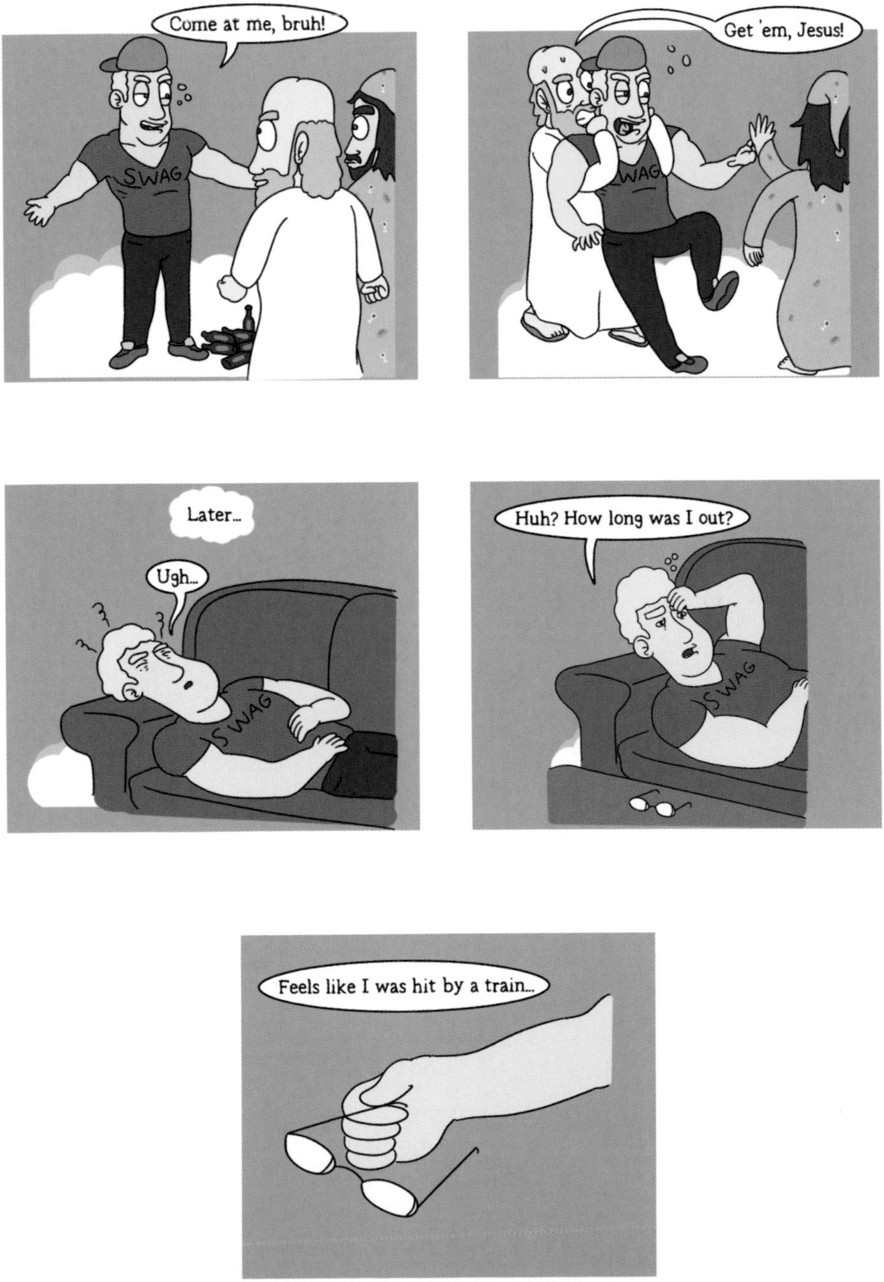
Come at me, bruh!
Get 'em, Jesus!
Later...
Ugh...
Huh? How long was I out?
Feels like I was hit by a train...

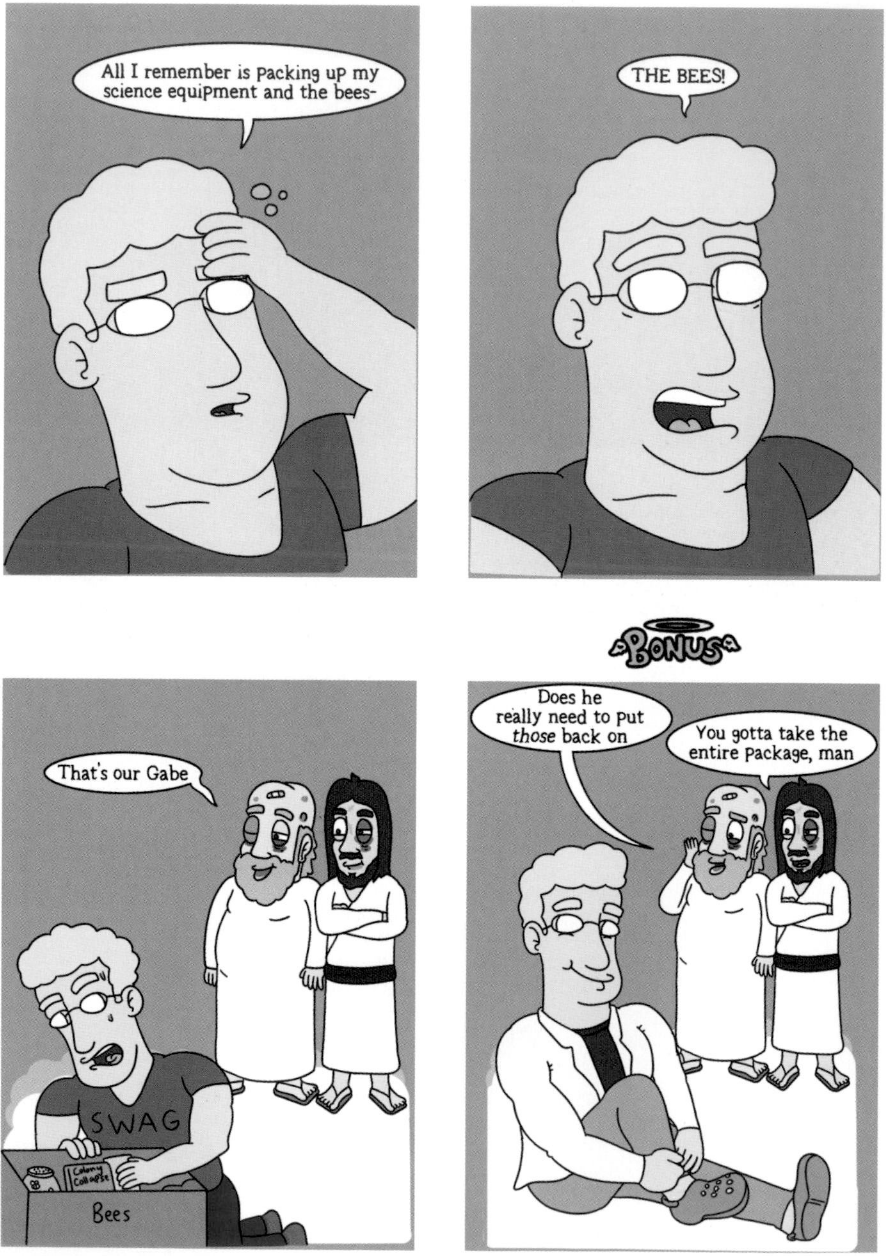
All I remember is packing up my science equipment and the bees-
THE BEES!
BONUS
That's our Gabe
SWAG
Colony Collapse
Bees
Does he really need to put *those* back on
You gotta take the entire package, man

Ashley's Cat

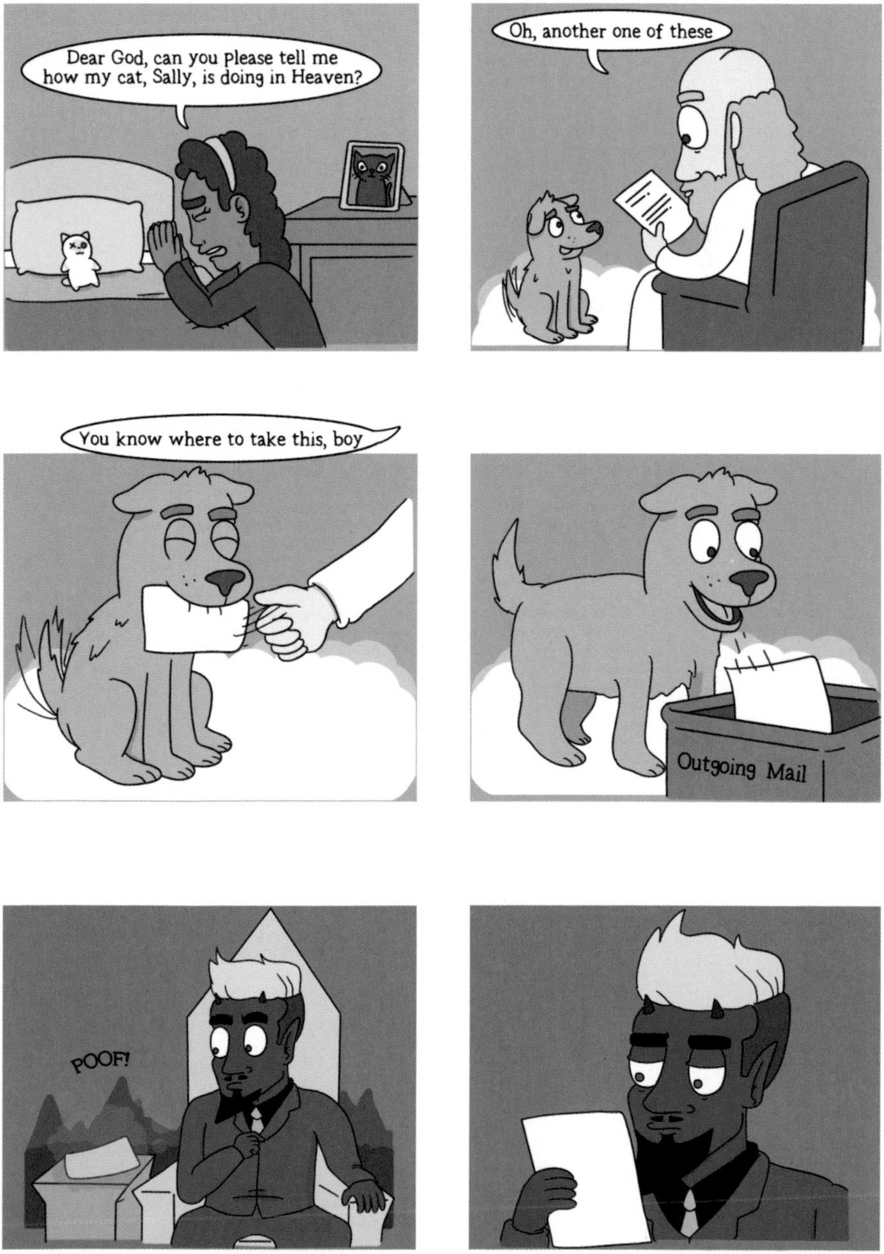
Dear God, can you please tell me how my cat, Sally, is doing in Heaven?
Oh, another one of these
You know where to take this, boy
Outgoing Mail
POOF!

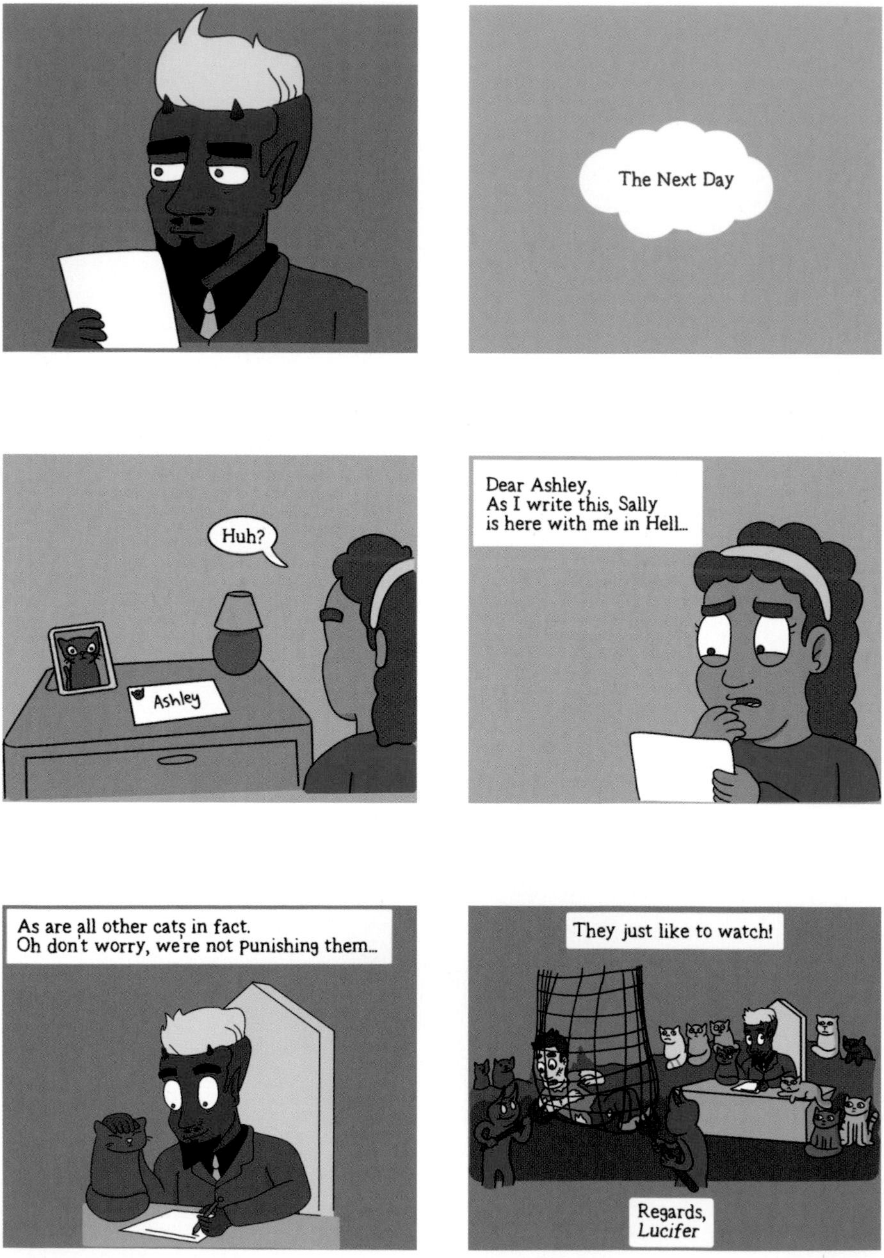
The Next Day
Huh?
Ashley
Dear Ashley,
As I write this, Sally
is here with me in Hell...
As are all other cats in fact.
Oh don't worry, we're not punishing them...
They just like to watch!
Regards,
Lucifer

BONUS

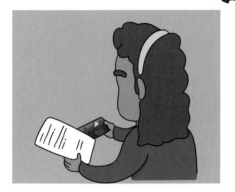

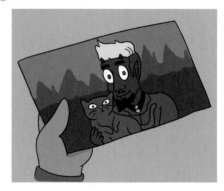

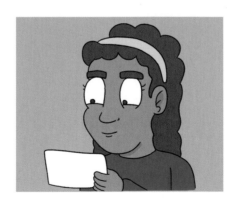

The Talk Show

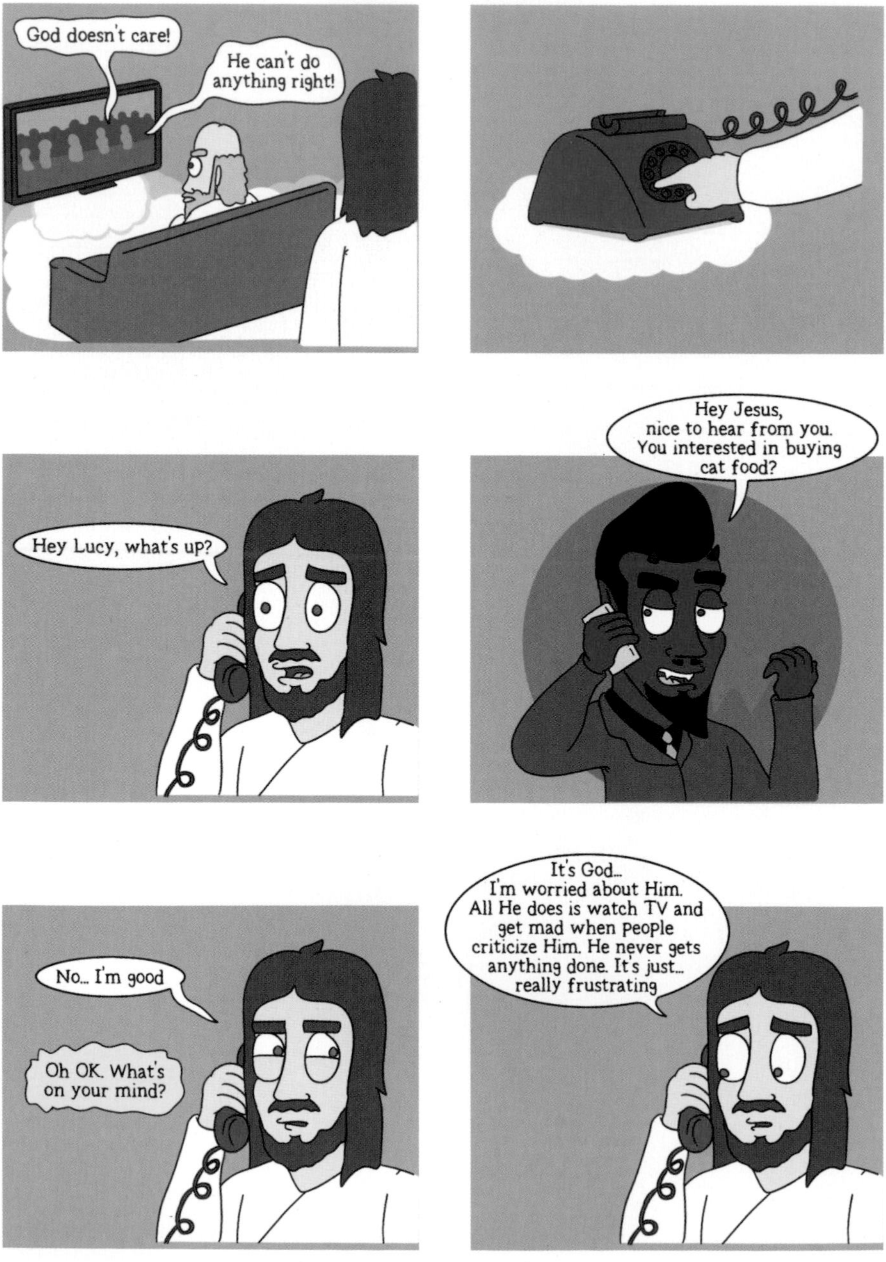
God doesn't care!
He can't do anything right!
Hey Lucy, what's up?
Hey Jesus, nice to hear from you. You interested in buying cat food?
No... I'm good
Oh OK. What's on your mind?
It's God... I'm worried about Him. All He does is watch TV and get mad when people criticize Him. He never gets anything done. It's just... really frustrating

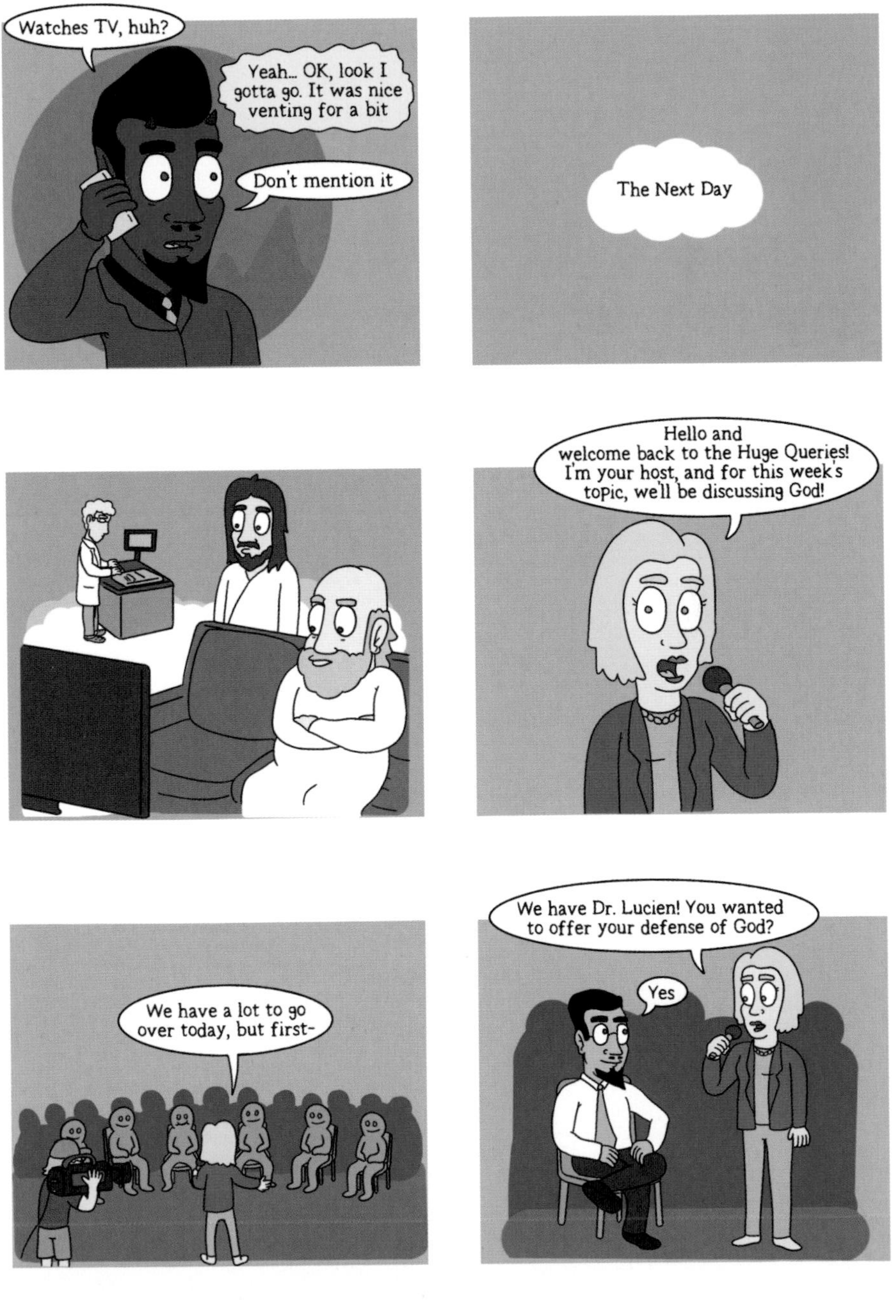
Watches TV, huh?
Yeah... OK, look I gotta go. It was nice venting for a bit
Don't mention it
The Next Day
Hello and welcome back to the Huge Queries! I'm your host, and for this week's topic, we'll be discussing God!
We have a lot to go over today, but first-
We have Dr. Lucien! You wanted to offer your defense of God?
Yes

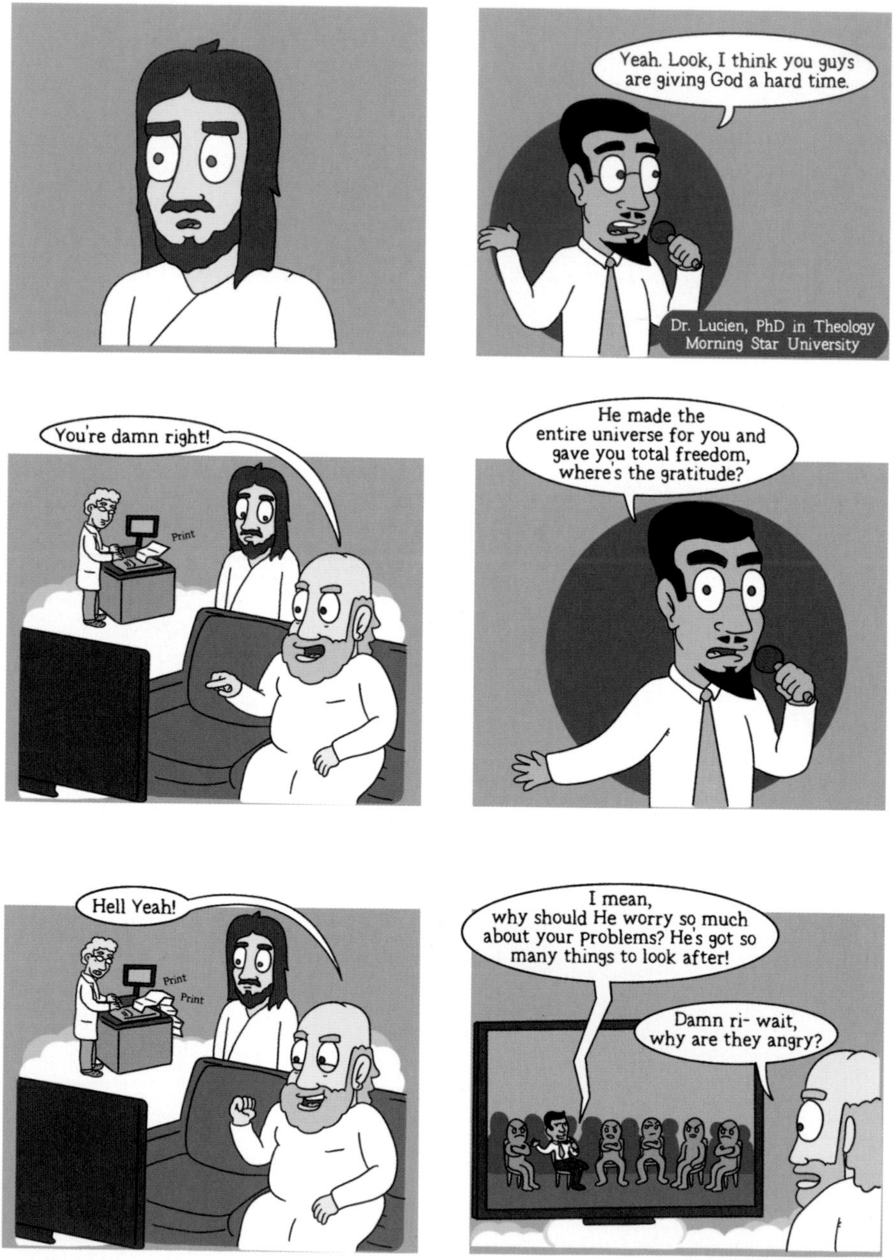
Yeah. Look, I think you guys are giving God a hard time.
Dr. Lucien, PhD in Theology
Morning Star University
You're damn right!
Print
He made the entire universe for you and gave you total freedom, where's the gratitude?
Hell Yeah!
Print
Print
I mean, why should He worry so much about your problems? He's got so many things to look after!
Damn ri- wait, why are they angry?

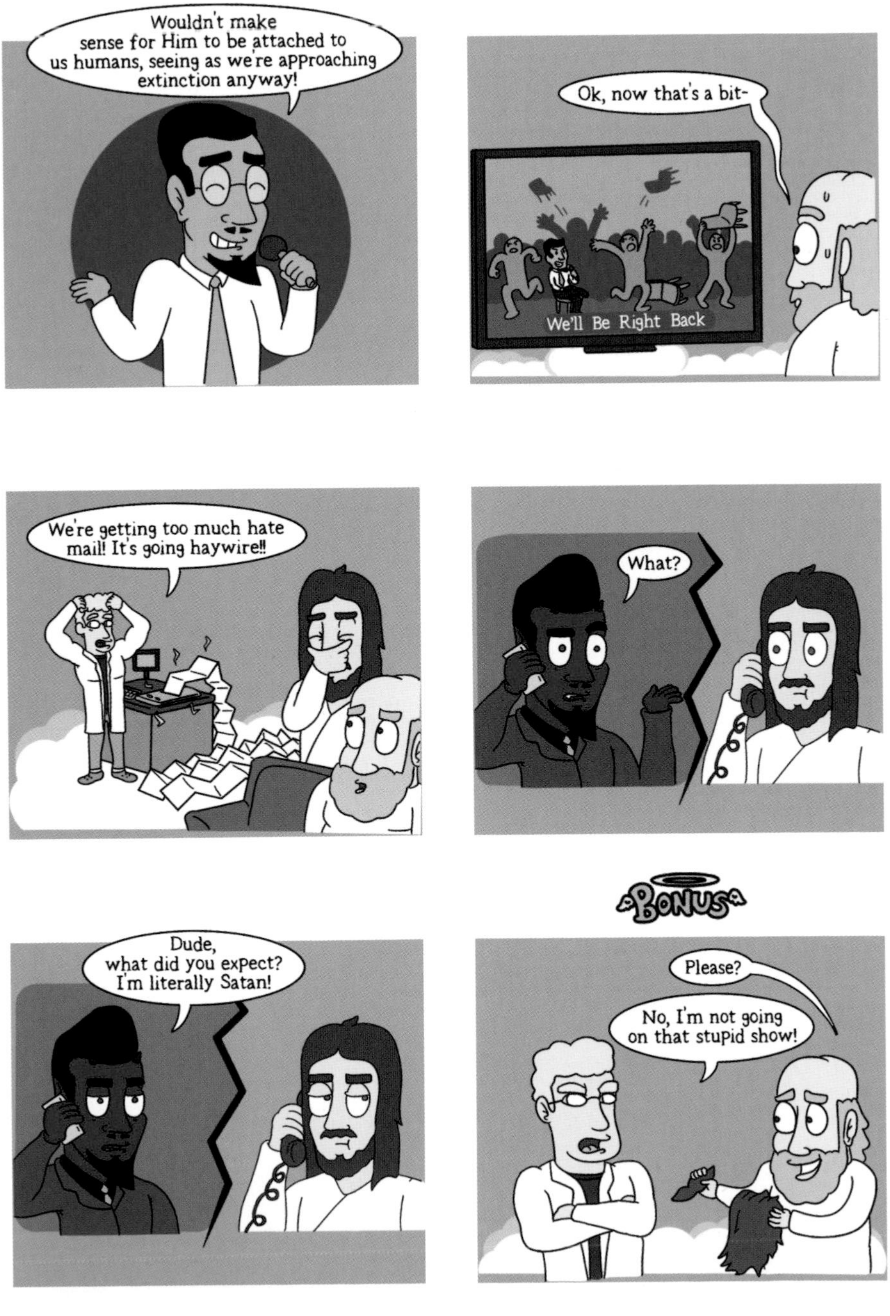
Wouldn't make sense for Him to be attached to us humans, seeing as we're approaching extinction anyway!
Ok, now that's a bit-
We'll Be Right Back
We're getting too much hate mail! It's going haywire!!
What?
Dude, what did you expect? I'm literally Satan!
BONUS
Please?
No, I'm not going on that stupid show!

Land

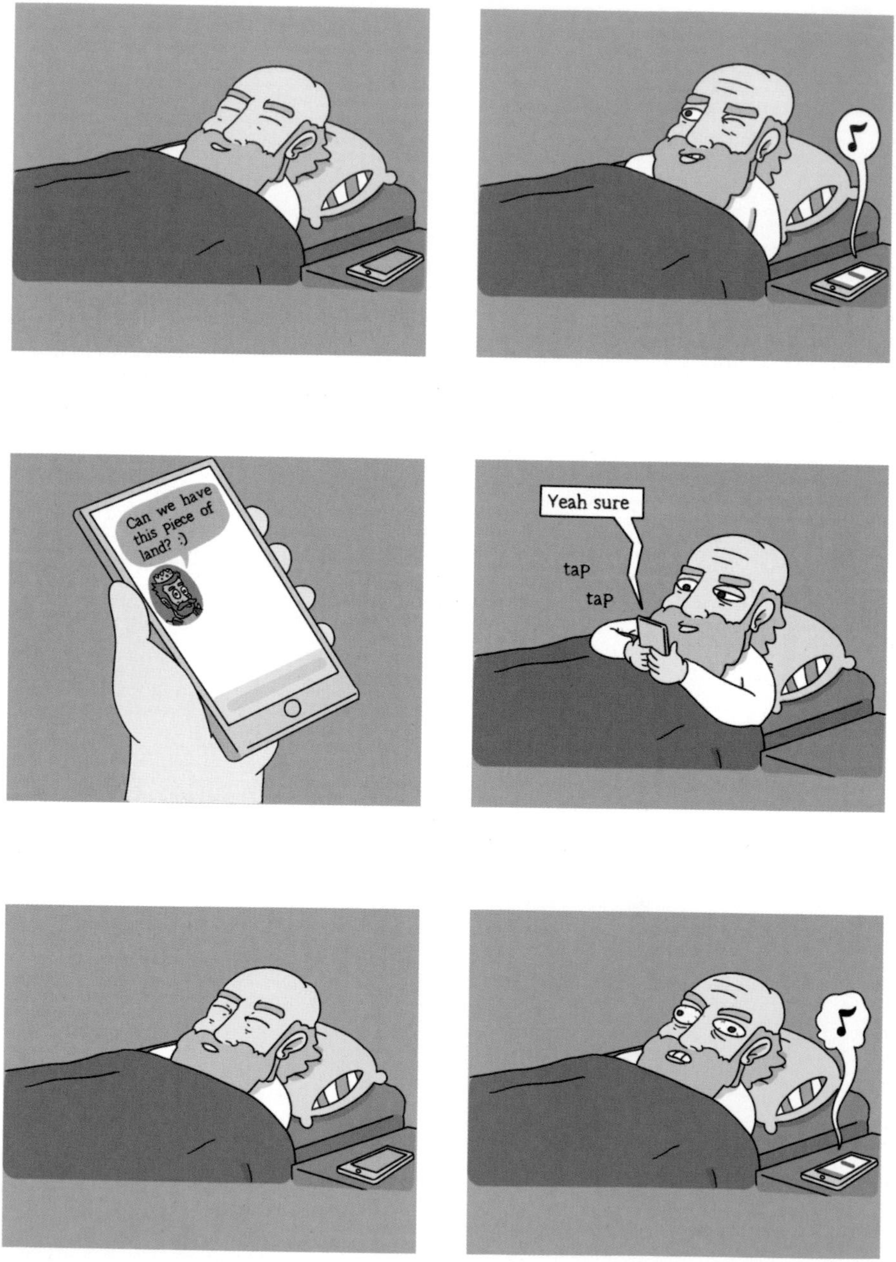
Can we have this piece of land? :)
Yeah sure
tap
tap

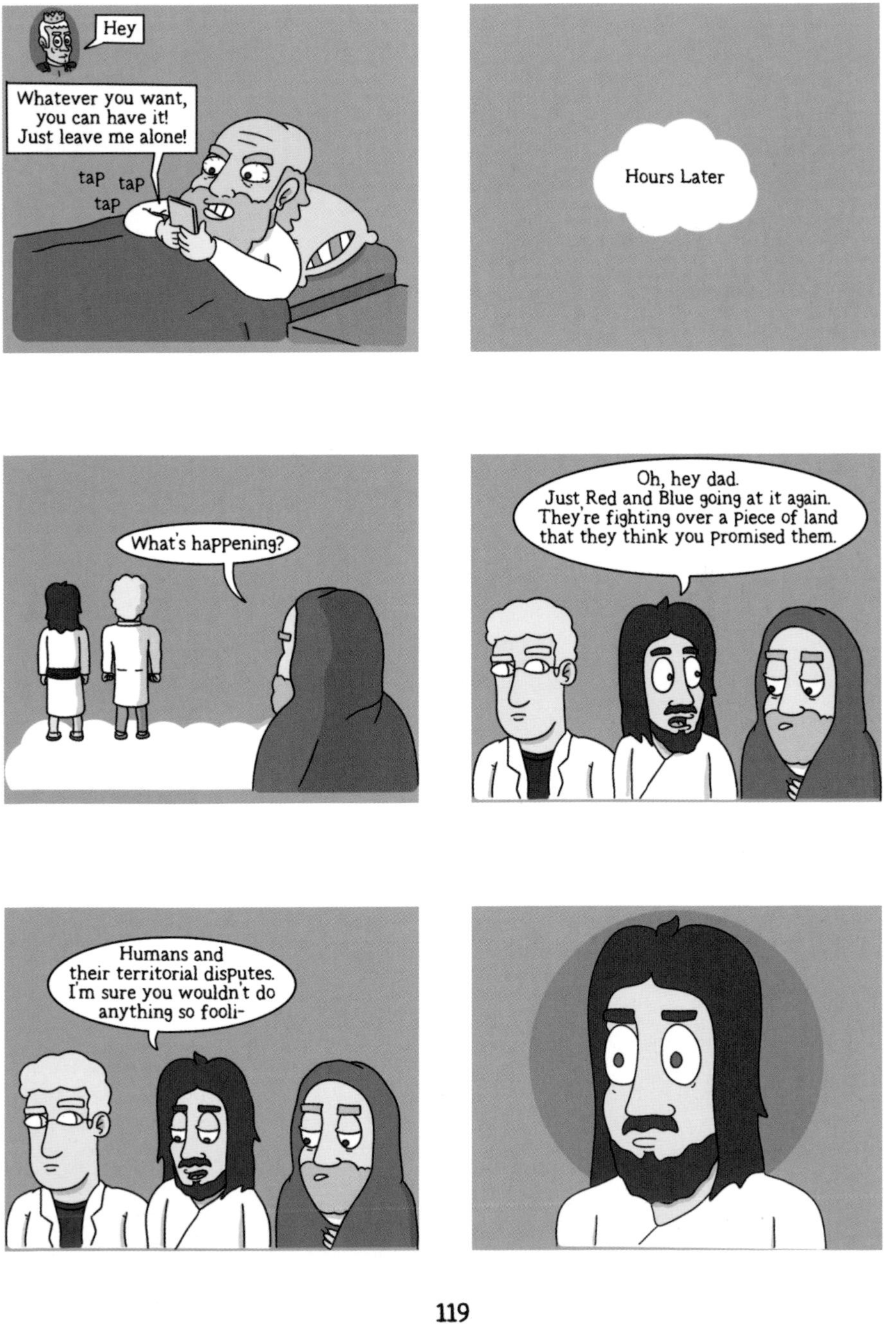
Hey
Whatever you want, you can have it! Just leave me alone!
tap tap tap
Hours Later
What's happening?
Oh, hey dad. Just Red and Blue going at it again. They're fighting over a piece of land that they think you promised them.
Humans and their territorial disputes. I'm sure you wouldn't do anything so fooli-

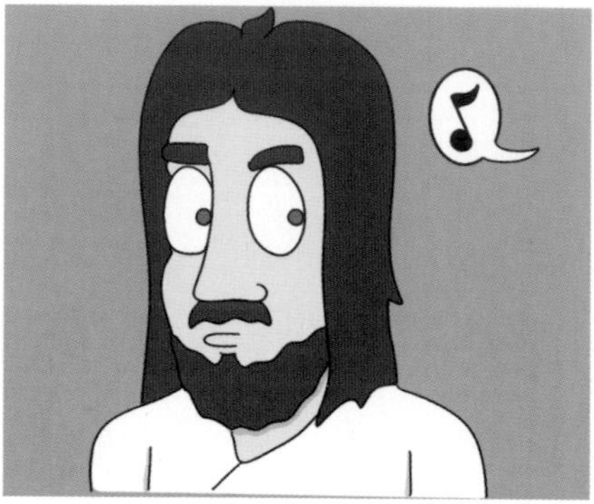

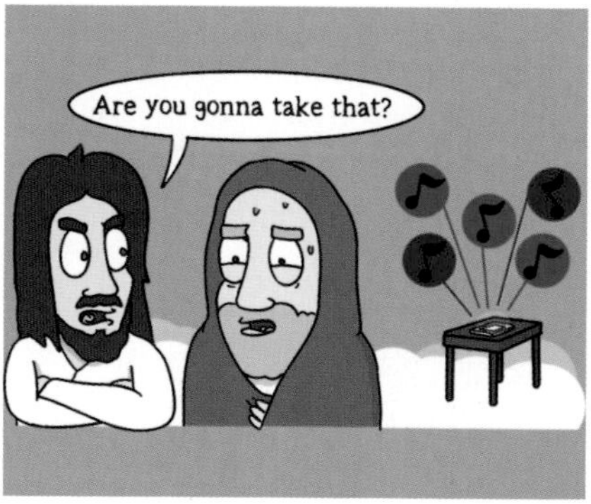
Are you gonna take that?

BONUS

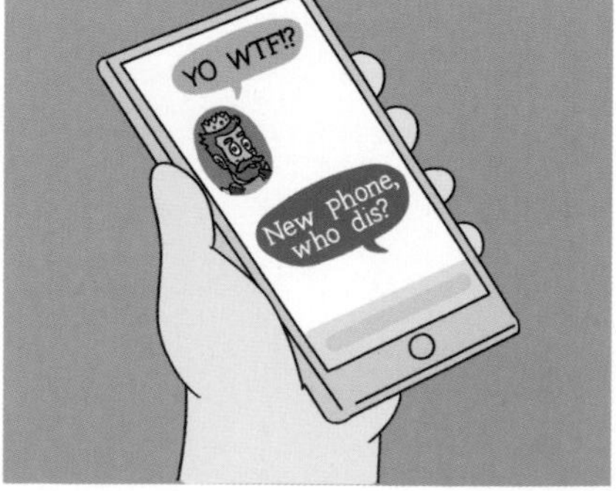
YO WTF!?
New phone, who dis?

Jesus?

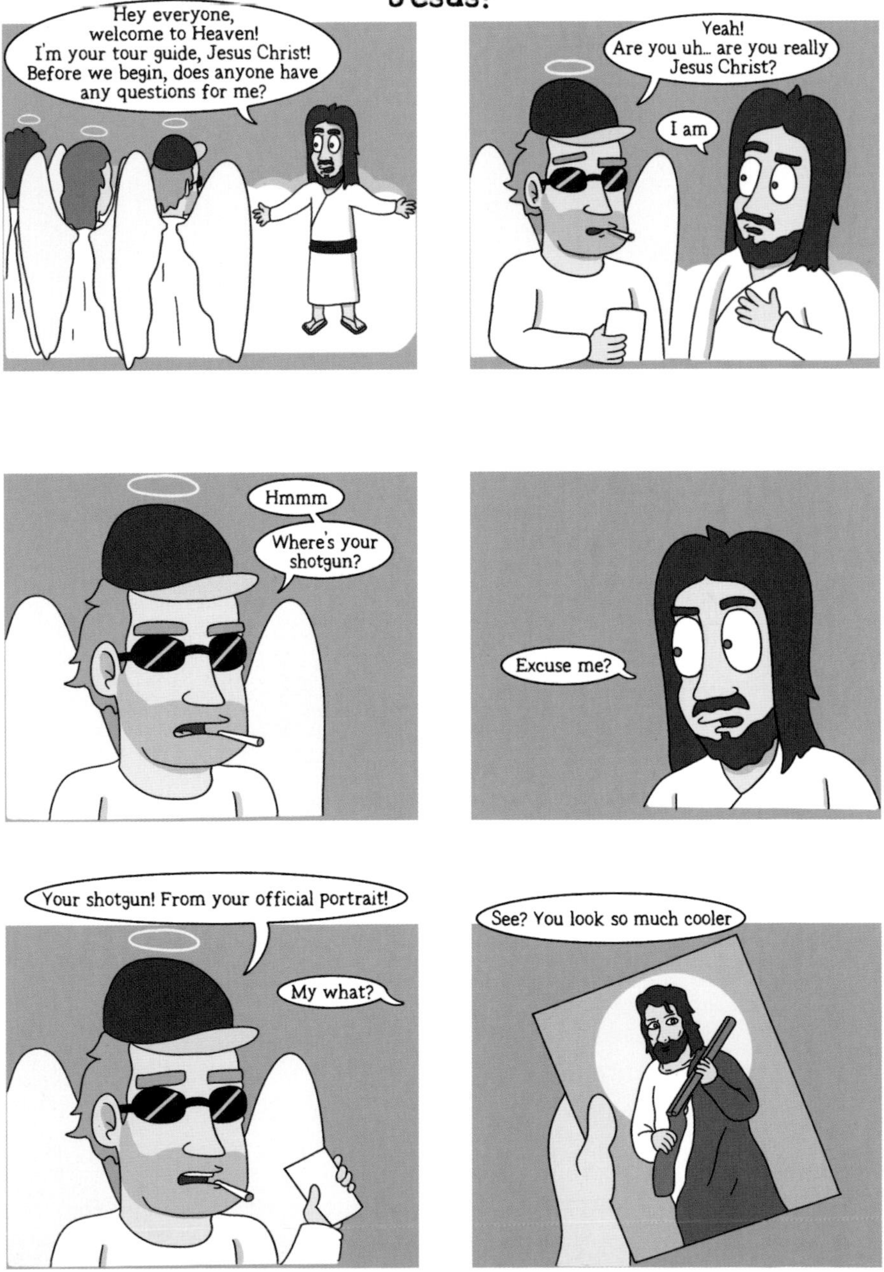

Hey everyone, welcome to Heaven! I'm your tour guide, Jesus Christ! Before we begin, does anyone have any questions for me?
Yeah! Are you uh... are you really Jesus Christ?
I am
Hmmm
Where's your shotgun?
Excuse me?
Your shotgun! From your official portrait!
My what?
See? You look so much cooler

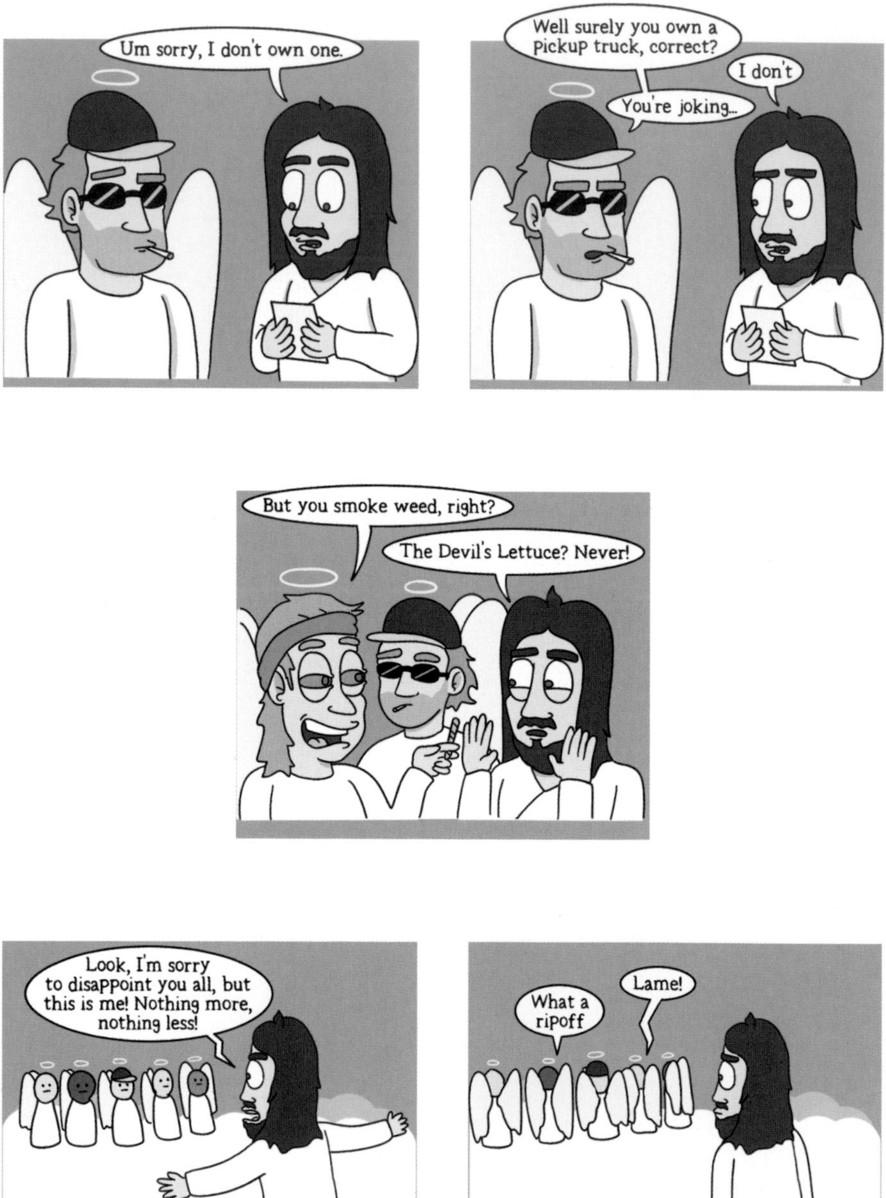
Um sorry, I don't own one.
Well surely you own a pickup truck, correct?
I don't
You're joking...
But you smoke weed, right?
The Devil's Lettuce? Never!
Look, I'm sorry to disappoint you all, but this is me! Nothing more, nothing less!
What a ripoff
Lame!

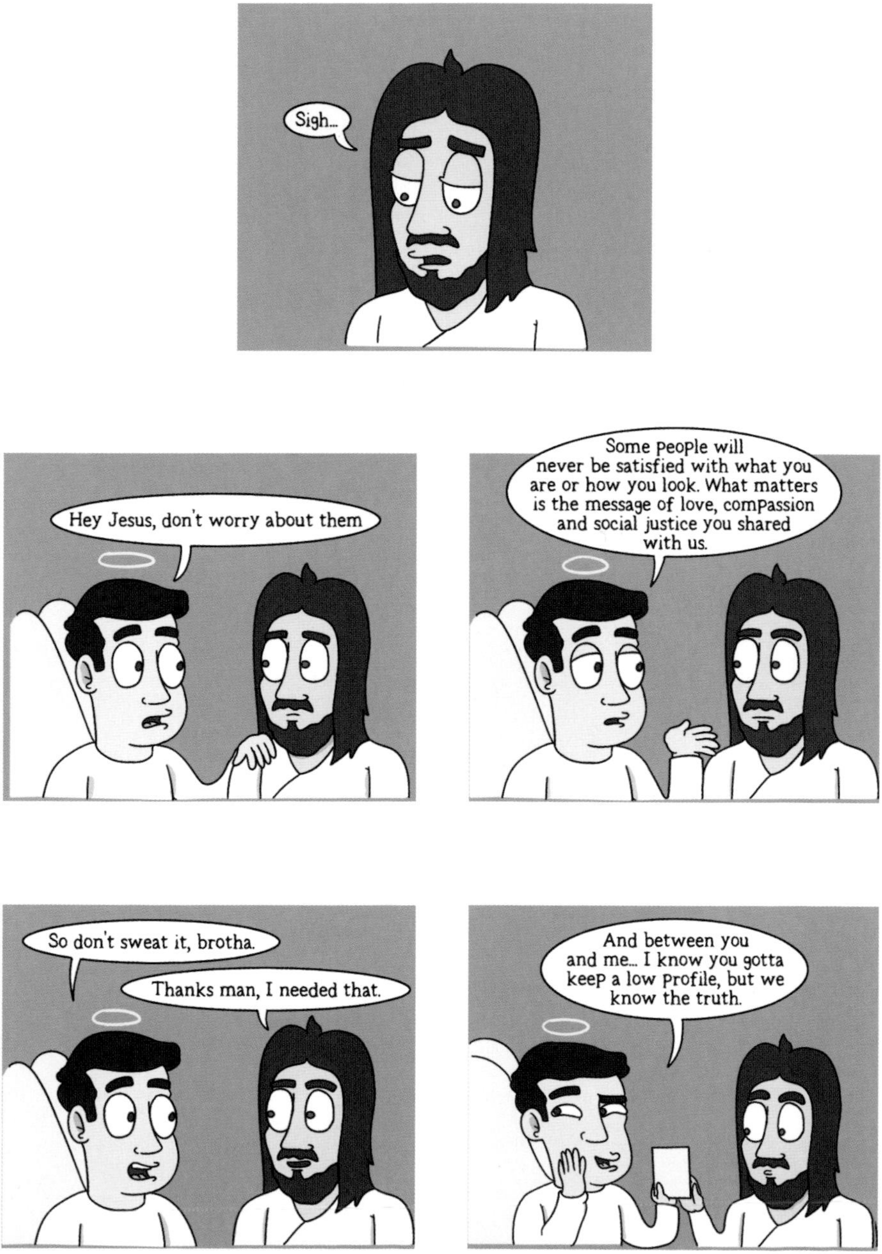
Sigh...
Hey Jesus, don't worry about them
Some people will never be satisfied with what you are or how you look. What matters is the message of love, compassion and social justice you shared with us.
So don't sweat it, brotha.
Thanks man, I needed that.
And between you and me... I know you gotta keep a low profile, but we know the truth.

BONUS

Who am I?

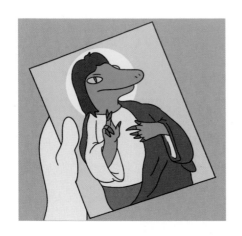

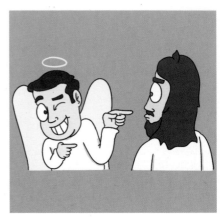

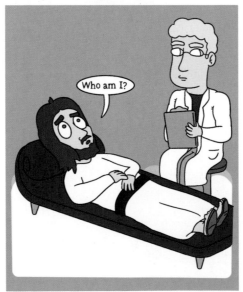

Work

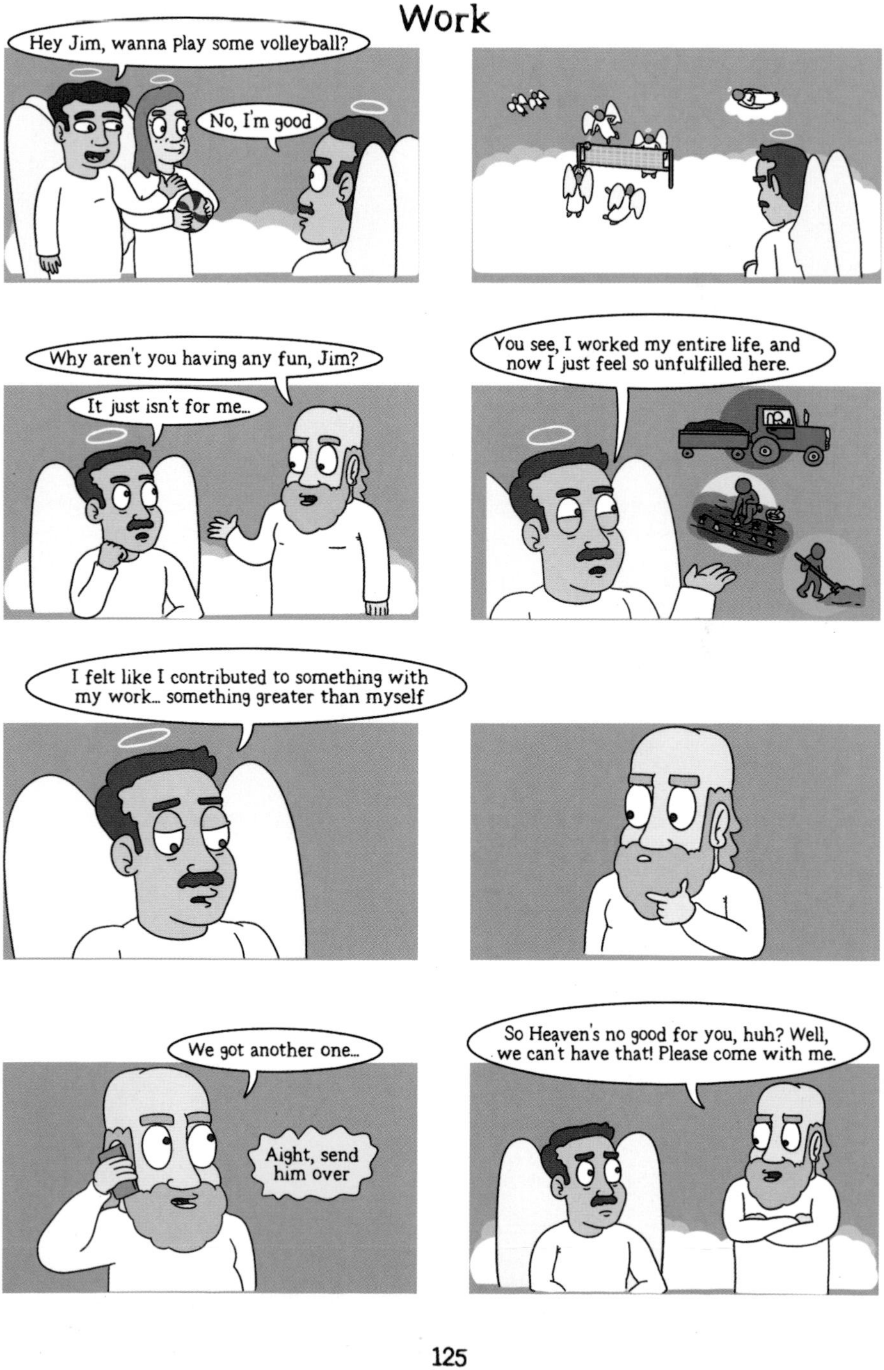
Hey Jim, wanna play some volleyball?
No, I'm good
Why aren't you having any fun, Jim?
It just isn't for me...
You see, I worked my entire life, and now I just feel so unfulfilled here.
I felt like I contributed to something with my work... something greater than myself
We got another one...
Aight, send him over
So Heaven's no good for you, huh? Well, we can't have that! Please come with me.

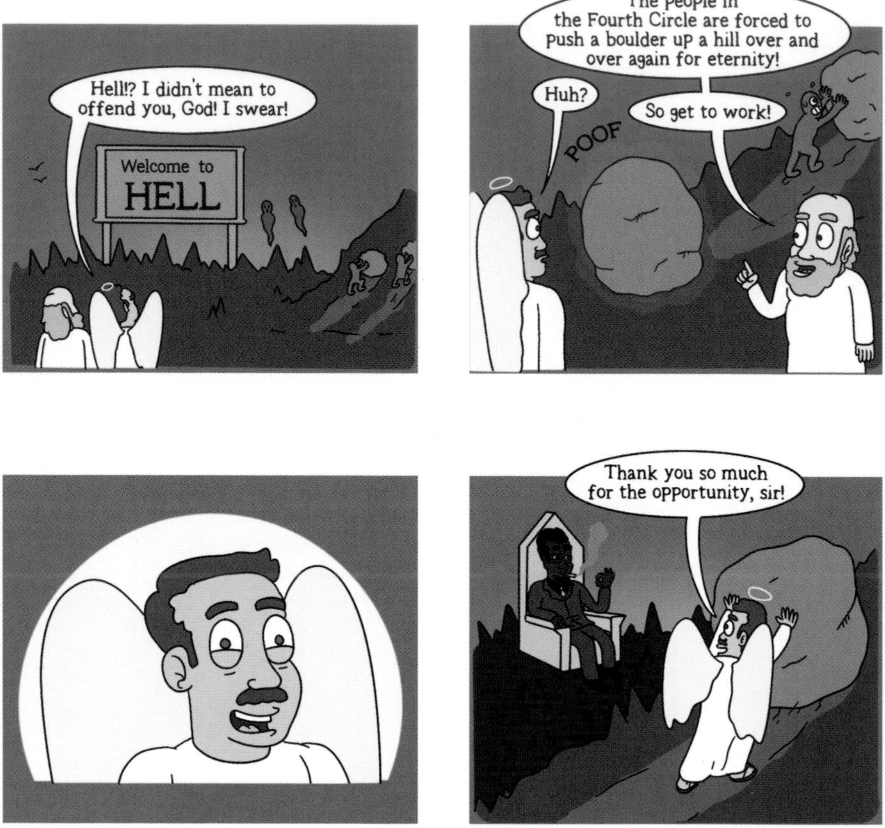
Hell!? I didn't mean to offend you, God! I swear!
Welcome to HELL
The people in the Fourth Circle are forced to push a boulder up a hill over and over again for eternity!
Huh?
POOF
So get to work!
Thank you so much for the opportunity, sir!

BONUS

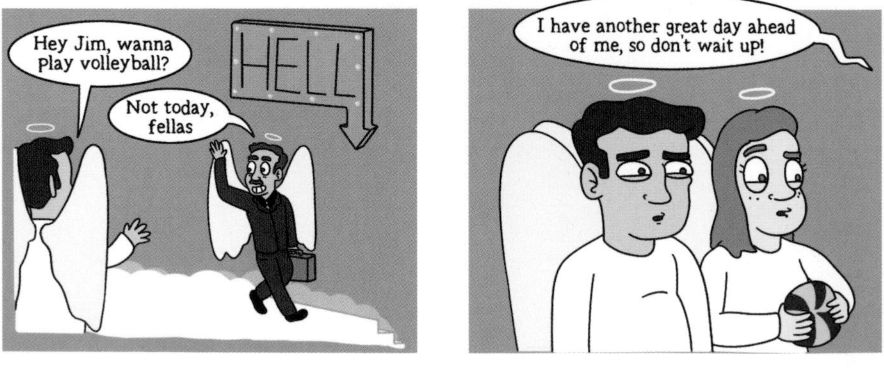
Hey Jim, wanna play volleyball?
HELL
Not today, fellas
I have another great day ahead of me, so don't wait up!

The End

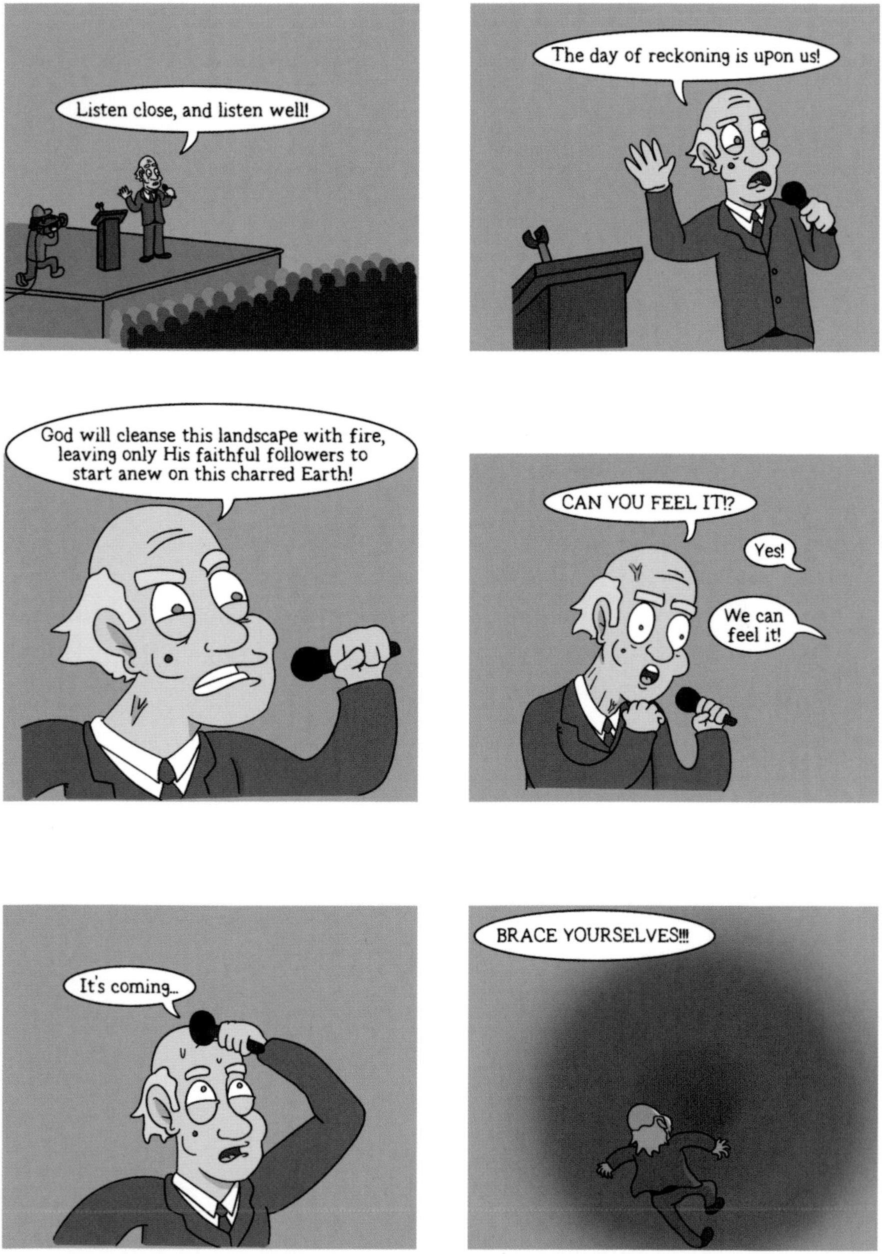
Listen close, and listen well!
The day of reckoning is upon us!
God will cleanse this landscape with fire, leaving only His faithful followers to start anew on this charred Earth!
CAN YOU FEEL IT!?
Yes!
We can feel it!
It's coming...
BRACE YOURSELVES!!!

The church is gone. Everything's gone!
That means...
The apocalypse has come... and God has spared me!
As your faithful follower, I will lead this new apocalyptic world and share the word of GOD!

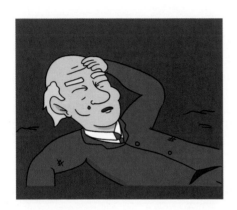

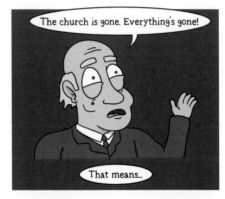

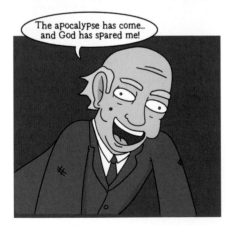

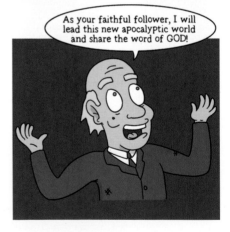

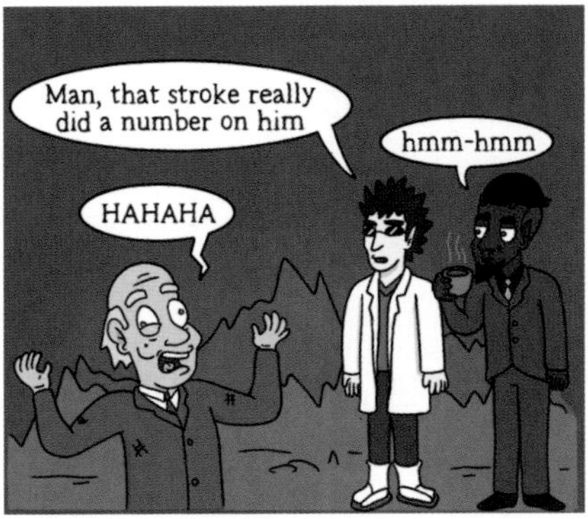
Man, that stroke really did a number on him
hmm-hmm
HAHAHA

BONUS

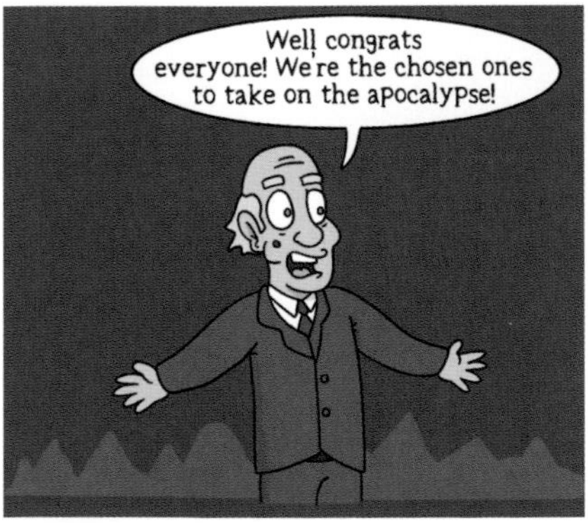
Well congrats everyone! We're the chosen ones to take on the apocalypse!

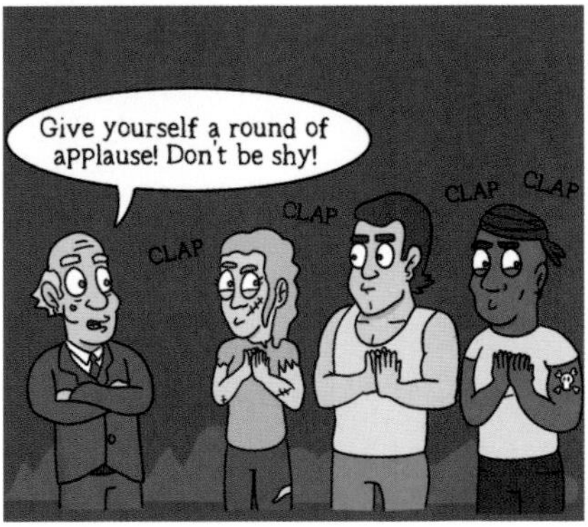
Give yourself a round of applause! Don't be shy!
CLAP
CLAP
CLAP
CLAP

The Beginning

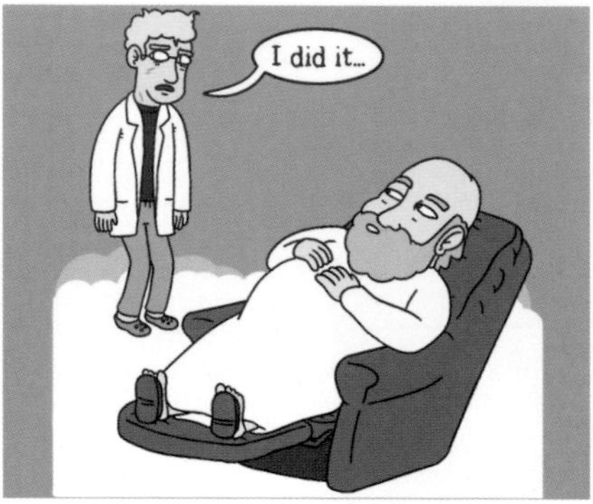
I did it...

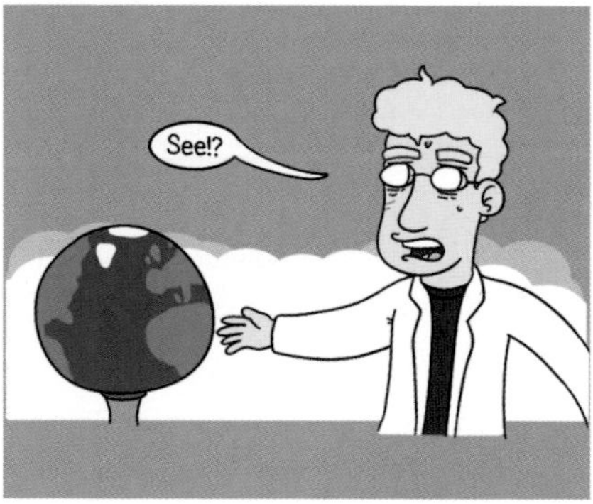
See!?

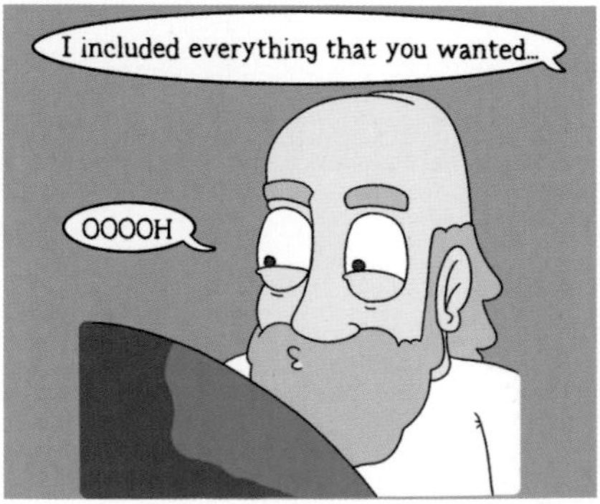
I included everything that you wanted...
OOOOH

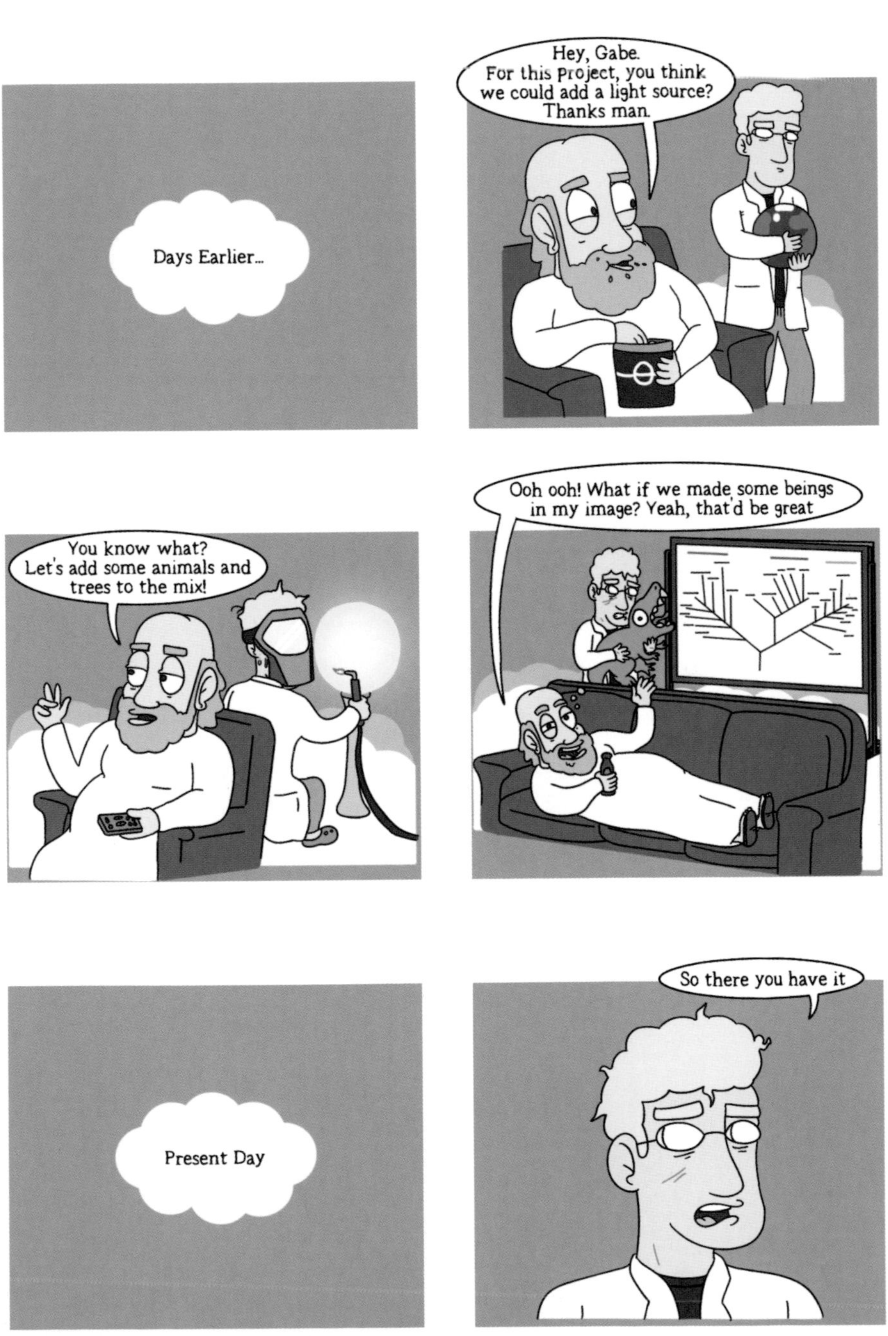
Days Earlier...
Hey, Gabe.
For this project, you think
we could add a light source?
Thanks man.
You know what?
Let's add some animals and
trees to the mix!
Ooh ooh! What if we made some beings
in my image? Yeah, that'd be great
Present Day
So there you have it

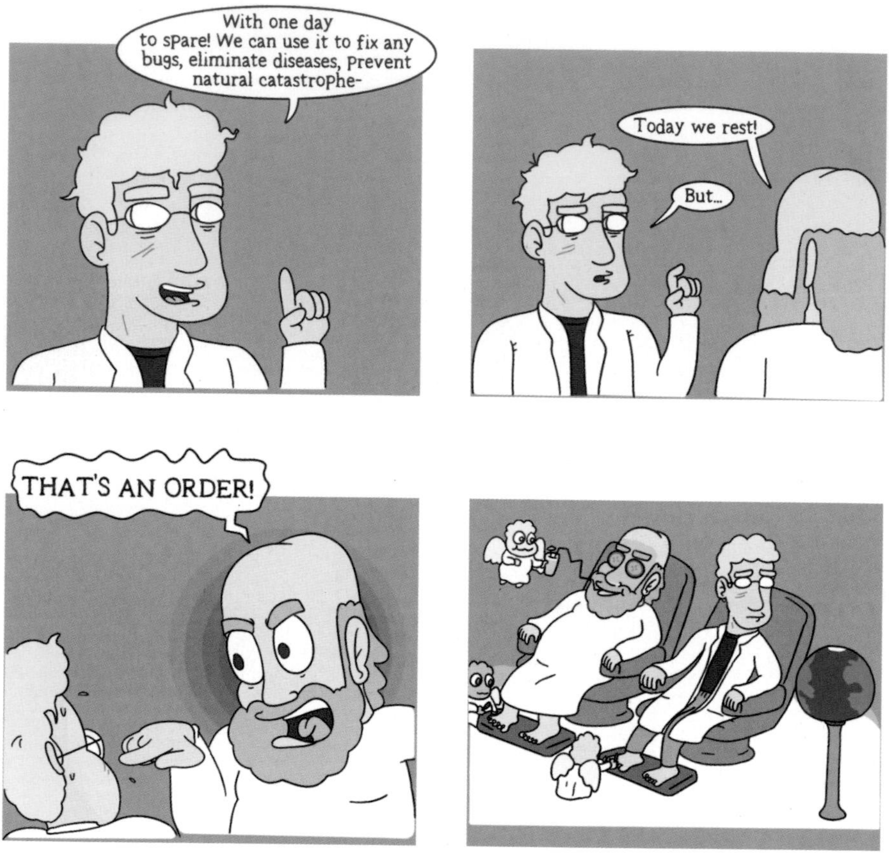
With one day to spare! We can use it to fix any bugs, eliminate diseases, prevent natural catastrophe-
Today we rest!
But...
THAT'S AN ORDER!

BONUS

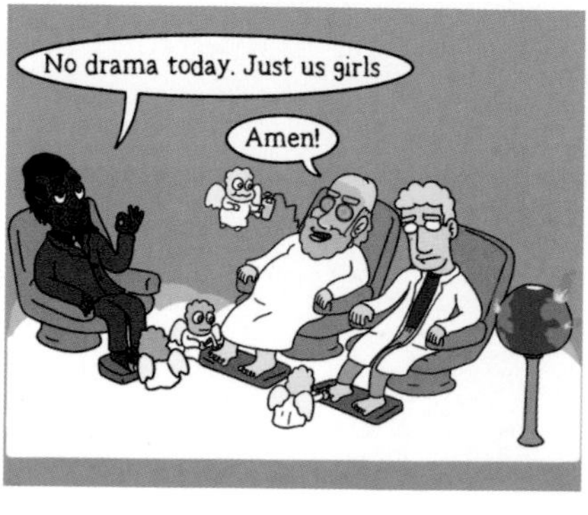
No drama today. Just us girls
Amen!

Jesus??

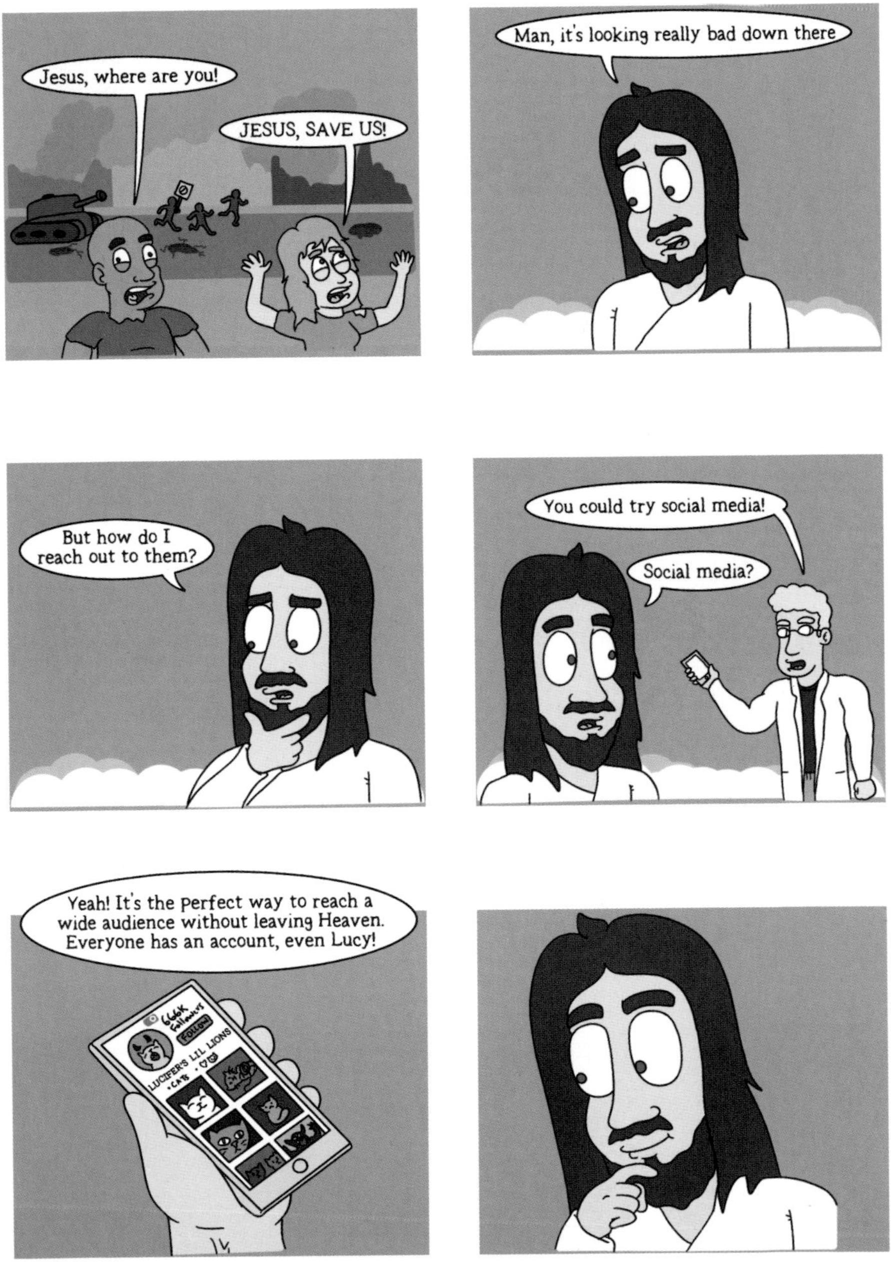

Jesus, where are you!
JESUS, SAVE US!
Man, it's looking really bad down there
But how do I reach out to them?
You could try social media!
Social media?
Yeah! It's the perfect way to reach a wide audience without leaving Heaven. Everyone has an account, even Lucy!
666K followers
Follow
LUCIFER'S LIL LIONS

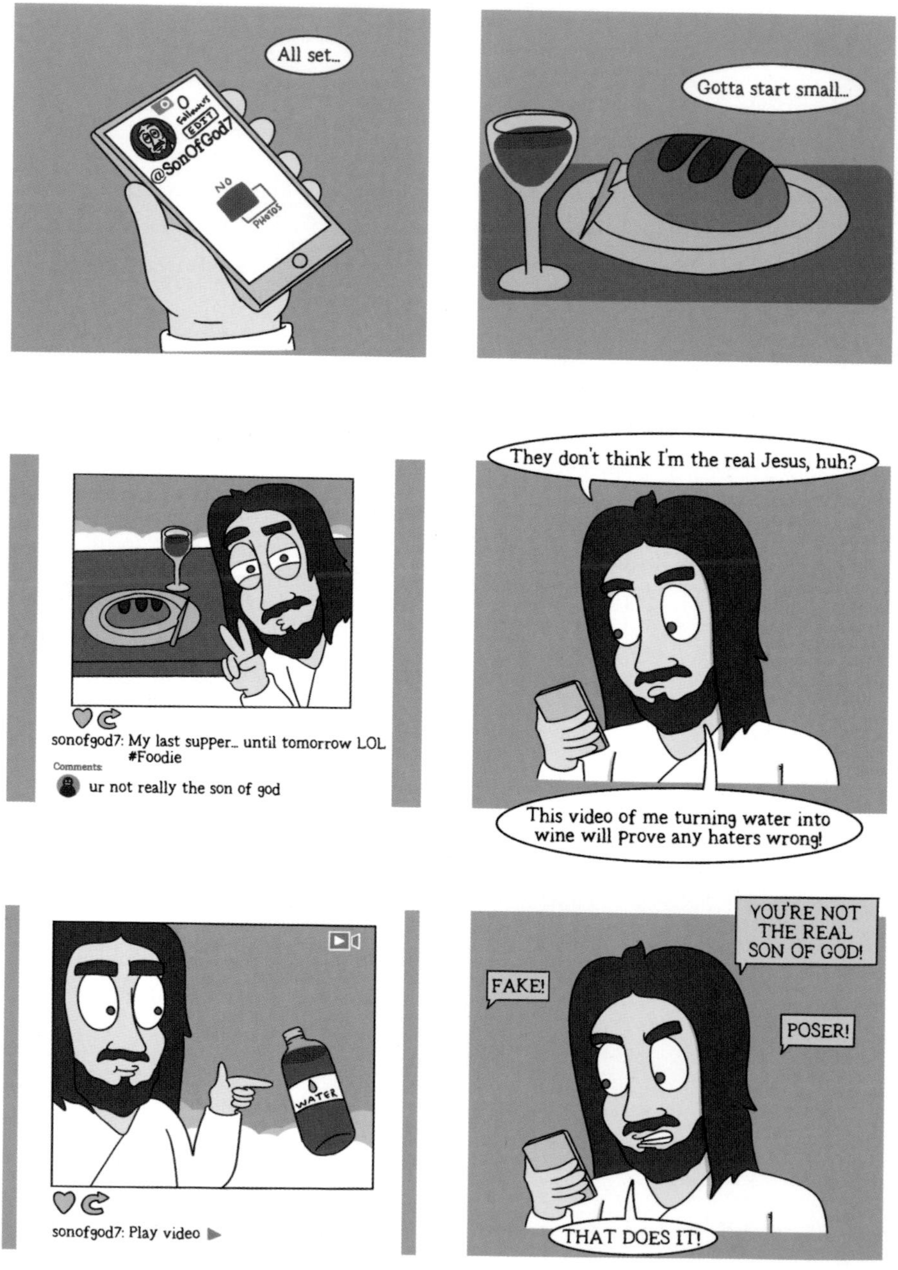
All set...
EDIT
@SonOfGod7
NO PHOTOS
Gotta start small...
sonofgod7: My last supper... until tomorrow LOL #Foodie
Comments:
ur not really the son of god
They don't think I'm the real Jesus, huh?
This video of me turning water into wine will prove any haters wrong!
WATER
sonofgod7: Play video
YOU'RE NOT THE REAL SON OF GOD!
FAKE!
POSER!
THAT DOES IT!

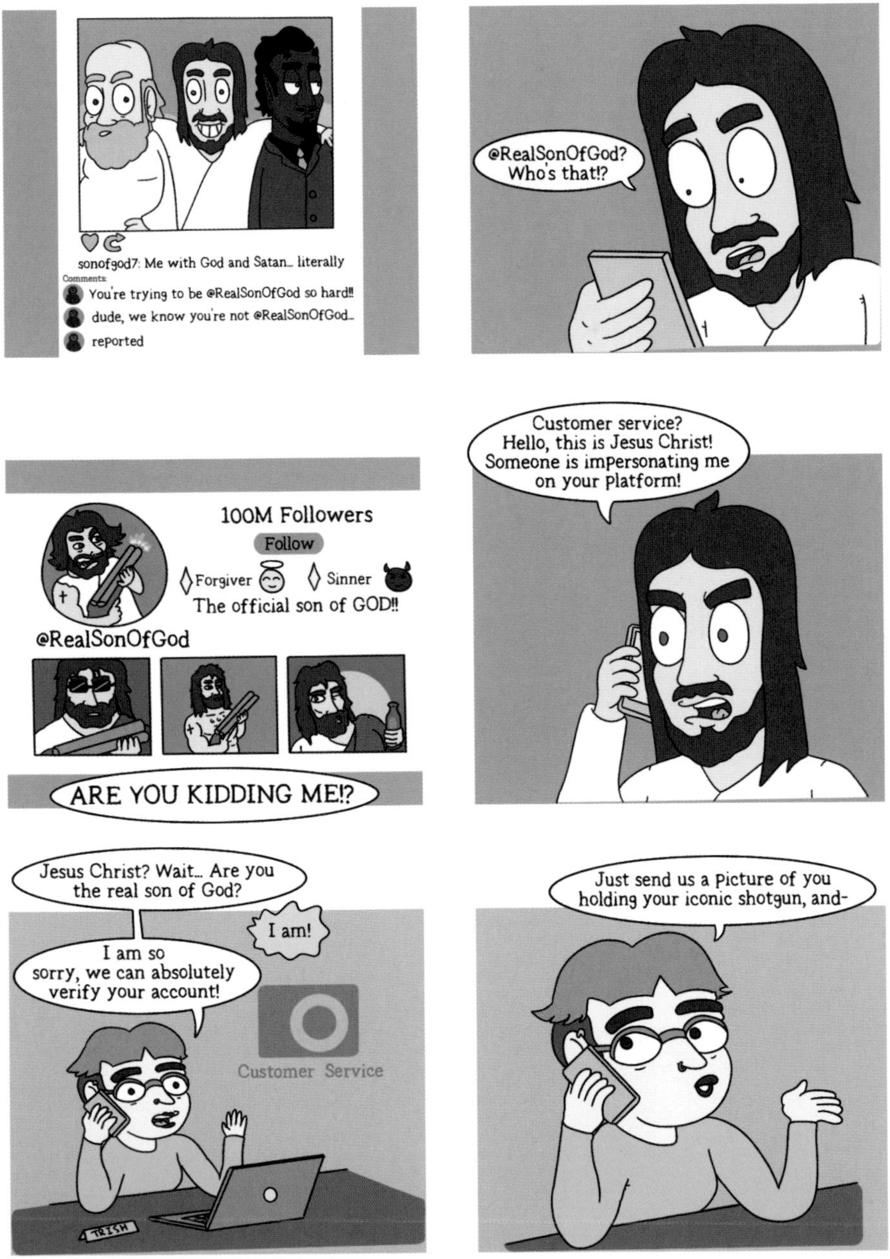
sonofgod7: Me with God and Satan... literally
Comments:
You're trying to be @RealSonOfGod so hard!!
dude, we know you're not @RealSonOfGod...
reported
@RealSonOfGod? Who's that!?
100M Followers
Follow
Forgiver
Sinner
The official son of GOD!!
@RealSonOfGod
ARE YOU KIDDING ME!?
Customer service? Hello, this is Jesus Christ! Someone is impersonating me on your platform!
Jesus Christ? Wait... Are you the real son of God?
I am!
I am so sorry, we can absolutely verify your account!
Customer Service
TRISH
Just send us a picture of you holding your iconic shotgun, and-

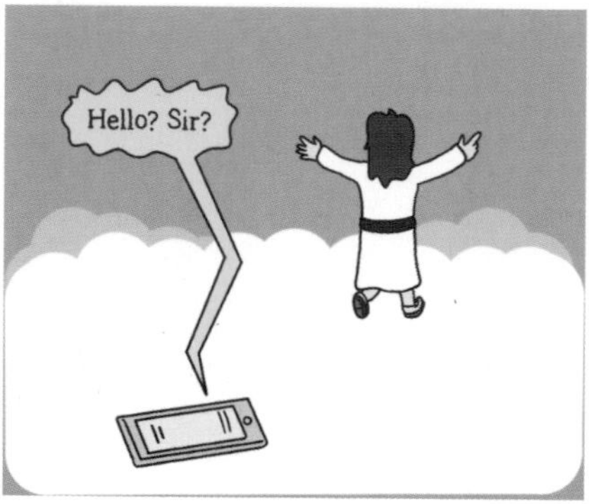
Hello? Sir?

BONUS

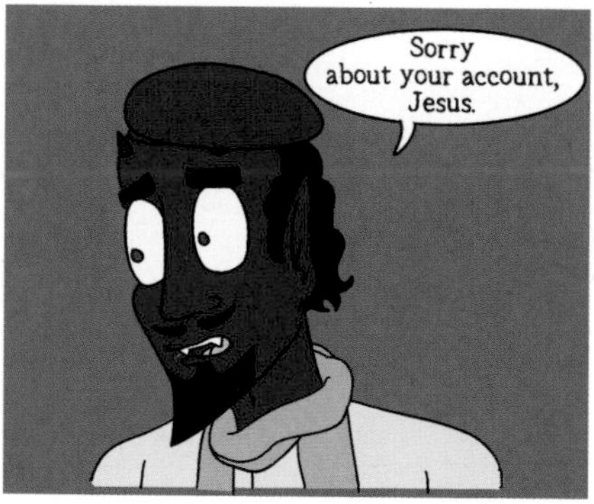
Sorry
about your account,
Jesus.

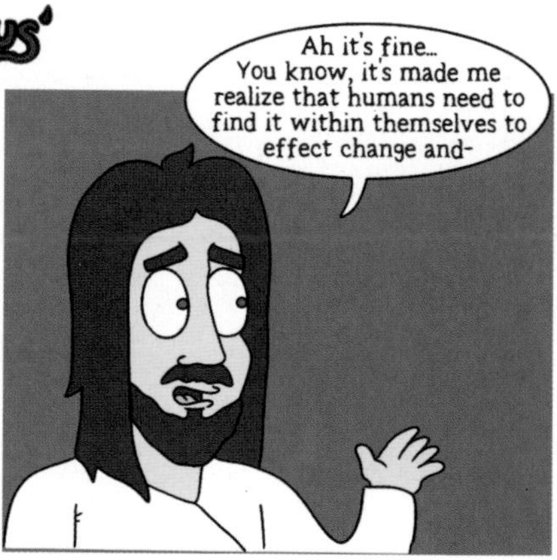
Ah it's fine...
You know, it's made me
realize that humans need to
find it within themselves to
effect change and-

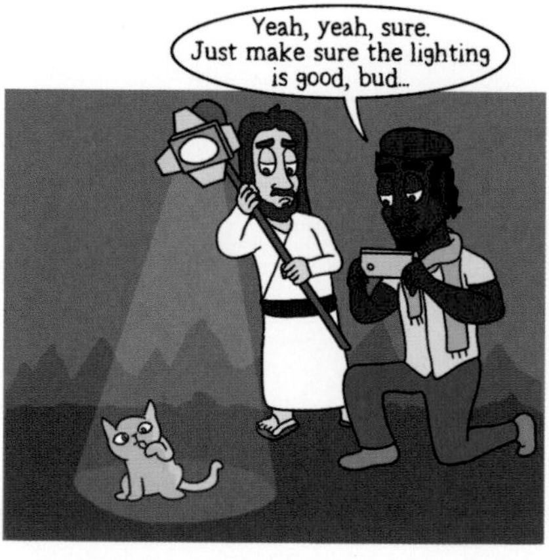
Yeah, yeah, sure.
Just make sure the lighting
is good, bud...

Bucky

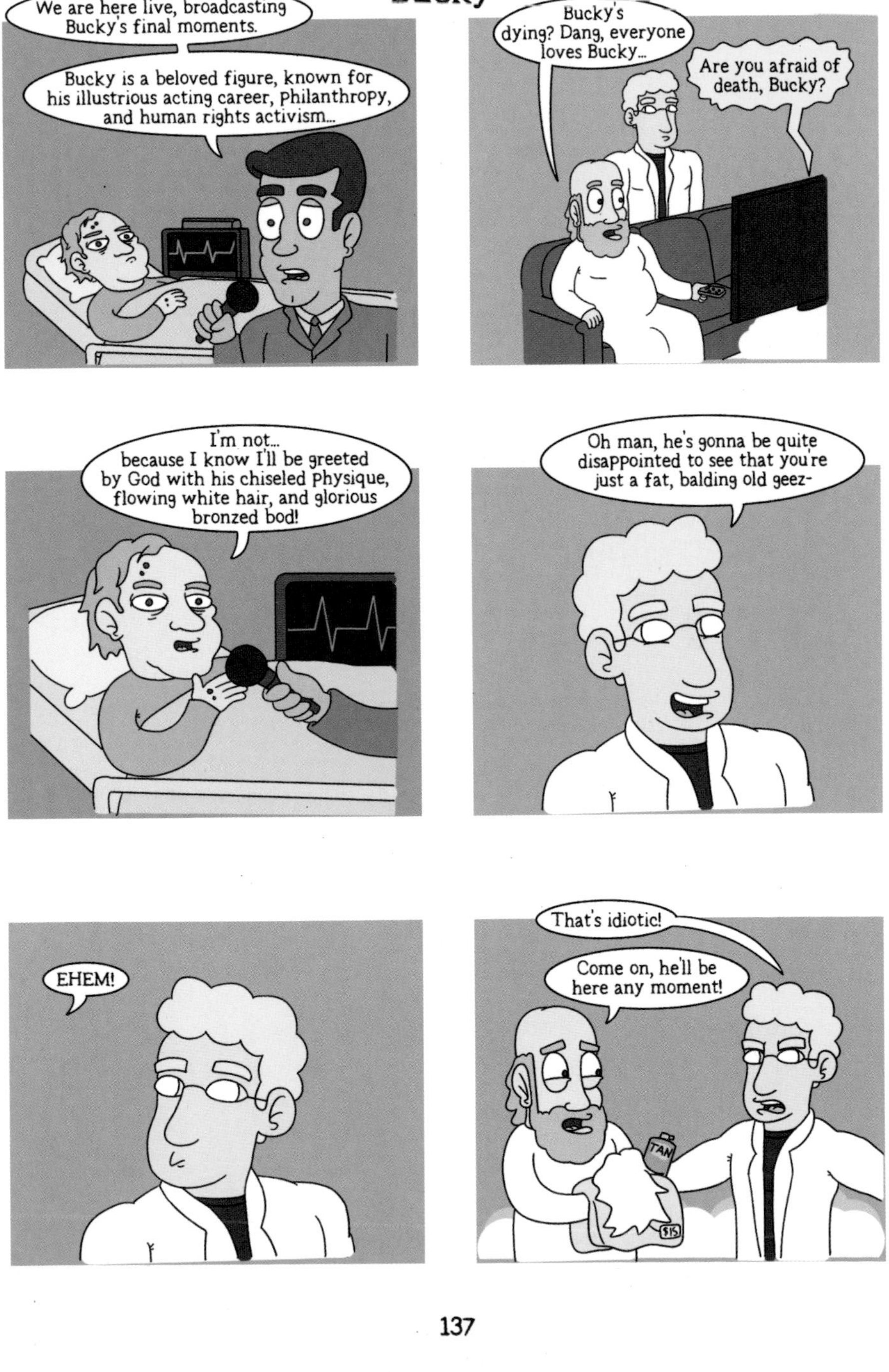

We are here live, broadcasting Bucky's final moments.
Bucky is a beloved figure, known for his illustrious acting career, philanthropy, and human rights activism...
Bucky's dying? Dang, everyone loves Bucky...
Are you afraid of death, Bucky?
I'm not... because I know I'll be greeted by God with his chiseled physique, flowing white hair, and glorious bronzed bod!
Oh man, he's gonna be quite disappointed to see that you're just a fat, balding old geez-
EHEM!
That's idiotic!
Come on, he'll be here any moment!
TAN
$15

BONUS
And I know God will have his trusty sidekick, the Lizard King of Dixie
What's going on y'all?
No time to explain, just put this on

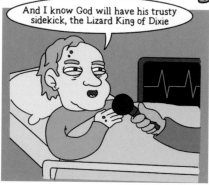

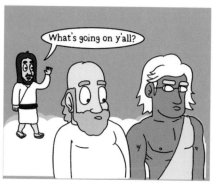

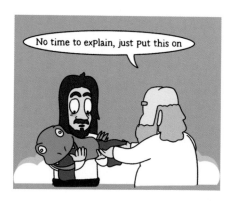

Noah's Ark: The Pre-prequel

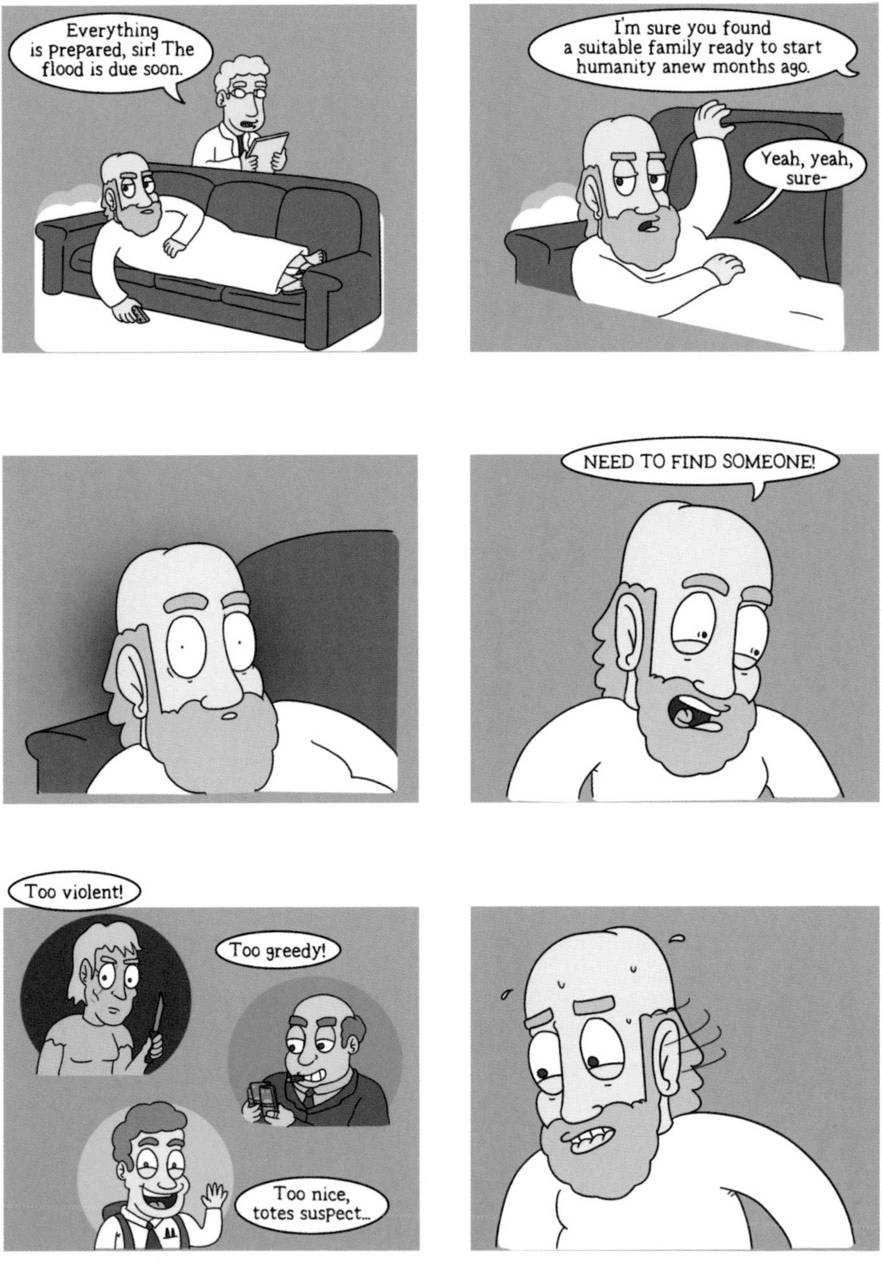

Everything is prepared, sir! The flood is due soon.
I'm sure you found a suitable family ready to start humanity anew months ago.
Yeah, yeah, sure-
NEED TO FIND SOMEONE!
Too violent!
Too greedy!
Too nice, totes suspect...

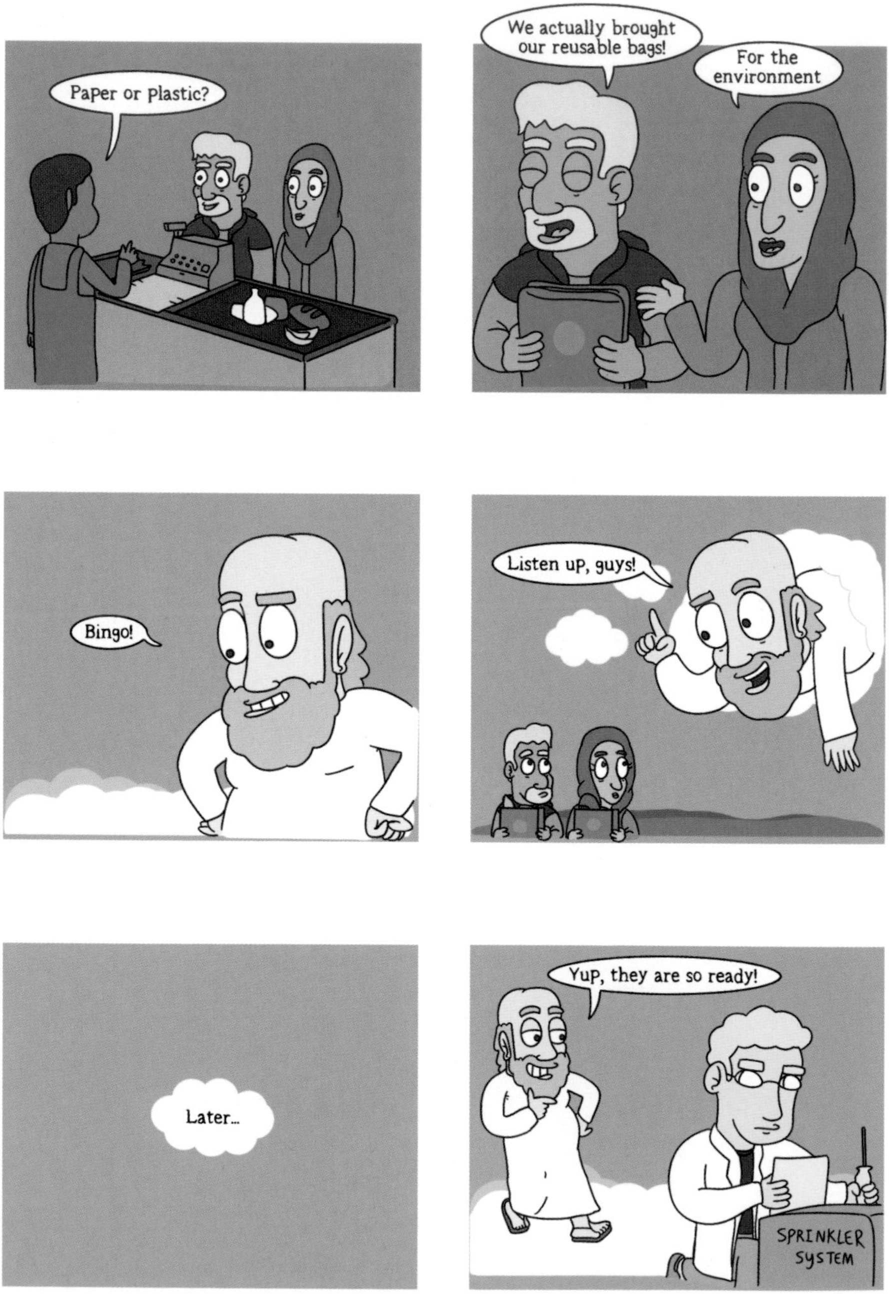
Paper or plastic?
We actually brought our reusable bags!
For the environment
Bingo!
Listen up, guys!
Later...
Yup, they are so ready!
SPRINKLER SYSTEM

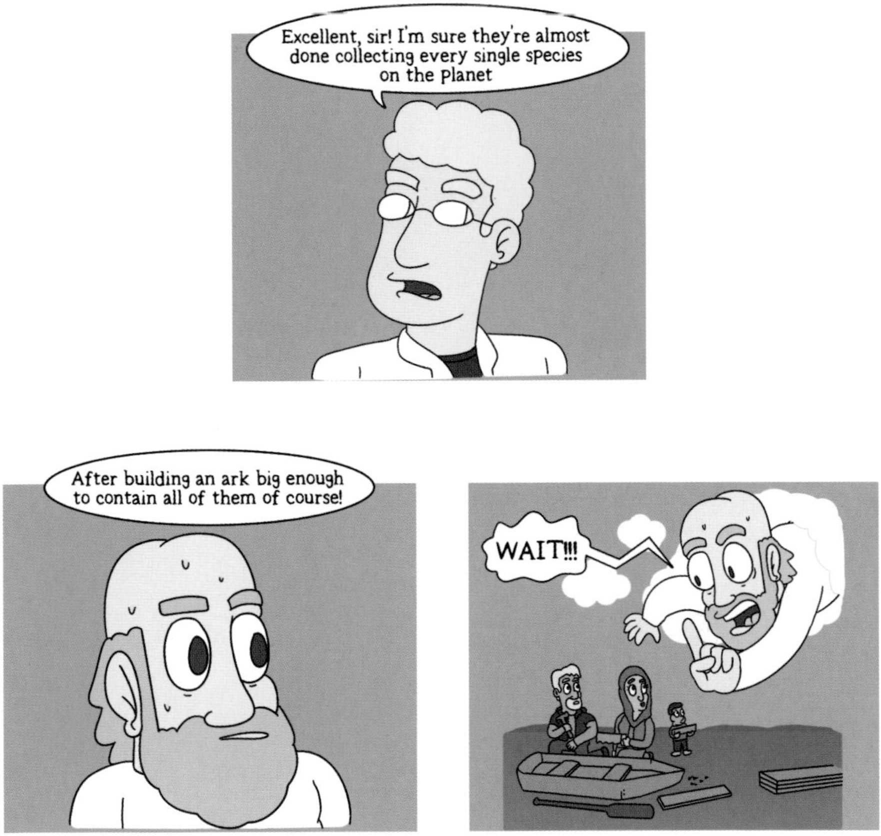
Excellent, sir! I'm sure they're almost done collecting every single species on the planet
After building an ark big enough to contain all of them of course!
WAIT!!!

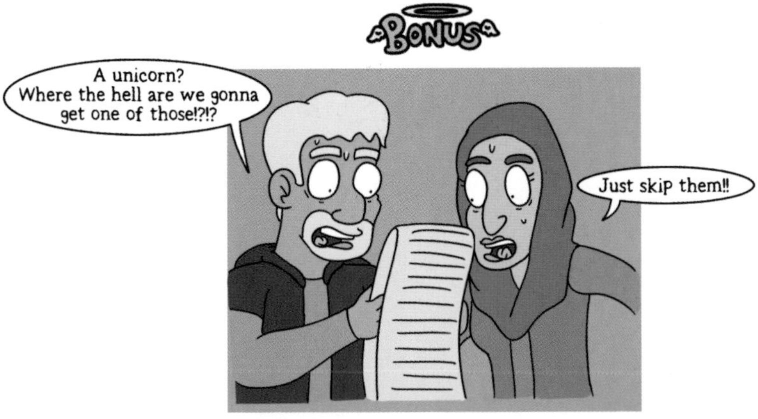
BONUS
A unicorn? Where the hell are we gonna get one of those!?!?
Just skip them!!

Jesus???

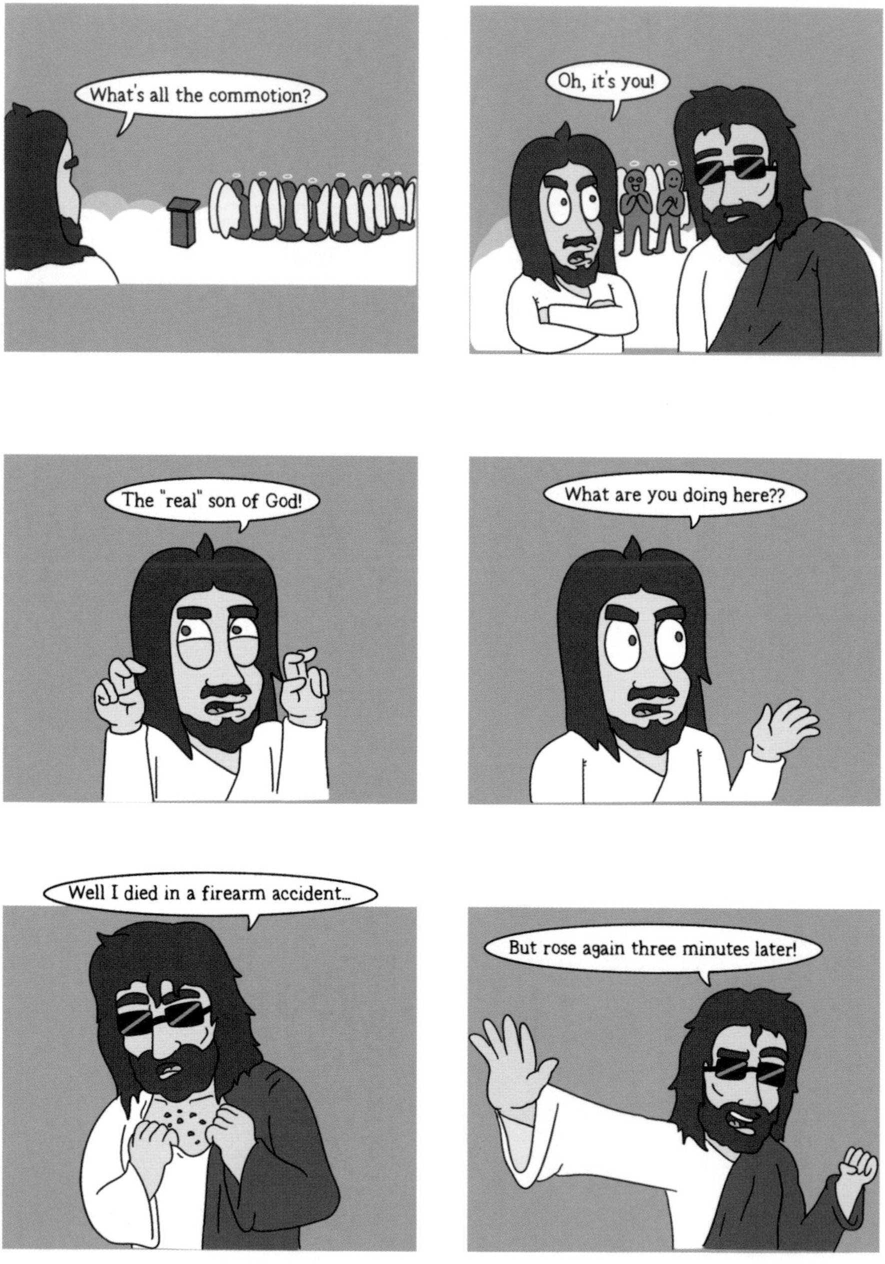
What's all the commotion?
Oh, it's you!
The "real" son of God!
What are you doing here??
Well I died in a firearm accident...
But rose again three minutes later!

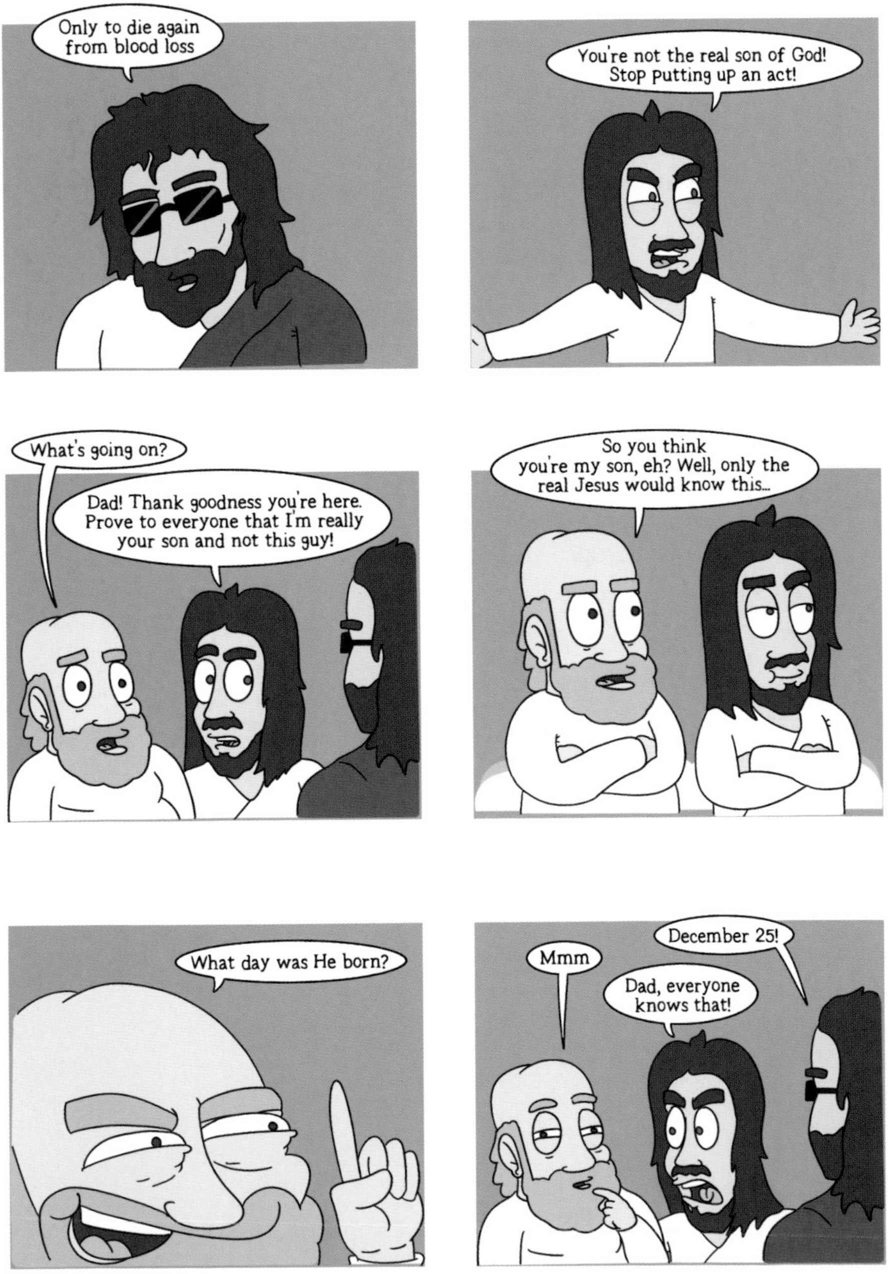

Only to die again from blood loss
You're not the real son of God! Stop putting up an act!
What's going on?
Dad! Thank goodness you're here. Prove to everyone that I'm really your son and not this guy!
So you think you're my son, eh? Well, only the real Jesus would know this...
What day was He born?
Mmm
December 25!
Dad, everyone knows that!

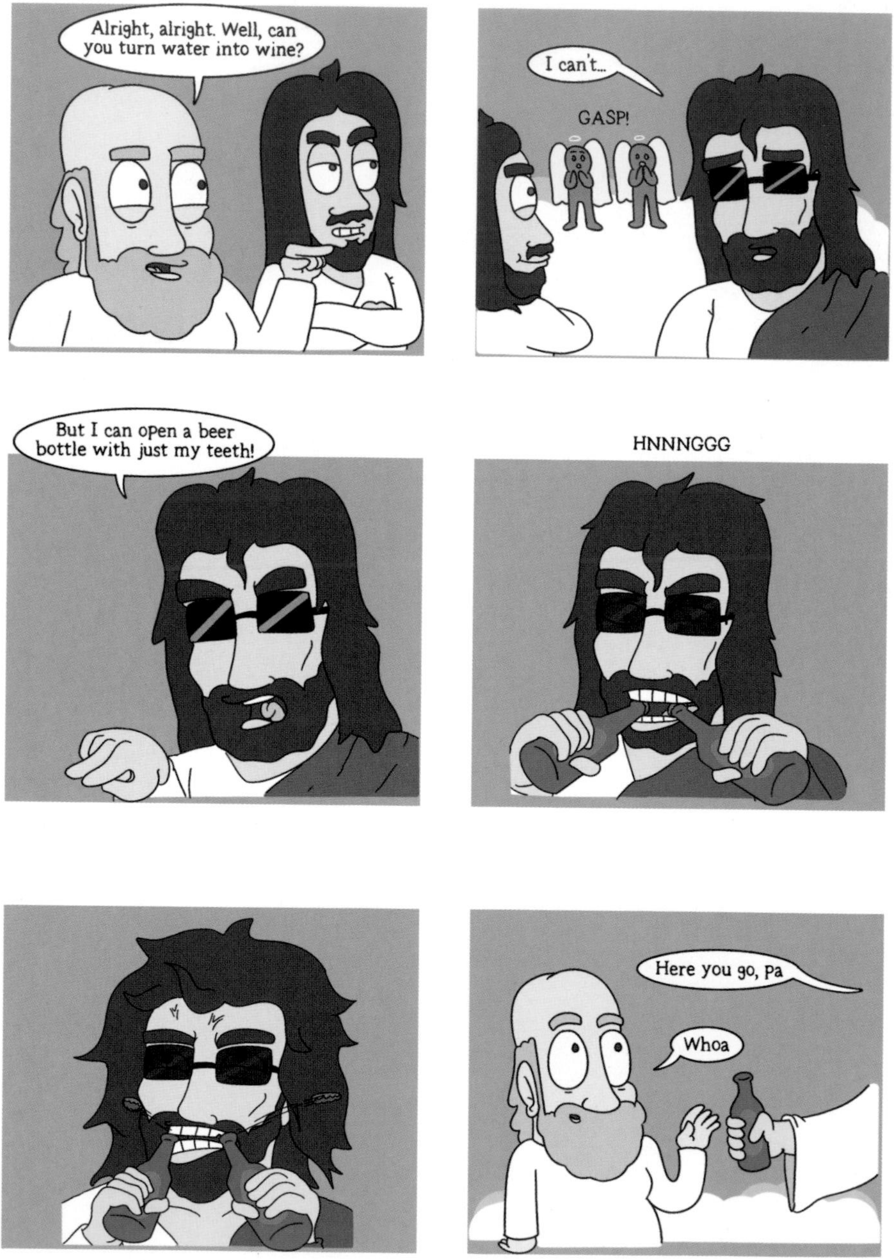
Alright, alright. Well, can you turn water into wine?
I can't...
GASP!
But I can open a beer bottle with just my teeth!
HNNNGGG
Here you go, pa
Whoa

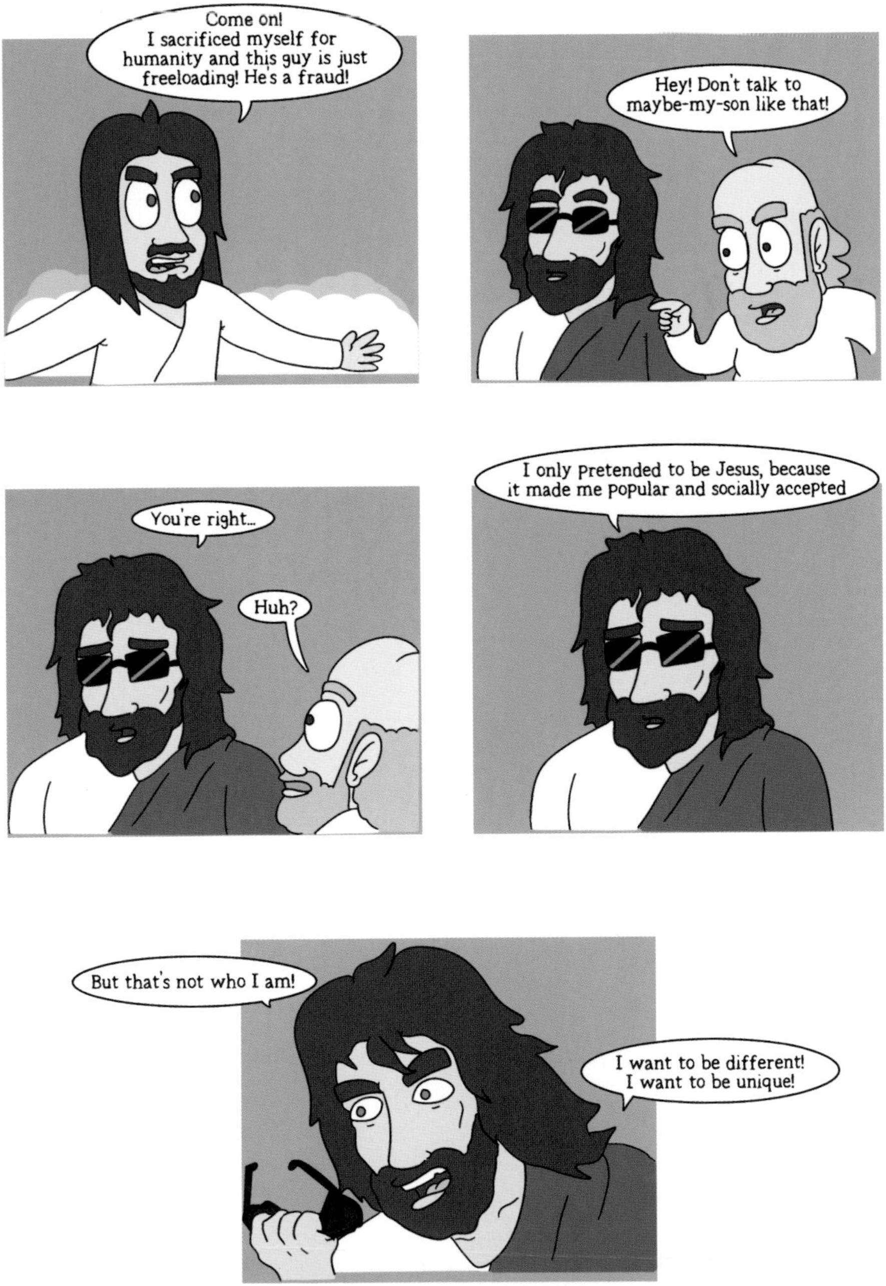
Come on! I sacrificed myself for humanity and this guy is just freeloading! He's a fraud!
Hey! Don't talk to maybe-my-son like that!
You're right...
Huh?
I only pretended to be Jesus, because it made me popular and socially accepted
But that's not who I am!
I want to be different! I want to be unique!

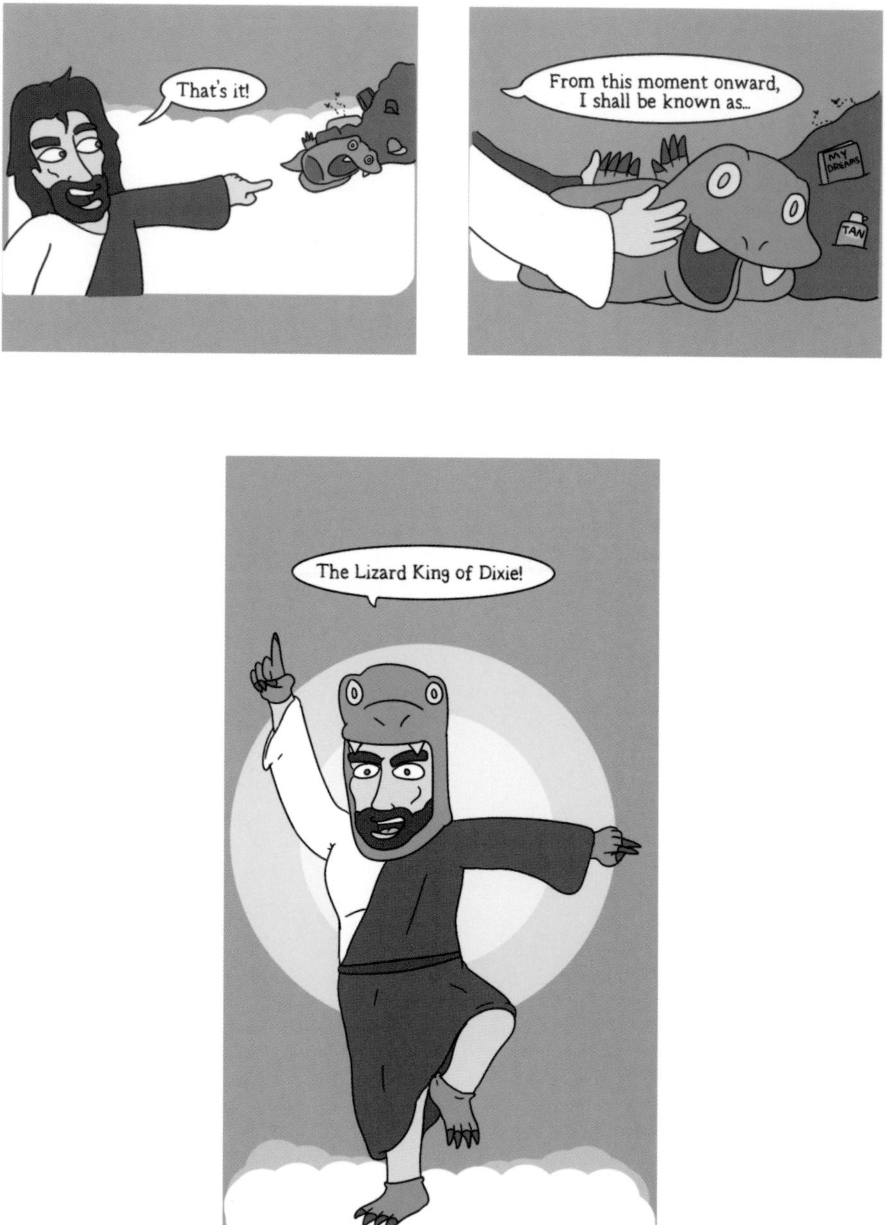
That's it!
From this moment onward, I shall be known as...
MY DREAMS
TAN
The Lizard King of Dixie!

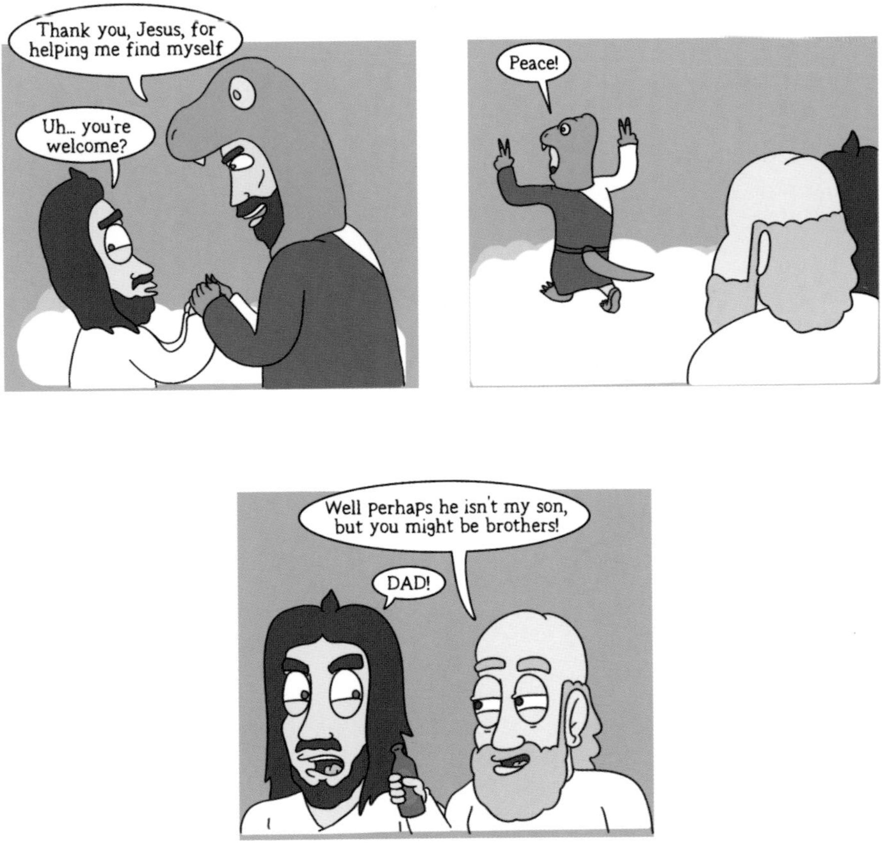
Thank you, Jesus, for helping me find myself
Uh... you're welcome?
Peace!
Well perhaps he isn't my son, but you might be brothers!
DAD!

BONUS

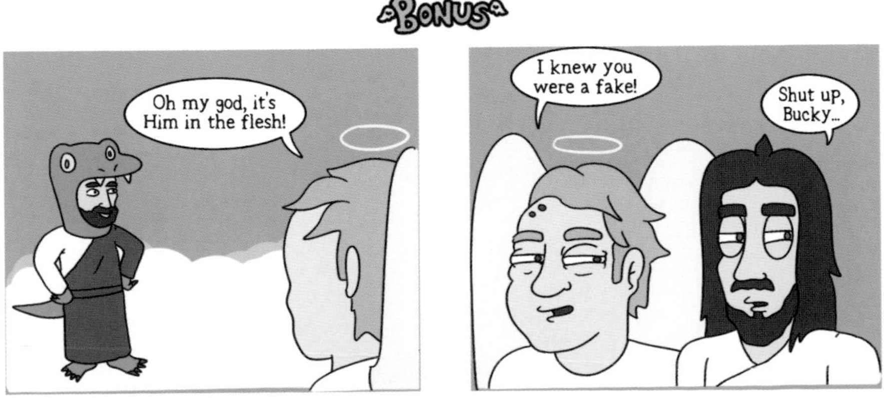
Oh my god, it's Him in the flesh!
I knew you were a fake!
Shut up, Bucky...

Smite

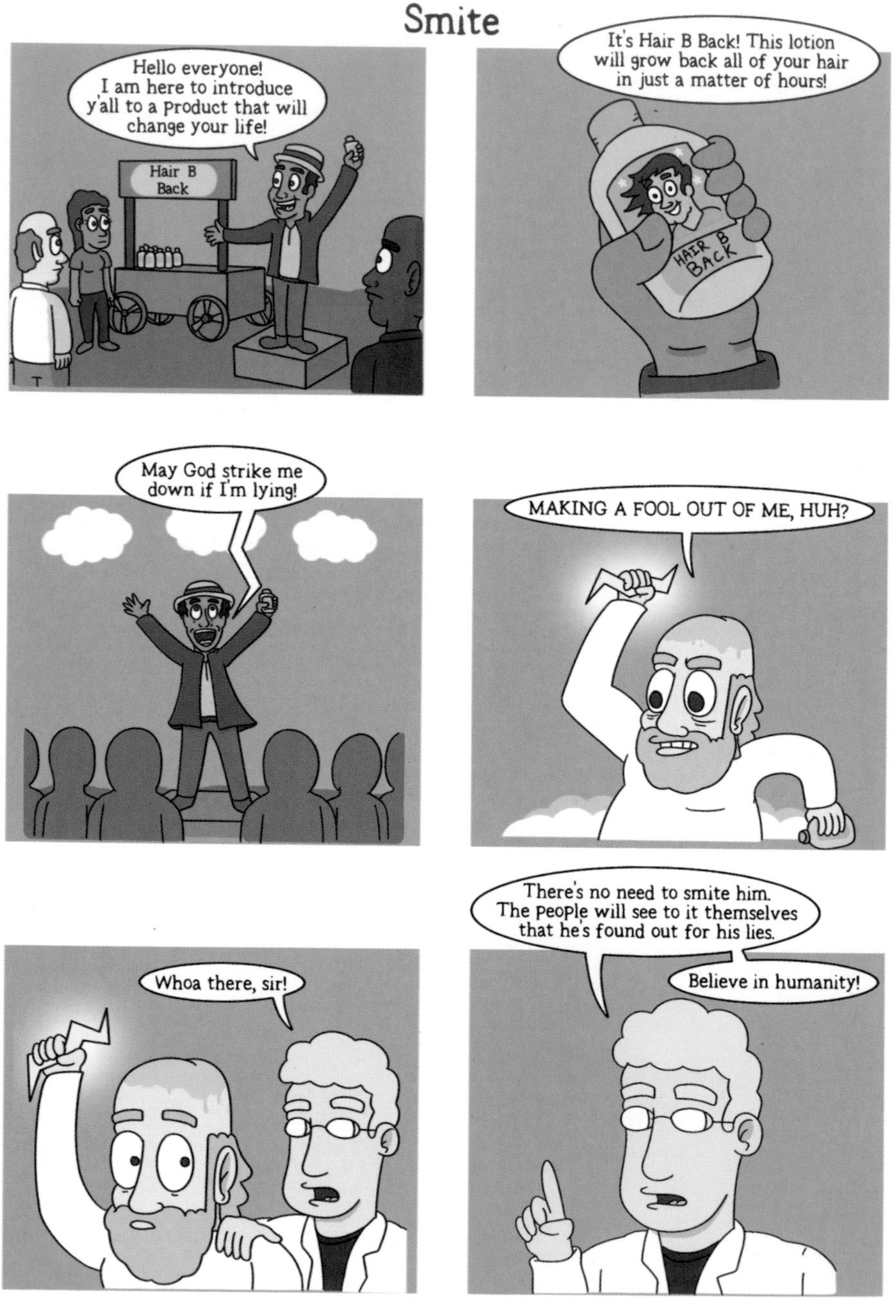
Hello everyone! I am here to introduce y'all to a product that will change your life!
Hair B Back
It's Hair B Back! This lotion will grow back all of your hair in just a matter of hours!
HAIR B BACK
May God strike me down if I'm lying!
MAKING A FOOL OUT OF ME, HUH?
Whoa there, sir!
There's no need to smite him. The people will see to it themselves that he's found out for his lies.
Believe in humanity!

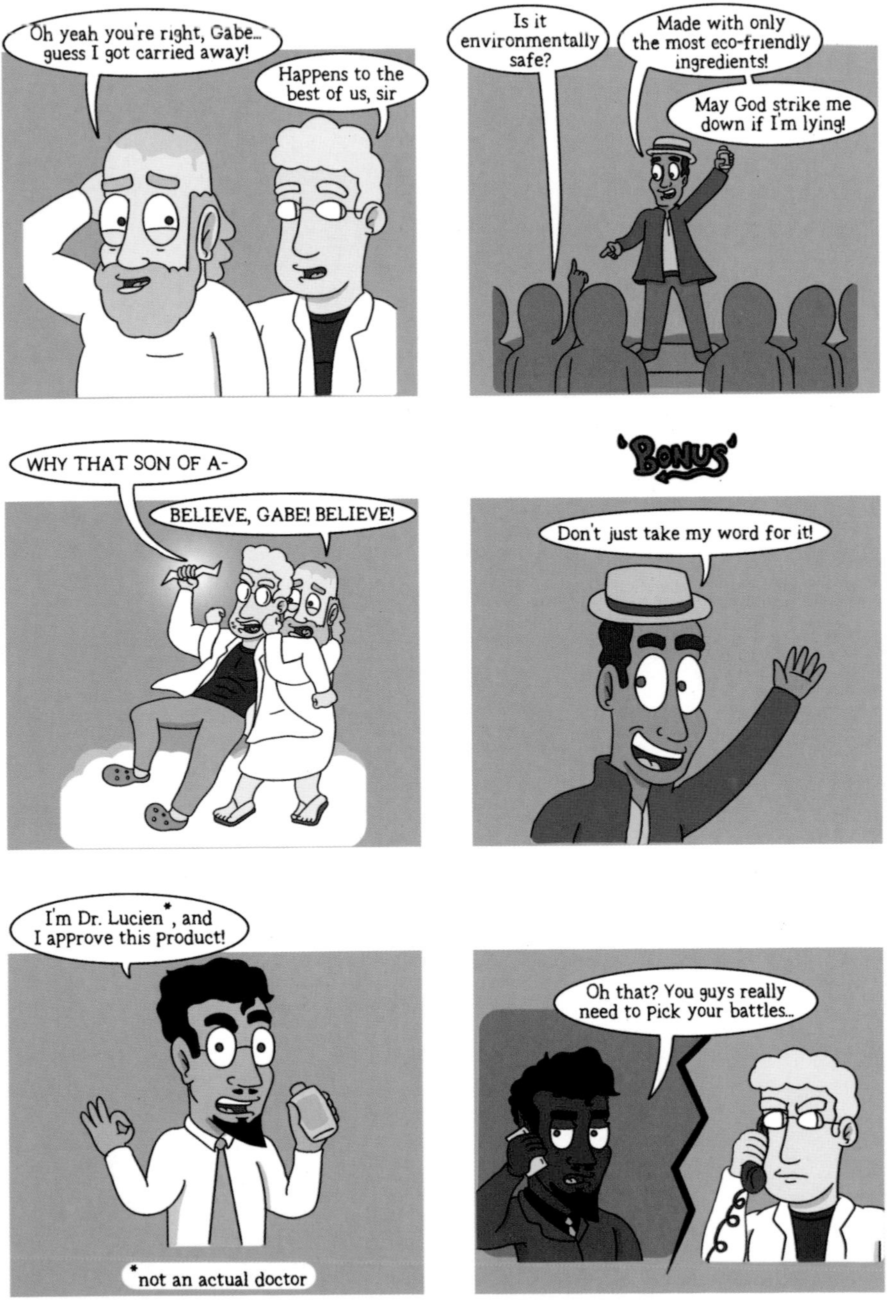
Oh yeah you're right, Gabe... guess I got carried away!
Happens to the best of us, sir
Is it environmentally safe?
Made with only the most eco-friendly ingredients!
May God strike me down if I'm lying!
WHY THAT SON OF A-
BELIEVE, GABE! BELIEVE!
BONUS
Don't just take my word for it!
I'm Dr. Lucien*, and I approve this product!
*not an actual doctor
Oh that? You guys really need to pick your battles...

Greetings from
PURGATORY

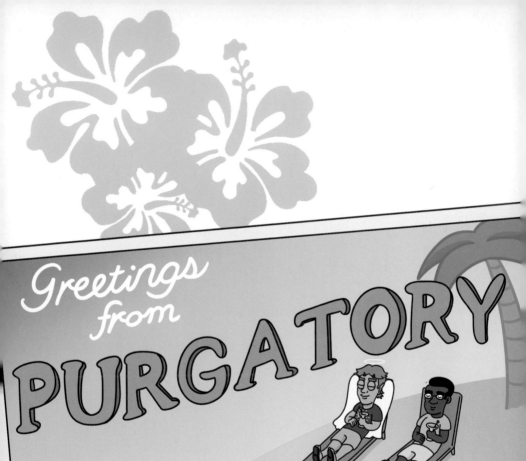

Outtakes

Sometimes, an idea isn't a good fit for Adventures of God, no matter how funny it is. Sometimes it's too provocative; sometimes it's out of character; sometimes it's simply too weird, or includes references too obscure for the public to get.

Here you will find some rough drafts that didn't get made, for one reason or another. Who knows, maybe they will appeal to your very specific sense of humor?

Rejected Idea: Miss Call

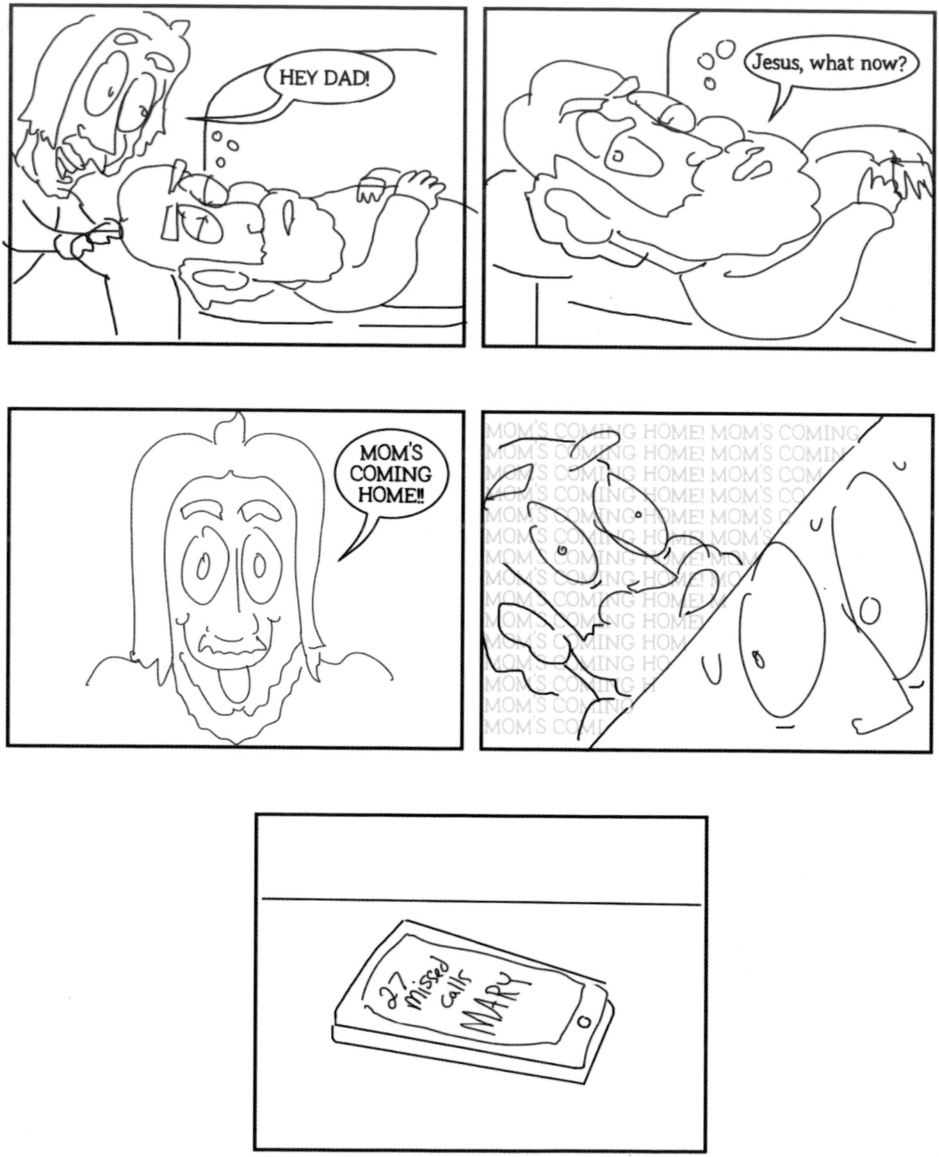
HEY DAD!
Jesus, what now?
MOM'S COMING HOME!!
MOM'S COMING HOME! MOM'S COMING
27 missed calls
MARY

Rejected Idea: Simulation

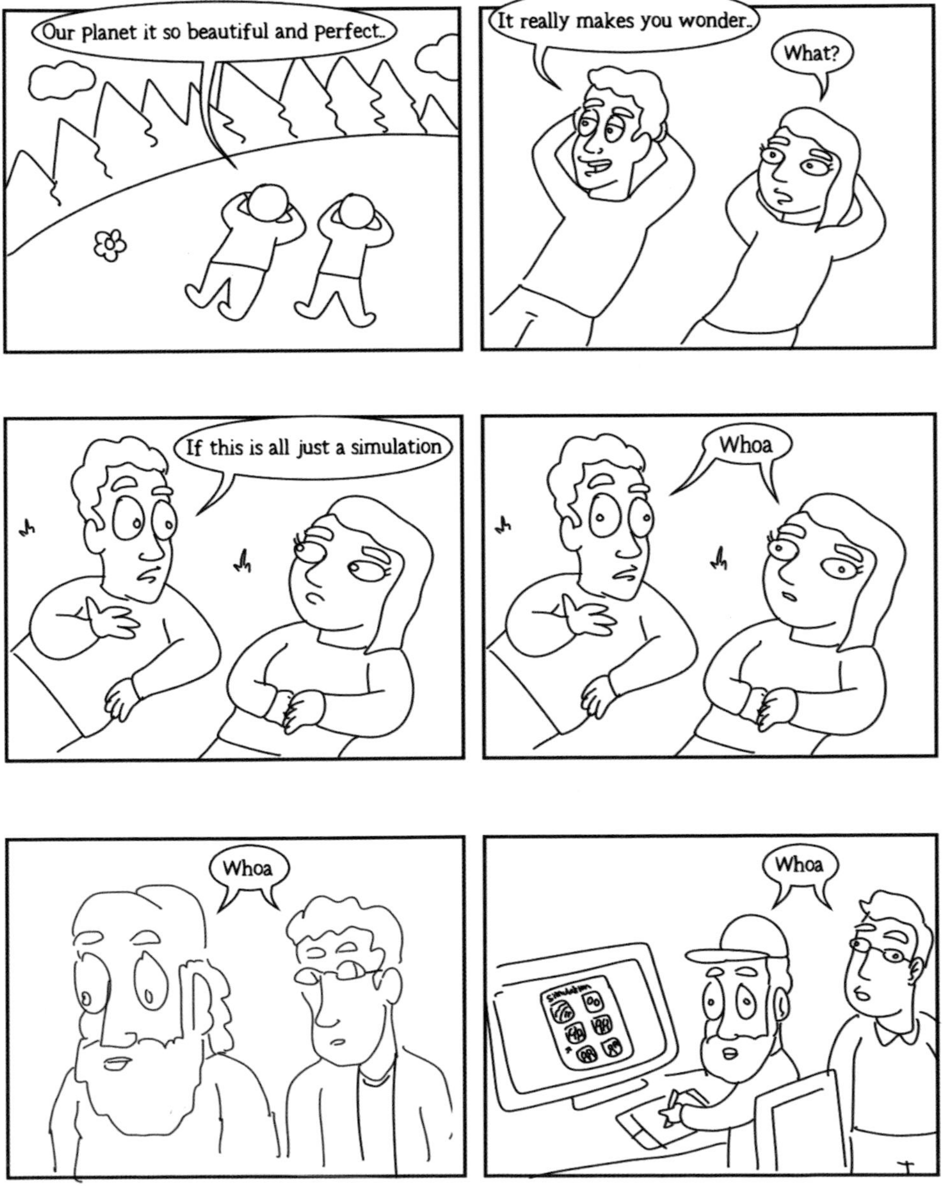
Our planet it so beautiful and perfect..
It really makes you wonder..
What?
If this is all just a simulation
Whoa
Whoa
Whoa

REJECTED IDEA: SELF-AWARE

Jesus, take the wheel!
Poof
Huh
AAAHHH
TITANIC

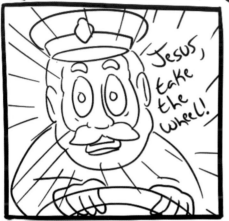

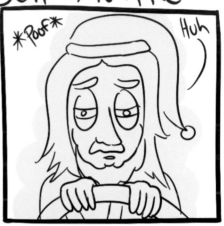

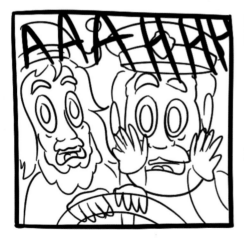

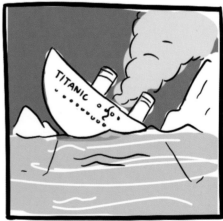

REJECTED IDEA: ZEUS

I smite people
HA! I do that too!
I can turn into a horse and seduce women

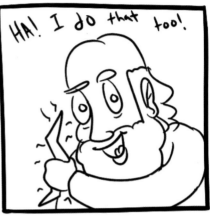

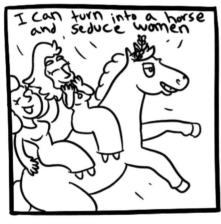

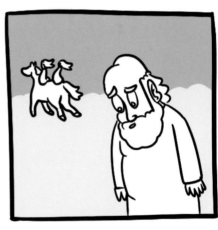

Corey's Pre-Adventures Period

Before he started making Adventures of God with Teo, Corey was already fascinated with God, the afterlife, and other religious topics.

He frequently visited Heaven and Hell in his gag comic, *Down The Upward Spiral*, and some of those episodes were adapted for Adventures of God. Here are a few!

What differences do you notice? Some lines had to be rewritten to fit the nature of our characters - for example, God needed more wacky non-sequiturs :)

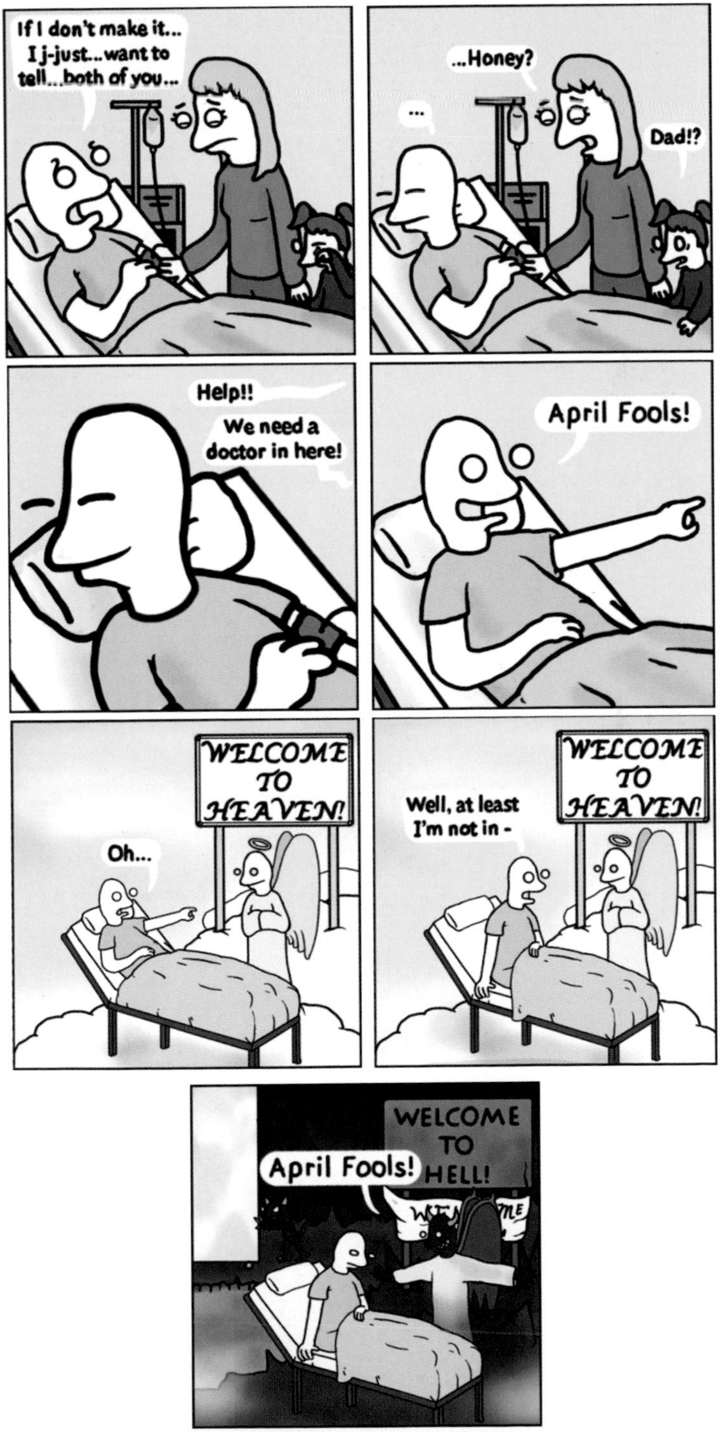
If I don't make it... I j-just...want to tell...both of you...
...Honey?
...
Dad!?
Help!!
We need a doctor in here!
April Fools!
WELCOME TO HEAVEN!
Oh...
WELCOME TO HEAVEN!
Well, at least I'm not in -
WELCOME TO HELL!
April Fools!

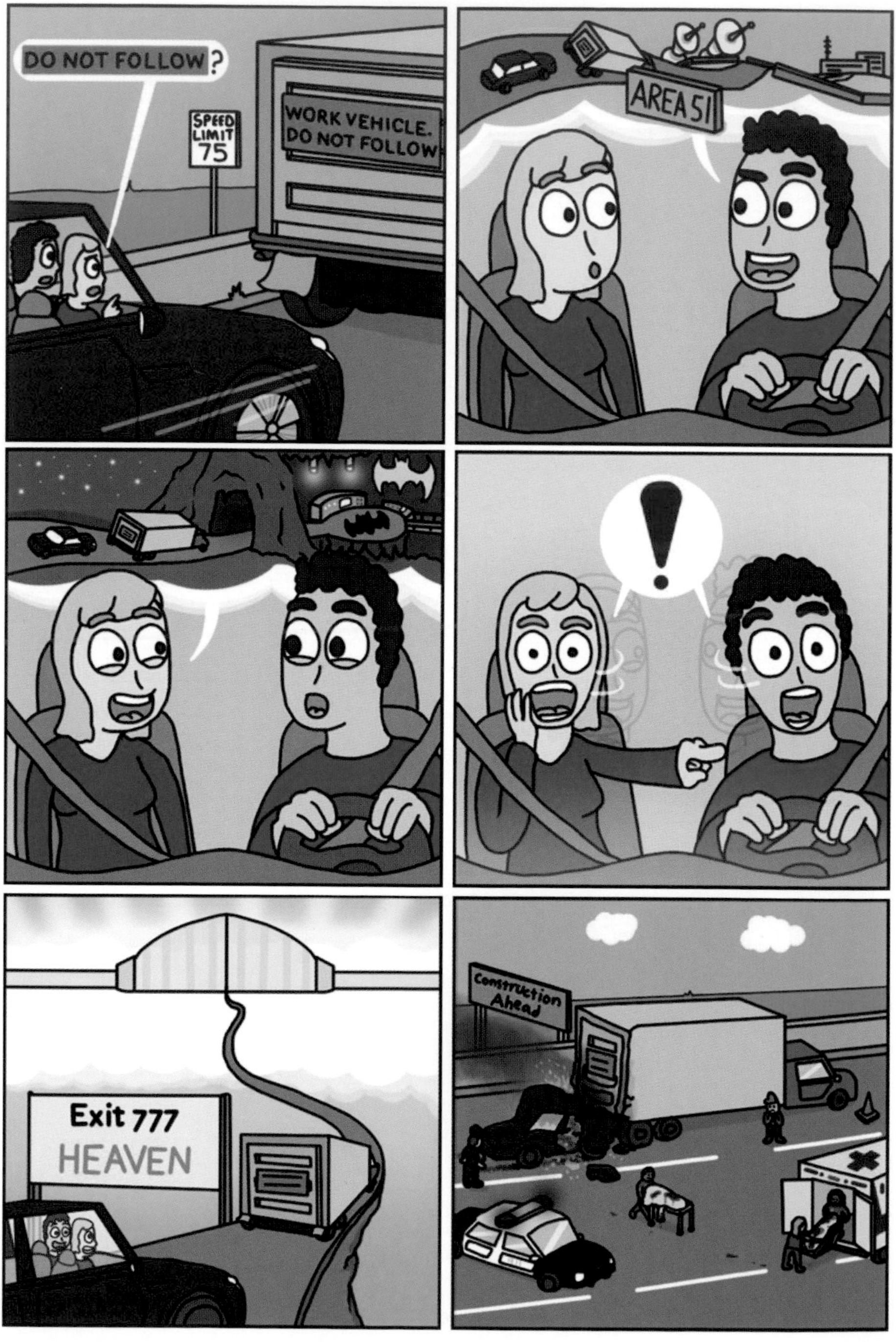

DO NOT FOLLOW?
SPEED LIMIT 75
WORK VEHICLE. DO NOT FOLLOW!
AREA 51
Exit 777
HEAVEN
Construction Ahead

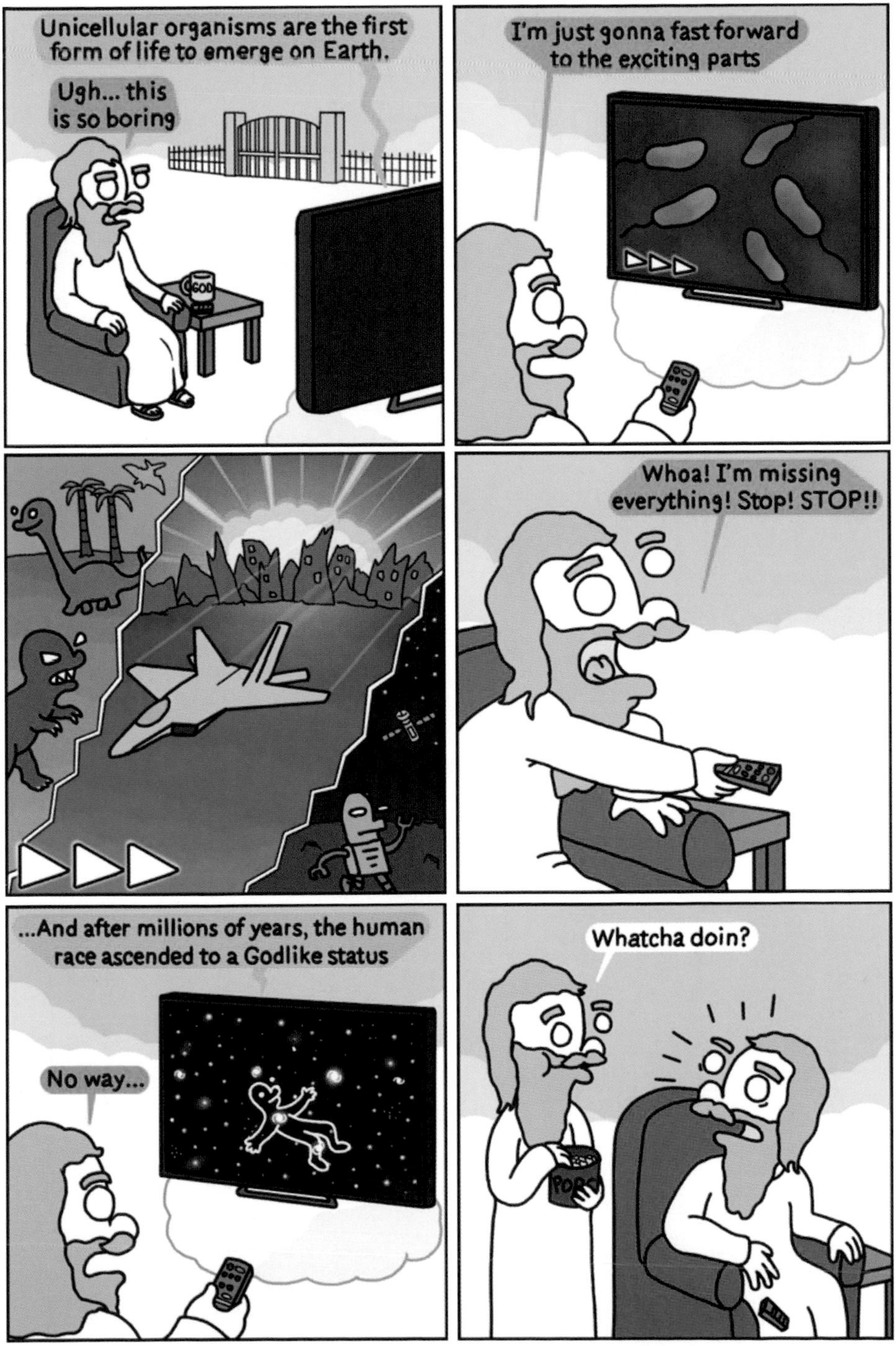
Unicellular organisms are the first form of life to emerge on Earth.
Ugh... this is so boring
GOD
I'm just gonna fast forward to the exciting parts
Whoa! I'm missing everything! Stop! STOP!!
...And after millions of years, the human race ascended to a Godlike status
No way...
Whatcha doin?
POPC

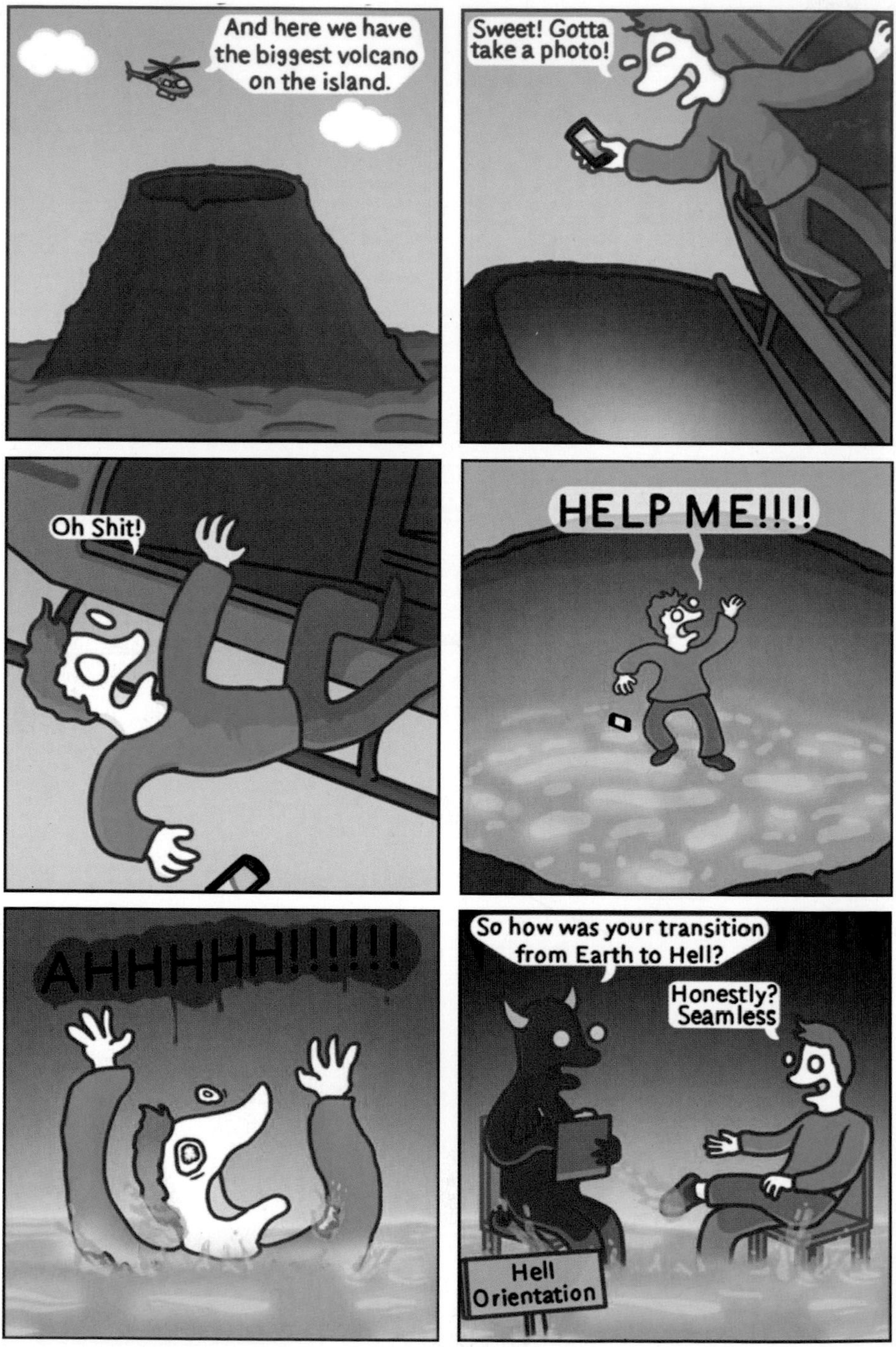
And here we have the biggest volcano on the island.
Sweet! Gotta take a photo!
Oh Shit!
HELP ME!!!!
AHHHHH!!!!!!
So how was your transition from Earth to Hell?
Honestly? Seamless
Hell Orientation

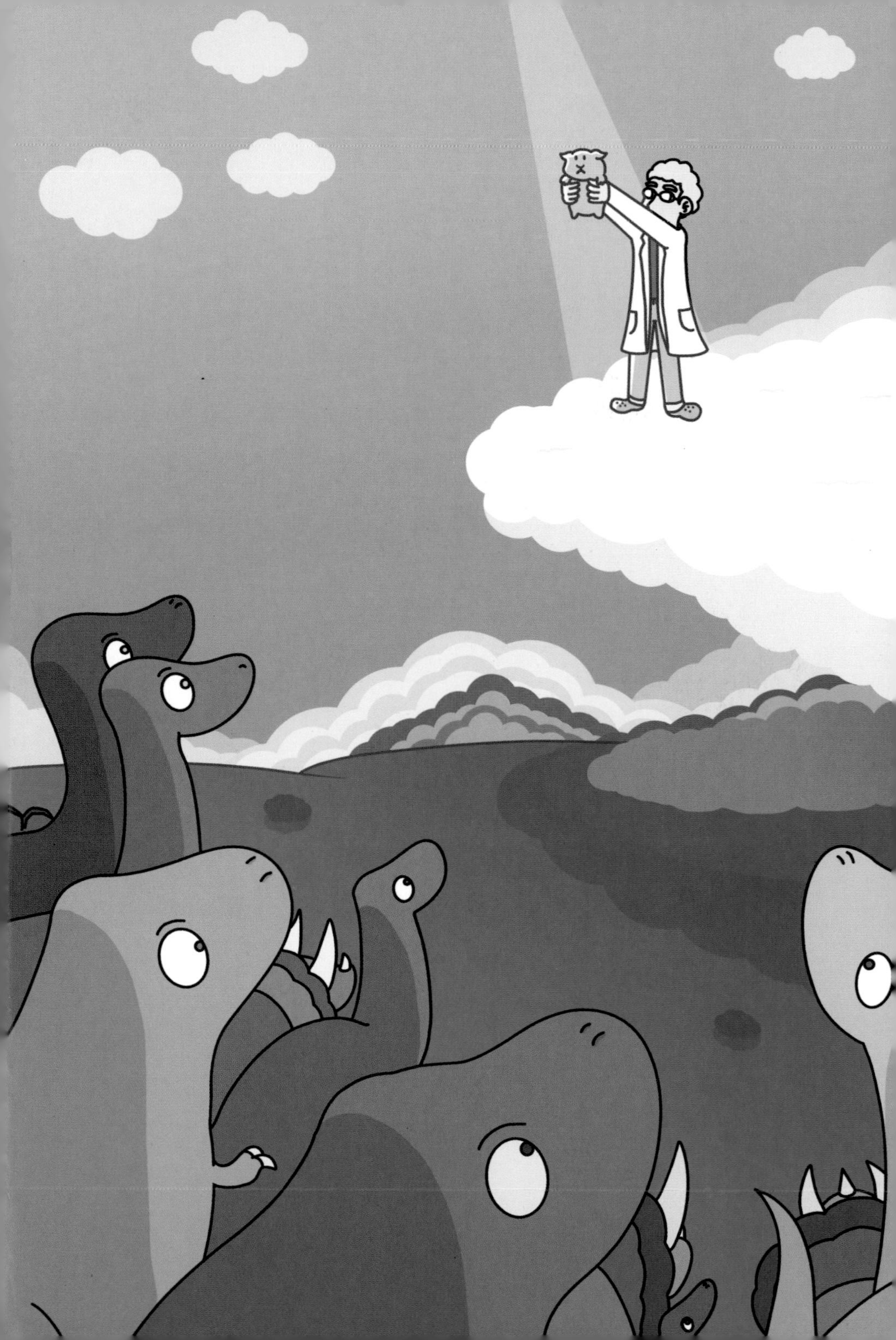

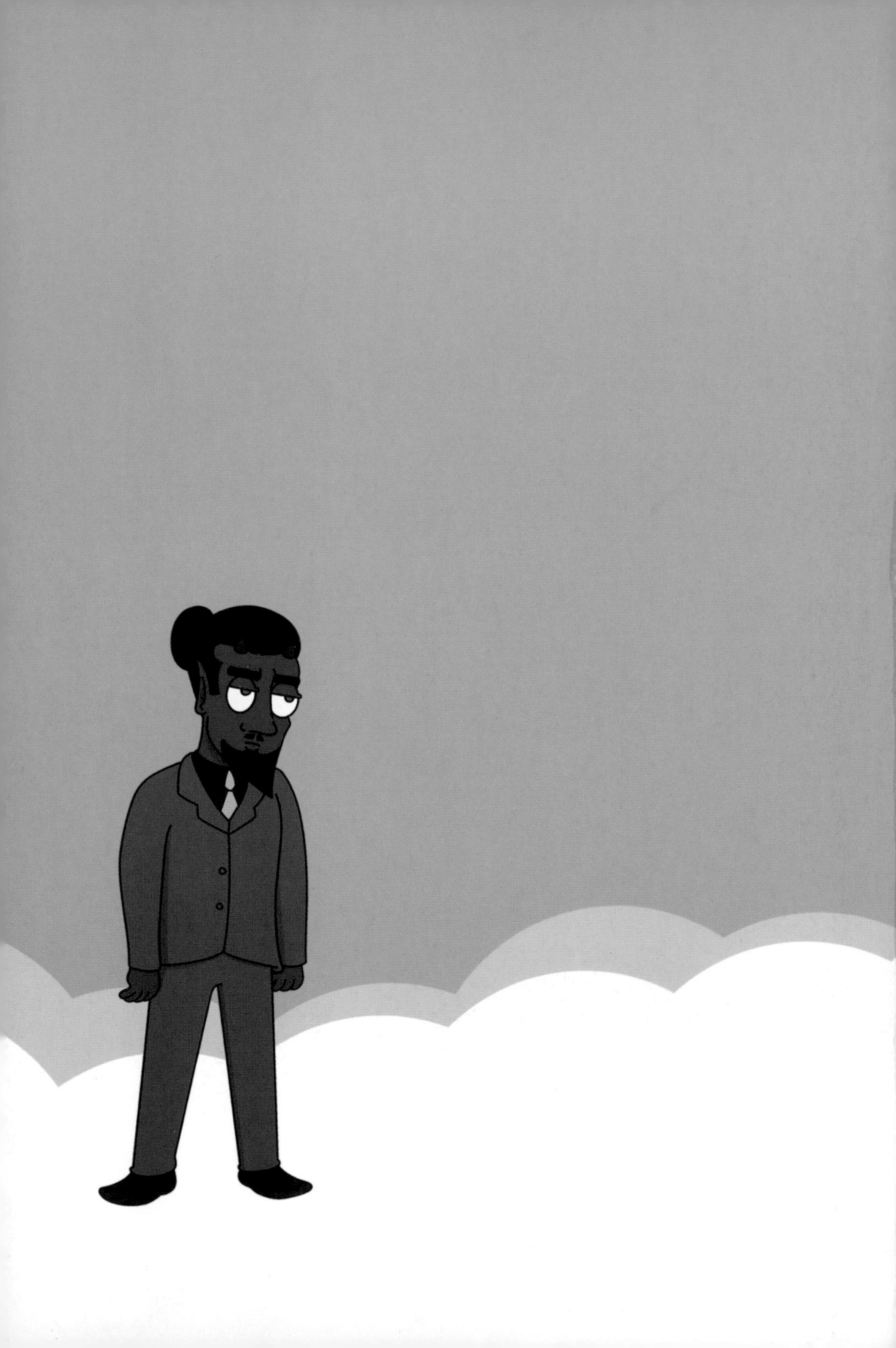